Taming
the Giant
Corporation

Ralph Nader

Mark Green

Joel Seligman

Taming the Giant Corporation

W · W · NORTON & COMPANY · INC · NEW YORK

FIRST EDITION

The text of this book was set by the variable input photosetter in the typeface Janson. Composition, printing, and binding are by the Vail-Ballou Press Inc.

Library of Congress Cataloging in Publication Data
Nader, Ralph.
      Taming the giant corporation.
      Includes bibliographical references and index.
      1. Corporation law—United States. 2. Incorporation—
United States. 3. Industry and state—United States.
I. Green, Mark J., joint author. II. Seligman, Joel,
joint author. III. Title.
KF1414.N34   346'.73'066   76–26113
ISBN 0 393 08753 0

1 2 3 4 5 6 7 8 9 0

Contents

Preface

TAMING THE GIANT CORPORATION examines the powers of giant corporations in the United States, and the ways they erode the rule of law and ethical precepts. For these massive institutions create serious adverse consequences for consumers, workers, shareholders, taxpayers, small businesses, and community residents; they operate without effective internal and external accountabilities to those persons so harmed. The growing damage—often latent, diffuse, or deferred—compounds the need to rethink and reshape the political economy away from these many forms of injustice.

Large corporations, commanding immense political, economic, and technological power, are different in kind and in degree from their smaller counterparts. They advance their control of political units by transcending the jurisdictions of these units, nationally and multinationally, and by financing or otherwise nourishing the political process. These corporations possess decisive market power, sometimes collusively with their giant brethren and sometimes unilaterally. Where smaller firms have to assume the bankruptcy option, these companies, controlling major resources, are considered too big to fail, despite their own mismanagement or corruption. Governments are thereby forced to socialize their losses and guarantee their tenure.

Moreover, the nonmarket impacts of giant corporations have become institutionalized. Pollution of the human environment is rationalized as an economic necessity. Subsidies have become an entrenched corporate welfare system inducing inefficiencies and political rewards. Such corporate excesses align big government and big business against public interests. As power begets power, large corporations are able to pursue their activities beyond the law, above the law, or against the law—a state of affairs clearly incompatible with democracy. Their ultimate influence is the capability to change the law in order to legalize their illegalities once the latter become widely known.

Historically, the principal restraint on corporate power has been the economic risks corporations have had to assume. In the past, investors in corporations were given limited liability. Now the corporations themselves want limited liabilities. The removal of traditional restraints, combined with the unprecedented hazards of corporate activities—one need only mention atomic power and toxic chemicals—make it imperative to examine closely how the consent of the governed, in both the marketplace and the polity, is rapidly reduced by corporate might.

The private governments of the megacorporations make the nominal government of state charters, whose measure is the Delaware corporation, a historic tragedy of far-reaching proportions. Through a federal charter instrument new rights and remedies can be accorded affected citizens by making the large corporate structure more anticipatory, self-correcting, and sensitive to public needs. This is essentially what we mean by the phrase "constitutionalizing the corporation."

All this is not to suggest that society must always depend on large corporations, even when they are made more responsive. There is something profoundly undemocratic about a "corporate state" run by a few without the informed consent and participation of the many. Fortunately, there are other ways of organizing major constituencies for the purpose of enabling individual pursuits of life, liberty, and happiness. There are also other forms of private and public property. For example, consumer-owned private enterprises at the community level can meet major needs presently ignored by corporate chains or conglomerates.

The attractiveness of such alternatives can be better discerned by first describing the many short and long term costs of centralized corporate power as it affects present and future generations.

This book is, then, but a step in the journey of understanding how to create efficient and democratic economic enterprise. It is a goal that invites the liberation of many minds and many initiatives.

Ralph Nader
Mark Green
Joel Seligman

Washington, D.C.
June, 1976

Acknowledgments

THE FORMULATION of this report—in preparation over parts of the past five years—was aided by the considerable help of many friends and colleagues. Irene Till and Jeffrey Nesvet did substantial work in developing Chapter V on "Corporate Disclosure." Beverly Moore, Jr., Harvey Goldschmid, Donald Petrie, and Donald Schwartz devoted substantial effort and time reading and commenting on earlier drafts. Also, Russell Stevenson, Ernest Folk, Detlev Vagts, Myles Mace, David Ratner, Joseph Bishop, Alice Tepper Marlin, John Tepper Marlin, Vic Reinemer, Peter Petkas, Walter Adams, Willard Mueller, Alan Morrison, Elliot Weiss, and Christopher Griffiths made valuable comments on specific portions of this report. None of them, of course, is responsible for the content that follows. Michael Rubin, Peter Rothberg, Rob Bildner and Craig Kubey helped track down elusive cases, sources, and arguments. And, finally, we owe our gratitude to Pamela Meyer and Cecilia Kelly for their support in producing, proofing, and researching the manuscript as it progressed.

Ralph Nader
Mark Green
Joel Seligman

The Case for Federal Chartering

I

The Corporate

Impact

[T]he corporation is a creature of the state. It is presumed to be incorporated for the benefit of the public. It receives certain privileges and franchises, and holds them subject to the laws of the state and the limitations of its charter. . . .

—United States Supreme Court in *Hale v. Henkel* (1906)

I F THE Constitutional Convention were convened in 1976 instead of 1787, can we imagine that this time the Founding Fathers would fail to mention the business corporation?

Two centuries ago Americans were keenly aware of the tyrannical potential of unlimited governmental power. In rejecting the undemocratic abuses of King George III, the colonists embraced the philosophical premises of Locke and Montesquieu in their constitution: power would be dispersed among countervailing institutions; political officials would be elected, and hence personally accountable for their actions; delegations of power would be limited to those specified in written law. What began as a novel experiment in self-government has endured the erosion of time, becoming the world's model for constitutional democracy.

With one glaring exception: the Constitution of the United States does not explicitly mention the business corporation. It neither explicitly defines the relation of the individual to the business corporation nor the relation of the business corporation to the federal government. For the Founding Fathers, reacting to the immediate problems of their time, were far more worried about political oligarchy than corporate oligarchy. As a result, while the United States Constitution today governs every federal, state, county, and local authority, no matter how small, it is effectively silent about the giant corporations which rule our economy. The fact of their impact is not difficult to trace. In 1974 the 500 largest industrial corporations accounted for 66 percent of the sales of all U.S. industrial firms—and 72 percent of the profits. Of *Fortune*'s top 1,000 corporations, the ten largest firms had 16 percent of the workforce, 20 percent of the profits, and 23 percent of the assets. Exxon had greater sales in 1974 than each of the GNPs of Austria, Denmark, and South Africa. General Motors employs more people—734,000—than are employed in the states of California, New York, Pennsylvania, and Michigan combined.

Mere brobdingnagian size, however, only begins an analysis of corporate power. Herbivorous dinosaurs were also huge—but weak, dumb, and helpless before predators. Our giant firms, on the other hand, have both size *and* power. A couple of hundred corporate managers, who could fit comfortably into a small auditorium, can make decisions controlling most of our industrial economy. How many billions of dollars will be paid out in dividends and wages; how many billions will be invested in various kinds of capital investment or research and development? It is an exercise in power when an electronics firm in a depressed eastern city shifts production to a newly built Mexican plant; when U.S. Steel decides to raise its price substantially in the face of slackening demand, thereby accelerating inflation; when B. F. Goodrich in the 1960s decides to sell an aircraft brake which its technicians know will fail under normal stress; when the American auto industry in the 1950s commits itself to bulky chariots rather than safer, fuel-efficient vehicles; or when General Motors in 1929 refuses to install shatterproof glass on its cars. In all these instances, consumers, workers, shareholders, and citizens can be very dramatically affected by Corporate America.

Theory, however, has lagged behind reality. Classical economists still appear to assume that if the government would only mind its own business we could have a self-correcting, perfectly allocating market. Many businessmen—of the sort who inveigh against "Big Government" at annual meetings—treat the *Fortune*

500 as if they were competing Ma and Pa groceries, just like small firms, only larger. But a giant corporation is not merely an inflated version of a small business firm, any more than a man is just an oversized infant or an elephant simply a large mouse. For corporations, as well, a vast increase in size transforms the nature of the enterprise.

Thus, prominent analysts like A. A. Berle, Walton Hamilton, Robert Dahl, John Kenneth Galbraith, Earl Latham, Richard Eells, and Arthur S. Miller have correctly perceived the largest corporations to be more like private governments. "The corporate organizations of business," wrote Columbia Professor Wolfgang Friedmann, "have long ceased to be private phenomena. That they have a direct and decisive impact on the social, economic, and political life of the nation is no longer a matter of argument." Often these private governments produce costly side-effects, or what economists call "externalities." As K. William Kapp argued in his prescient 1950 book, *The Social Costs of Private Enterprise*, GNP and production data usually "leave out important social costs of production borne by third parties and future generations. . . . [T]he institutionalized system of decision-making in a system of business enterprise has a built-in tendency to disregard those negative effects on the environment that are 'external' to the decision-making unit."

For those who simply assume that big business is what has made America great and that there is no need for a major redesign of our large corporations, it is useful to catalogue some of the social and economic costs of the giant corporations. Our focus is on the largest 700 or so industrial, retail, and transportation companies, those that annually sell $250 million or more in goods and services. In brief fashion, this catalogue describes the invisible taxes these private governments levy on all Americans.

Industrial Pollution—Until the recent environmental movement caught much of business short, industrial pollution was considered a free form of waste disposal. Free, that is, for the business corporation. Society inevitably pays the bill in impaired health, damaged property, and aesthetic despoliation. In the early 1970s, as companies such as Reserve Mining Company dumped 67,000 tons of waste rock and asbestos fibers a day into Lake Superior, as

American Cyanamid poured six million gallons of waste water into the Savannah River daily, and as U.S. Steel released 225 tons of pollutants into the air each day at its Clairton coke plant near Pittsburgh, the link between industrial production and environmental pollution became clear. "A factory dumps its wastes into an adjoining river," observes economist Anita Summers, "and consequently fishermen no longer fish, sailors no longer sail, and nature lovers search for another retreat. Urban centers swarm with autos, the pollution index soars, eyes burn, shirts get dirtier, and the view from the city's highest point is no longer a source of delight."

Between 1946 and 1971, levels of pollution in many industries rose from 200 percent to 2,000 percent, though production grew only 126 percent in the same period. Industrial pollution today directly accounts for one-third of all solid waste, one half of all air pollution, and more than one half of total water pollution. The deadly consequences of this ecological assault are now increasingly understoood. Both the National Cancer Institute and the World Health Organization have estimated in separate studies that up to 90 percent of all human cancers are caused by environmental factors, including industrial pollution. For example, The Cancer Institute computer analysis of death certificates from 1950 to 1969 found an extremely high incidence of bladder cancer in heavily industrialized areas around Newark, Chicago, St. Louis, and New Orleans. The Environmental Protection Agency calculates that health and property damage from industrial air pollution alone will cost Americans $23 billion in 1977. This $23 billion social cost could have been cut almost in half—except for industry opposition to employing $3.9 billion in added abatement gear.

Toxic Substances—Business not only often pollutes its surrounding environment but its internal environment as well. The chemicalization of the workplace threatens the well-being of millions of American workers. The 1972 *President's Report on Occupational Safety and Health* said that perhaps 100,000 deaths annually are caused by occupational disease. For example, in January 1974 the B. F. Goodrich Company reported to the National Institute of Occupational Safety and Health that several employees had died of a rare form of liver cancer, angiosarcoma. The workers had been exposed to vinyl chloride, a colorless gas used in the production of the common plastic, polyvinyl chloride. At the Johns-Manville plant in Manville, New Jersey, writes reporter Phil Greer, "people are dying of diseases virtually unknown elsewhere; they are dying, medical experts agree, because they work in the biggest asbestos processing plant in the world." A 1970 PHS survey showed that over 30,000 workers are routinely exposed to beryllium, which can produce severe inflammation of the lungs, nose, and throat, chest pains, congestive heart failure, enlargement of liver and spleen, and discoloration of skin from oxygen deficiency.

Still, in the view of a lawyer in a silicosis compensation case in 1970, "with a maximum liability of only $12,500 plus medical and funeral expenses, it has been so inexpensive to disable and kill a man . . . that it has not been worthwhile to clean up."

Discrimination—Although many large corporations appear today to be in a race to place on their boards of directors women and blacks (or better yet, black women), the record behind the window-dressing is unimpressive. In 1973 alone, the Equal Employment Opportunity Commission moved against nine of the largest 25 firms in the nation for alleged discrimination against black and/or female employees. A 1975 survey of the 2,500 most senior executives of this country's major corporations found only 15 women; a study of the 1008 directors of the 67 largest California corporations found no blacks and six women (three being the wives of the company's chairman or president).

It should not be surprising, then, that black male workers earned 69 percent of the salary of their white counterparts in 1972 and that full-time female workers had a median income only 60 percent of their male counterparts in 1973. Dr. Andrew F. Brimmer, a former governor of the Federal Reserve Board, points out that in the past five years black families have suffered a new "drift toward inequality" with income levels relative to white families down from 1969 levels. This trend is largely due to the fact that black unemployment rates are today twice as high as whites.

White Collar Blues—Most students of the business world are familiar with the phenomenon of "blue-collar blues," where worker powerlessness and alienation lead to job dissatisfaction and hostility to management. But a comparable despair has begun to afflict executives as well. Based on a survey of 2,800 corporate executives, the

American Management Association observes that job alienation "has not merely spread to, but may even thrive in, the managerial suites of American business." Though businessmen may maintain an image of rugged individualistic enterprise—a cross between *Cash McCall* and Sir Andrew Undershaft in *Major Barbara*—William H. Whyte Jr.'s *The Organization Man* appears the more apt characterization.

Consider John DeLorean who, with a $550,000 salary and a shot at the presidency of General Motors at age 48, suddenly quit. He complained that one simply couldn't be an innovator, a planner, on the 14th floor of the G.M. building in Detroit. "You were too harassed and oppressed by committee meetings and paperwork. It [GM] has gotten to be a total insulation from the realities of the world." At a May 1972 conference in Wilmington, Delaware, on business management structures in major countries, Charles Wilson, a historian at Cambridge University, thought that the drive for more security through mergers and diversification was blotting out individuality and self-determination. *Washington Post* reporter William Jones, summarizing the conference's findings, wrote that "Many large business enterprises around the world are being turned into bland, unimaginative [institutions]. . . . And the men who run the large corporations follow similar patterns in their management direction, seeking to avoid controversy or competition and striving for perpetual security." Elsewhere, *Business Week* magazine has pointed to "no-risk supercautious management" as "the prime villain" in the "breakdown of U.S. innovation."

Political Power—In the political marketplace powerful corporations by the weight of their wealth can overwhelm the voices of individuals. This link between corporate power and political power existed long before Dita Beard held center stage for two months in 1972, but ITT's self-inflicted anguish over its antitrust problems spotlighted the problem for all to see: too often when a major company has much at stake, it possesses the resources and contacts to lobby the government into acquiescence.

The techniques of converting economic strength into political strength are reasonably clear. First, campaign contributions can help put sympathetic legislators into office. As Senator Boies Penrose candidly explained to a group of his business patrons at the turn of the century, "You send us to Congress; we pass laws under which you make money; . . . and out of your profits you further contribute to our campaign funds to send us back again to pass more laws to enable you to make more money." The 1925 Campaign Finance Act notwithstanding, Penrose's ethic prevailed and was the source of much of the Watergate Special Prosecutor's business; and since the Federal Election Commission decided to allow corporations to raise money in political action committees, the 1974 Federal Campaign Finance Act may have encouraged what Fred Wertheimer of Common Cause called an "explosion" of corporate money in politics.

Second, there is the benefit of having friends in high places. President Gerald Ford regularly golfs with the U.S. Steel lobbyist William Whyte, not Common Cause chairman John Gardner. When Elmer Bobst, chairman of Warner-Lambert and godfather to Tricia Nixon, had an antitrust problem, he felt free to bypass the Justice Department. "I never opened my mouth to the President about the case," protested Bobst, adding, however, "I did talk to other people in the White House about it, though."

Third, prominent businessmen enter and exit prominent government positions with rapid-fire regularity. Large contingents of oil men at the Federal Energy Administration; generals in defense firms; businessmen like Roy Ash, William Simon, Peter Flanigan, and Bryce Harlow in Cabinet level posts—the examples are many. Equally prominent are the number of senior government officials, such as onetime Environmental Protection Agency chief William Ruckelshaus, who have left government to represent big business.

Fourth, large companies can employ fleets of lobbyists to push for favorable policies and call upon affiliated interests to reinforce their positions; thus, GM in early 1975 sent a letter to 1.3 million shareholders, 13,000 dealers, and 19,000 suppliers asking them to press their Congressmen to postpone safety and emissions standards for five years. Finally, big business can possess the kind of technical data that the federal government does not have, or does not want to have—natural gas reserve data, for example.

Together the above methods create an unhealthy dependence by government on business, or what a July 4, 1972 *New York Times* editorial called "The Corporate State." The editorial concluded that "the overriding issue is how to prevent powerful special interests from frustrating the democratic process."

• *The Corporate Welfare State*—An extensive system of direct and indirect federal subsidies to the largest firms costs American taxpayers many billions of dollars annually. For example, a consumer group's analysis of President Ford's $357 billion budget in 1975 found that $3.2 billion was paid directly to the largest corporations in the agribusiness, air and shipping industries. The federal government currently pays up to 39 percent of the cost of building a U.S. ship and 70 percent of merchant marine labor costs, although studies by economist Allen Ferguson and others have forcefully argued that "there appears to be little net economic contribution to the U.S. by the subsidized liner firms." Another $21.2 billion in direct or indirect tax subsidies went to all corporations; the bulk, according to Rep. Charles Vanik's studies, were garnered by the very largest corporations. The 1971 Domestic International Sales Corporation (DISC) plan, for example, exempts large corporations from paying federal taxes on one-half of their export profits as a device to increase exports. Yet U.S. exports in 1971 totaled roughly $40 billion and DISC was only expected to increase exports by $1.5 billion. So 96 percent of the exports DISC would subsidize would have occurred anyway, which means that taxpayers lose $2 in revenues (a total of $1.3 billion in 1976) for every $1 in new exports.*

A trait common to many corporate subsidies is inefficiency—

---

* Corporate welfare programs must also include contract and regulatory "subsidies." Seventy-five billion dollars of President Ford's 1975 budget went to companies in the form of procurement, research and development and consulting contracts—most going to the biggest American corporations. Some 70 percent of the Defense Department's $39.5 billion procurement budget, for instance, went to the hundred largest prime contractors. The well-documented and massive waste in such programs understandably induce corporations to be the recipients of these contracts.

Federal regulatory policies have been noteworthy more for the way they have entrenched oligopoly power than for the way they have promoted competition—with the result that air fares, for instance, are up to 50 percent higher than competition would provide. The aggregate cost to consumers from regulation by the Interstate Commerce Commission, the Civil Aeronautics Board and the Federal Communications Commission was $16–24 billion a year according to a collection of economic studies in 1973. These subsidies are discussed in detail in Green (ed.), *The Monopoly Makers: The Nader Report on Regulation and Competition* (*1973*).

the inefficiency natural to programs created because of corporate political power rather than genuine economic need. After a comprehensive eight part study of federal subsidy programs in 1974, Congress's Joint Economic Committee concluded, "On the whole these studies showed that many subsidies do not work well economically, they are often directed at out-moded or non-existent objectives. They redistribute income to the affluent, and in too many cases their costs far exceed their benefits to society as a whole."

Privacy Invasions—Confronted by employee theft or suspicions of disloyalty, overzealous companies have at times fulfilled George Orwell's worst fears. During the labor conflicts in the 1930s—three decades before Vincent Gillen began investigating Ralph Nader—General Motors' "spy system was one of the most vicious in the country," according to William Manchester in *The Glory and the Dream*. Hearings before Senator Edward Long's Subcommittee on Administrative Practices and Procedures in 1965 documented a pattern of "eavesdropping techniques": corporations testified to monitoring telephone conversations, placing hidden microphones in washrooms and lounge areas, deploying company spies, installing false ceilings with peepholes, and bribing the employees of rival companies. In 1975, the Senate Subcommittee on Constitutional Rights heard estimates that up to one-fourth of the major U.S. corporations require polygraph tests as a condition of employment. Reported questions probed the applicant's sex life, political preferences, and relationships with his family—questions that even the FBI is prohibited from asking its applicants. But most job seekers, hostage to their need for employment, can do little about such intrusions.

Local Sway—Perhaps the most obvious hostages of corporate power are those communities which depend on large companies for their existence, even as these companies tax these communities in numerous ways.

Local plants can provide employment—and pollution, as Gary, Indiana, understands about U.S. Steel. Subsidiaries of giant firms can exploit and damage local services: when a Union Camp manager was asked whether his company's heavy industrial pumping might dry up Savannah, Georgia's underground water supplies, he replied, "I don't know. I won't be here." Large companies possess and often exploit their leverage to bargain down the amounts of local tax they must pay. The Mayor's office in Gary estimated that U.S. Steel properties there had been underassessed by about $140 million in 1971, enabling the firm to avoid paying $16–23 million in taxes. "Avoidance of state tax liabilities by America's largest corporations," concludes Byron Dorgan, North Dakota's tax commissioner, "has reached scandalous proportions."

Especially in company towns, such as St. Marys, Georgia, or Pullman, Illinois, the dominant corporation can control public opinion and political activities—a syndrome which can apply as well to "company states" like Delaware. In January 1974, four editors at Wilmington's *The Morning News* and *The Evening Journal*, both run by DuPont interests, either resigned or were fired; the editors said that their boards of directors opposed news stories that embarrassed or reflected adversely on the DuPont family. While locally dominant corporations can be oppressive, absentee corporations with national interests can be indifferent to community needs. For many plant managers at local subsidiaries, their town is a temporary station on the way to success in New York City or Los Angeles. "IBM is famous for never allowing anyone to take up roots . . . they're constantly moving people around the country," complains Congressman Hamilton Fish (R.–N.Y.), who has IBM facilities in his district. Sociological, economic, and congressional studies have documented this lack of civic involvement and its erosive effects on community well-being.

To take one example, Professor C. Wright Mills in 1946 compared three pairs of cities: in each pair was a "big-business city," where a few large absentee-owned firms provided most of the industrial employment, and a "small business city," where many smaller, locally owned firms comprised the community's economic life. Using such variables as unemployment rates, suburban sprawl, income distribution, the frequency of home ownership, the number of libraries, and per capita expenditures for schools, Mills concluded that "big business tends to depress while small business tends to raise the level of civic welfare."

Deceptive Information—Large corporations also possess, in Richard Neustadt's description of American presidents, "the power to persuade." The average American adult sees 40,000 commercials *a year* on television. The top 100 national advertisers spent $3.6 billion in 1974 in the effort to favorably shape their corporate image and consumer purchasing decisions, an effort which to a large extent succeeds: one study concluded that if advertising expenditures were limited to 3 percent of the sales revenues for 14 specific industries that exceeded that level, their aggregate sales would have declined by 16.7 percent.

Ideally, informational advertising can educate consumers about best buys and hence encourage the intelligent allocation of economic resources. All too often, however, corporate advertising is the inane, misleading, or deceptive fare we digest daily on television. Instead of advertising about price and quality, leading companies strive to associate their products with alluring superstars or seductive moods—Catherine Deneuve and Chanel, or the Marlboro Country. In the food industry, ads as informative as "Mmm, Mmm good" and "anyone can be a Frito bandito" prevail, as the least nutritious foods tend to be the most heavily advertised. Potlatch Forests illustrated its environmental concern by a nationwide advertisement showing a picture of a spanking clean Clearwater River in Idaho, where Potlatch has a pulp mill, with the caption, "It cost us a bundle, but the Clearwater still runs clear." The photograph, however, had been taken many miles *upstream* from its polluting pulp mill. When a public interest law firm affiliated with Georgetown University studied advertising submissions by television manufacturers to the Federal Trade Commission, it found that nearly 60 percent of the ads were inadequately substantiated.

Product Safety—Perhaps it is a lingering belief in caveat emptor, or the knowledge that judicial hurdles make successful suits unlikely, but American business has a poor record on product safety. Too often its products add to the GNP in two ways: in manufacturing output *and* in increased expenditures for those injured, maimed, or killed.

There are several gauges to measure this consumer cost. The 1966 Traffic Safety Act has led to the recall of 35 million cars between 1967 and 1974. Recent data indicate that overprescription promoted by drug companies leads to 60,000 to 140,000 deaths each year. Cosmetics injure 60,000 people annually, mostly women who suffer skin eruptions, loss of hair, severe allergic reactions, and burns. Then there was the engineering director at General Dynamics who sent the following memorandum to his superior a few years ago: "It seems to me inevitable that, in the 20 years ahead of us, DC-10 cargo doors will come open and cargo compartments will experience decompression for other reasons and I expect this to usually result in loss of the airplane"; he added that floor changes would be costly, but "may well be less expensive than the cost of damages resulting from the loss of one plane-load of people." This advice was ignored, and two years later a Turkish Airlines DC-10 crashed in France after its cargo door blew open, killing all 346 passengers.

In 1968, the National Commission on Product Safety reported that each year 20 million Americans were injured severely enough in product related accidents to require medical treatment; 585,000 were hospitalized, another 110,000 permanently injured, and 30,000 died—at a cost to the economy of $5.5 billion. This grim rollcall led to the creation of the Consumer Product Safety Commission in 1973.

The Price of Technology—Luddites notwithstanding, advancing technology can of course greatly enhance the quality of life. Which is why the Greek word *"techne,"* from which technology is derived, meant "art." From penicillin to transistorization, the benefits of research and development can be seen all around us. "Modern technology is creating a society of such complex diversity and richness," observes Buckminster Fuller, "that most people have a greater range of personal choice [and] wider experience than ever before."

On the other hand, technology is also quite capable of exacting a catastrophic price from society. This is especially true given the complexity and interconnection of modern life—e.g., a power failure at a single switching station in Canada throws the east coast of the United States into darkness. It was one thing when an individual consumer bought and drank some noxious snake oil potion from a traveling salesman a century ago; but when thousands of pregnant women abroad consume Thalidomide, leading to horribly deformed babies, it is quite another.

When problems involving nuclear power or pesticides or aerosol cans become public, those industries with financial interests in these technologies often simply assert that they are the experts and that their technology is safe. But when the health and safety of hundreds of millions of citizens are at stake, pure assertions of reliability are not enough—especially given how wrong self-serving experts can be. The Titanic was supposedly unsinkable; it sank. The Maginot Line was a supposedly impregnable barrier; it was outflanked in three days.

Corporate Concentration—National and state laws regarding the economy assume the existence of a competitive enterprise system. Judge Learned Hand best appreciated the virtue of competition and evil of monopoly when he wrote, in 1946, "Many people believe that possession of unchallenged economic power deadens initiative, discourages thrift and depresses energy; that immunity from competition is a narcotic, and rivalry a stimulant, to industrial progress; that the spur of constant stress is necessary to counteract an inevitable disposition to let well enough alone." Yet by 1976, in John Kenneth Galbraith's useful dichotomy, the American economy could be functionally divided into two economies: the market system and the planning system. In the former, small businessmen and service firms compete among themselves according to the model of the marketplace. But the planning system, by and large the financial, manufacturing and mining sectors, is dominated by our giant corporations—Alcoa, Reynolds and Kaiser in aluminum; IBM in computers. Beyond specific markets, huge conglomerate firms such as Textron and Gulf & Western have acquired holdings in numerous industries.

In 1955 it was estimated that 44.5 percent of those working in manufacturing worked for the top 500 companies; in 1970 it was 72 percent. Between 1948 and 1968, the largest 200 U.S. industrial firms increased their share of all industrial assets by 25 percent. Today, these 200 control two-thirds of all industrial production. Thus, in much of American industry, a few giant firms jointly act as would a monopolist or cartel. There are higher prices: the Federal Trade Commission has estimated that car and camera consumers overpay, respectively, nine and eleven percent for their products due to the concentrated structure of their industries. There are higher profits, as studies by Joe Bain and Leonard Weiss have documented. There is the frustration of federal monetary and fiscal policy, since our large corporations will maintain their high prices even if demand falls during periods of tight money. There is waste: without the "stimulus" of competition, economist Frederic Sherer estimates monopoly waste and inefficiency at 10 percent of costs.

Like many consumer problems, the high cost of monopoly is invisible to the naked eye. If it could be transmuted into black children riding school buses into white neighborhoods, or a comatosed consumer kept alive by life-saving devices as an overreaching businessman threatens to pull the plug, perhaps the subject would work its way into the headlines. But Professor Walter Adams understands the problem even without these dramatics. "It poses the No. 1 domestic problem of our time—the prevalence of private socialism in what we like to think of as a free enterprise economy."

Multinational Corporations—As the world GNP increases at about 5 percent annually and the world's multinational community grows by some 10 percent annually, one can understand why the U.S. Chamber of Commerce predicts that by the year 2000 a few hundred multinational corporations will own $4 trillion in assets, or 54 percent of the projected world wealth. To the managers of American-based worldcorps—and 13 of the largest 20 in the world are American—this is an encouraging development toward world peace and prosperity.

But there are vigorous dissenters. To the American labor movement, these companies are the modern version of the runaway shop: they flee to nonunionized, low-paying outposts like Singapore (Gulf) or Spain (Ford), thereby exporting jobs (the AFL-CIO has estimated that multinationals cost 900,000 American workers their jobs between 1966 and 1971). Labor is also anxious that it may lose its ability to strike—and hence its collective bargaining leverage—if multinationals can move abroad when American labor increases its demands or can increase production in their foreign facilities when they are struck in the United States. As Henry Ford II said after Ford's English workers at Dagenham began organizing, "Behave yourselves or we will go elsewhere."

These worldcorps cite the multiple benefits they bestow on underdeveloped countries, though often the benefits flow in the opposite direction. They often merely buy out existing local firms rather than build new facilities, use local capital rather than import U.S. capital, and, between 1960 and 1968, according to a U.N.-sponsored study, were able to take 79 percent of their profits out of Latin America. Between 1950 and 1965, the profit inflow to the United States from third world investments was 264 percent of capital outflow. The multinationals, with subsidiaries in many countries, can manipulate their charges for services and transactions via intrafirm transfer payments to disguise earnings and minimize tax payments to their host countries. For example, the United Kingdom Monopolies Commission recently discovered that while the Hoffman La Roche drug firm had earned 25 million pounds between 1966 and 1972, it declared only three million pounds—passing on the difference from high-tax Britain to low-tax Switzerland.

Multinationals may use underdeveloped countries as dumping grounds for products thay have trouble marketing elsewhere due to strict regulatory laws. Hazardous drugs are marketed abroad that are either prohibited in the U.S. or that require warning labels regarding their use. Finally, however benevolent their intentions, multinational corporations often fail to adapt their technology to the needs of their underdeveloped host nations. They may insist on capital-intensive production rather than the labor-intensive facilities needed in densely populated areas. Or they may unwittingly promote a cultural imperialism which perverts local custom for "Western progress." Richard Barnet and Ronald Müller, in their *Global Reach*, write that "It is not uncommon in Mexico, doctors who work in villages report, for a family to sell the few eggs and chickens it raises to buy Coke for the father while the children waste away for lack of protein."

Concentration of Wealth and Income—Business managers proclaim a "People's Capitalism" in which 25 million Americans are shareholders, while labor leaders—whose unions represent under 25 percent of all workers—understandably extol their own influence on maintaining decent wages. The large companies, to be sure, are our major disbursers of income in the form of dividends, interest, and wages. But a concentration of ownership and income misdirects these benefits toward an elite who are already wealthy and away from most Americans who are not. According to a 1962 Federal Reserve System study, one percent of all shareholders held 72 percent of all corporate stock. Based on Census data, the top 5 percent of Americans hold 53 percent of net private wealth, and the bottom 60 percent hold only 7.5 percent. While the poorest fifth of the U.S. earned 3.7 percent of the nation's income, the top fifth earned 47.9 percent; the top one percent earned 10.5 percent of all income, or 51 times the per capita income earned by the poorest fifth.

Business Crime—"If the word 'subversive' refers to efforts to make fundamental changes in a social system," sociologist Edwin Sutherland wrote more than two decades ago, "business leaders are the most subversive influence in the United States." In the past that notion would either rankle or amuse most corporate managers, but today, in the midst of what can only be called a corporate crime wave, they cannot dismiss its accuracy.

The Special Prosecutor's Office has successfully prosecuted 22 individuals and 18 companies—Phillips Petroleum, 3M, American Airlines, Goodyear Tire, among others—for violations of the campaign finance laws. The Securities and Exchange Commission (SEC) has sued 17 firms for their failure to disclose, as required under the securities laws, the existence of political slush funds at home or bribes abroad. Admitted foreign law violations include a $4 million payoff by Gulf Oil to South Korea, a $1.25 million bribe by United Brands to reduce export taxes in Honduras, and a $450,000 bribe by the Northrop Corporation to two Saudi Arabian generals to obtain lucrative arms contracts. In March 1976, SEC Chairman Roderick Hills informed the Senate Banking Committee that the commission has examined or is examining some 75 other corporations. Hills indicated that 55 of the largest 500 industrial corporations, whose combined 1974 revenues equaled $220 billion dollars, may have made unlawful payments. In April, 1976, the Internal Revenue Service announced it had sent a questionnaire to 1200 corporations to investigate possible tax fraud in connection with foreign or U.S. bribes. So far over half a billion dollars in illegal bribes have been disclosed—and the story, as of this writing, is still unfolding.

Nor has the "Corporate Watergate" been limited to violations of the SEC and campaign finance laws. Joe Sims, an official at the Antitrust Division, complained in early 1976 that based on his

agency's record number of grand jury investigations and actual indictments, "price-fixing is a common business practice." Nine
major grain companies have been convicted of a conspiracy to
short-weigh—or steal from—wheat and rice shipments made by
the U.S. to foreign nations under the Food for Peace program. Executives at the now defunct W.T. Grant Company were charged
with taking hundred-thousand-dollar kickbacks on store sitings.
The Internal Revenue Service obtained an indictment of 3M for tax
fraud relating to its slush fund, and announced it was investigating
111 other companies for similar violations. The Civil Aeronautics
Board has uncovered how Braniff Airways failed to record the sale
of 3,626 tickets in order to finance its illegal campaign giving. And
press reports have disclosed how aerospace firms seeking Pentagon
contracts have lavished valuable benefits on procurement officials;
Northrup had Defense Department personnel to its duck hunting
lodge 144 times between 1971 and 1973—activities that appear to
violate Executive Order 11222, which prohibits procurement officials from accepting anything of monetary value from companies
seeking contracts.

It is difficult to believe that these cases are mere aberrations.
Many of the most important and established corporations in the
country are involved, firms apparently no more or less prone than
other firms to prevailing political and commercial pressures. These
companies include such diverse industries as aerospace, food processing, oil, sewing machines, airlines, banking, and office supplies. Indeed the prevalent rationales for these crimes—it's the way
business is done abroad; if we don't do it, our competitors will—
lead to the conclusion that this pattern of illegality is customary
and pervasive.

This conclusion is corroborated by the general empirical data
which exist on business crime and morality: in the 18 months ending in December 1974, the FBI announced that white collar convictions were up 30 percent; Public Citizen's 1974 Staff Report on
White Collar Crime reports that frauds and embezzlements have
increased 313 percent since 1969; in a study by the Corporate Accountability Research Group of the presidents of *Fortune*'s top 1000
firms, 60 percent of the 110 respondents agreed that "many price-
fix"; in a 1975 poll by University of Georgia professor Archie Car-

roll, three-fifths of corporate executives say that young managers in business would commit unethical acts to exhibit their loyalty to superiors. "At Carthage," said Greek historian Polybius, in words still echoing two millennia later, "nothing which results in profits is regarded as disgraceful."

Large business firms, to be sure, have been creators of wealth and jobs, a major reason why our real per capita income has tripled in the past forty years. Corporate philanthropy totals some $1 billion annually—or six percent of all philanthropy in the country. Still, invocations of corporate responsibility notwithstanding, the social balance sheet of big business contains enormous debits— economic, political and social. In the last decade alone, an avalanche of congressional, academic and journalistic reports on business abuses can lead only true believers or Dr. Pangloss to remain upbeat about corporate power in America.

Which leads naturally to the question: where is the law? When confronted with social or economic wrongdoing, presumably the law—the reflection of democratic will—can provide a remedy. Has it historically done so?

II

The Collapse of
State Corporation Law

We have nothing left but our great empty corporation statutes—towering sky-scrapers internally welded together and containing nothing but wind.

—Professor Bayless Manning

FROM ENGLAND the colonies inherited a corporate law very different from that we know today. Most strikingly, the earliest American corporation law made no distinction between a "public" corporation, such as a city or a hospital, and a "private" corporation, such as a bank. Since a corporation was considered an extension of the state, it could only be created by the state. In each instance, the colonial assembly enacted a compact or "special charter" which specified the terms of corporate existence. Typically, in return for the corporation agreeing to perform a service considered of general value, the legislature granted it the advantage of perpetual existence, the power to purchase and hold property collectively, and the right to sue or be sued collectively.

Since the earliest business corporations were also granted monopoly privileges, they were not very popular. As a result, at most forty business corporations had been chartered prior to the Constitutional Convention. "Puny institutions," Professor Eugene Rostow has called them. Local, restricted by their charters to designated lines of business, the earliest business corporations played a minor role in an economy "addicted to agriculture" and unaccustomed to the aggregation of capital outside of the family.

Yet almost overnight, the requirements of the new republic transformed the business corporation into an important instrument of economic development. The overriding concern of all levels of government in the first decades of the United States was to restore commerce. At the state level, this primarily meant the encouragement of inland transportation projects such as turnpikes, bridges, and canals and the establishment of bank and insurance facilities. Since the states, heavily burdened by Revolutionary War debts, could not directly finance internal improvements, they supplemented grants of incorporation with valuable privileges to encourage private investment. Not only were shareholders allowed to profit from administering essentially public enterprises, but their risk was further reduced by state loans or state purchases of shares, tax exemptions, rights to conduct fund-raising lotteries, and, on rare occasion, direct state bounties.

So bolstered, the number of incorporations soared. In the ten years 1790–1800, the total number of corporations chartered by the first 16 states increased from 37 to 334. Yet the functions of the corporation were little changed. In 1790 nearly half the charters were for the improvement of inland navigation; by 1800, 219 of the earliest corporations, or 65.4 percent, served this general need. In 1790, 11 corporations, or 30 percent, were engaged in banking or insurance; by 1800 67 corporations, or 20 percent, were so engaged. In 1790, exactly three manufacturing corporations had been chartered; by 1800, the number had increased negligibly to eight.

It was not until the War of 1812 and the tortuous British embargo that the number of manufacturing corporations increased significantly. "In this situation," explained Harvard Law School's late Professor E. Merrick Dodd, "some state governments appear to have adopted the view that the chartering of domestic manufacturing associations was a matter of patriotism. Between 1808 and 1815 New York issued more charters (165) to joint stock companies engaged in manufacturing than to all public utilities combined." By 1830, nearly 600 of the 1900 business corporations chartered in the New England states were engaged in manufacturing or mining.

Like the earlier colonial corporations, the state corporations of the 1790–1830 period were essentially "chips off the block of sovereignty." Traditional state powers such as those of eminent domain, road planning, or setting toll rates were liberally delegated to turnpike, bridge, and canal builders. But as the number of incorporations swelled, the corporate character also changed. New privileges such as limited liability exemplified this change. Initially, a great advantage of the corporation's quasi-public character had been its power to enforce unlimited assessment of its members in times of debt. Though unlimited shareholder liability certainly protected the fortunes of creditors, it was early recognized that it deterred incorporations. Beginning with New York in 1811, within the next two decades several state legislatures limited the liability of shareholders to the stated share value. Those capable of wrangling a special charter from the state legislature could then solicit capital with the assurance that a business failure would not endanger their other personal assets.

The ensuing proliferation of bank and manufacturing corporations ultimately undermined the quasi-public character of the business corporation. In its landmark *Dartmouth College* decision of 1819, the United States Supreme Court distinguished between the "private" corporation, whose property was employed primarily for the benefit of its shareholders, and the "public" corporation, which existed only for public purposes. More importantly, the Court held that all corporate charters were protected by the United States Constitution clause prohibiting a state "from impairing the obligation of contracts." Under that ruling, after granting a corporate charter, a legislature could no longer repeal or revise it.

THE JACKSONIAN REACTION

By the time of Andrew Jackson's presidency, the role of the private business corporation had become a matter of intense political dispute. Anticorporate sentiment crystalized around President Jackson's "War on the Bank." In 1836, the charter of the Second Bank of the United States was to expire. Although a private, profit-seeking corporation, the Bank performed many of the monetary and credit functions of the present Federal Reserve Board.

In 1832, Jackson vetoed the Act to extend the term of the Bank's charter principally because of the Bank's tendency to concentrate "power in the hands of a few men irresponsible to the people." His veto message emphasized themes applicable to all specially chartered business corporations:

Distinctions in society will always exist under every just government. Equality of talents, of education, or of wealth can not be produced by human institutions . . . but when the laws undertake to add to these natural and just advantages artificial distinctions . . . to make the rich richer and the potent more powerful, the humble members of society—the farmers, the mechanics, and laborers—who have neither the time nor the means of securing like favors to themselves, have a right to complain of the injuries of their government.

Within months, the "War on the Bank" had been broadened into an attack on all corporate privileges. William Gouge, then a leading egalitarian economist, summarized the Jacksonian position:

Against corporations of every kind, the objection may be brought that whatever power is given to them is so much taken from either the government or the people. As the object of charters is to give to members of companies power which they would not possess in their individual capacity, the very existence of monied corporations is incompatible with equality of rights.

The essence of the Jacksonian assault was not against the corporate form per se but against the monopoly privileges that so often accompanied the special charter. Rather than abolish the corporation, most Jacksonians sought to make its advantages freely available. Such "liberalism" harmonized well with the economic realities of the day. The industrialization of the United States began during the 1830–1860 decades. Textile manufacturing —our first domestic industry—was almost completely mechanized by 1860. Iron smelting matured; coal and steam power became widely used. Entrepreneurs applied machine tools to the fabrication of arms, clocks, sewing machines, rubber, glass and tin products on a factory scale. The railroad—"America's first big business"—grew from a local curiosity into an important local transportation. The 1850s, calculated historian Stuart Bruchey, "saw a phenomenal increase in incorporation, with nearly half of all corporations chartered between 1800 and 1860 appearing in that decade."

The effect of three decades of Jacksonian politics was to transform the nature of the business corporations. The constitutions of several states were amended to enjoin their legislatures from creating corporations by special act "when the object of the incorporation is attainable by general laws." Under the new general incorporation acts, the hated privileges of the special acts were abolished. The corporate form—once available only to those few capable of lobbying a legislature—became automatically available to everyone who satisfied certain minimum requirements.

At the same time, the general incorporation acts of this period imposed limitations on corporate size and activity. First, there were limitations upon authorized capital. Well into the nineteenth century, few states permitted corporations to aggregate more than $500,000 or $1 million. Similarly, severe limitations were imposed on the amount of indebtedness, and the power of one corporation to hold stock in another was neither conferred nor implied. Second, limitations upon the scope of a business corporation's powers were also universal. Until 1837 every state in the Union limited incorporation to a single purpose of a limited number of purposes, such as a particular transportation, mining, or manufacturing project. Third, corporate charters were limited to a term of years—generally 20, 30, or 50 years in duration. And corporations were limited geographically as well. Several states prohibited corporations from doing business or owning property outside the state of their creation.

The general corporation acts established the power of shareholders to direct the policy of their corporation as well. The shareholders meeting—much like a New England town meeting—became the critical decision-making forum. At the meeting, any proposal to change the corporation's assets, share structure, capitalization, or by-laws had to be *unanimously* approved. To assure strict conformity with their will, the shareholders annually chose directors by majority vote. The directors, in turn, appointed a manager or other agents to execute their business plans. For many years, shareholder control was further augmented by the common law principle that directors could be removed at will.

Underlying the Jacksonian statutes was a basic fear of corporate power. "First, there was the fear of monopoly," Justice

Brandeis would subsequently explain. "Then the fear of domination more general. Fear of encroachment upon the liberties and opportunities of the individual. Fear of the subjection of labor to capital. Fear that the absorption of capital by corporations, and their perpetual life, might bring evils similar to those which attended mortmain. There was a sense of some insidious menace inherent in large aggregations of capital."

This distrust of the corporation also appeared in the judicial decisions of the Jacksonian epoch. Most famously, Chief Justice Taney contravened the effect of the *Dartmouth College* case by holding in the 1837 case of *Charles River Bridge v. Warren Bridge* that monopolistic privileges were never to be implied, even if the grant, without such privileges, was of little use. "The continued existence of a government would be of no great value," Taney generalized, "if by implications and presumptions, it was disarmed of the powers necessary to accomplish the ends of its creation; and the functions it was designed to perform, transferred to the hands of privileged corporations." Thus where the *Dartmouth College* case tended to free the corporation from government regulation, the *Charles River Bridge* case decisively reduced corporate autonomy.

THE TRUSTS

The hallmark of the Jacksonian economy was its atomization. Business firms tended to be small, and bought their raw materials and sold their finished goods locally. "Vertical integration" was a concept barely known. Farmers and miners who produced raw materials were largely separate from the concerns which processed goods. When a firm manufactured for a market more than a few miles from the factory, it bought and sold through independent agents who handled the business of several other firms as well.

During the decades after the Civil War, the character of the United States economy was radically transformed. On May 10, 1869, the first transcontinental rail line was completed at Promontory Point, Utah. This linkage symbolized the great age of railway construction. In the next decade, a staggering 20 percent of United States capital formation was devoted to extending rail line systems. Trunk lines burgeoned in the Middle Atlantic states and the North

Central states and then across the Great Plains and finally into the South.

By greatly broadening the markets of an agrarian economy, the railroads quickened the growth of such established commercial centers as New York, Philadelphia and St. Louis, and helped populate such new centers as Chicago, Minneapolis, Kansas City, Dallas, and Atlanta. In the four decades prior to 1880, the proportion of urban population rose from 11 to 28 percent; by 1900, it had risen to 40 percent. This great urban expansion increased the demand for consumer goods such as clothing, food, and whiskey. At the same time, railroad construction created the first large market for producers' goods such as steel.

The genesis of a national transportation network and an expanding urban market made possible a new type of business corporation. For the first time, a single manufacturer could dominate not just a local market, not just a regional one, but an entire national market. To the corporation, the advantages of such a national monopoly were obvious. Risk would be reduced. No longer would rivals compete for markets, or raw materials, the best locations, or labor. Without competition, capital would be easier to secure. Money need not be squandered on advertising or independent salesmen or price wars. More importantly, without competition, profits would be increased. It was an insight as ancient as Aristotle that the merchant who controls a market may charge a monopoly price.

The great eastern railroad corporations were the first to secure important national monopolies. Exploiting their strategic position by discriminatory freight rates and refusals to deal, eight railroad corporations were able to wrest ownership of 95 percent of the anthracite coal industry by 1893. Similar monopolies were achieved in bituminous coal, kerosene, matches, stoves, furnaces, steam and hot water heaters, boilers, gas pipelines, and candles. As the journalist Henry Demarest Lloyd exclaimed:

A new law of industry is rising into view. Ownership of the highways ends in ownership of everything and everybody that must use the highways. . . .
The railroads compel private owners to sell them their mines or all the

product by refusing to supply cars, and by charging freight rates so high that every one but themselves loses money on every ton sent to market. When the railroads elect to have the output large, they furnish many cars; when they elect to have the output small, they furnish few cars; and when they elect that there shall be no output whatever, they furnish no cars.

Geopolitics was not, however, a business method reserved to railroads. Soon after the Civil War, producers of cordage, gunpowder, whiskey, upholstery felt, and other products organized "output pools" to regulate competition by apportioning production and setting prices. Occasionally pooling associations were successful. Often, however, these "gentlemen's agreements" were violated or monopoly profits attracted new competitors who were less "gentlemanly."

In 1871, John D. Rockefeller, who was decidedly less gentlemanly, set out to consolidate the oil refining industry under a more effective legal form. Already Rockefeller had become the leading refiner in Cleveland by combining several local refineries and then persuading two of three competitive railroad lines to secretly rebate 37½ percent of the freight tariff on crude oil shipments from the Pennsylvania oil region and on refined oil shipments to the eastern states. His Standard Oil Company was able to secure these advantages from the railroads because of its large capacity (4 percent of the oil refined in the nation) and because Cleveland's refiners could ship east or west by water if railroad rates were not to their liking.

In late 1871, Rockefeller met with the leading refiners of Philadelphia and Pittsburgh to form a corporation capable of monopolizing the entire oil refining industry. By contract, dated January 18, 1872, their concerns merged into the "South Improvement Company." Although the Company possessed less than 10 percent of the refining capacity of the nation, the strategic locations of its refineries enabled Rockefeller to persuade each of the three regional railroads to sign contracts, to cooperate "as far as it legally might to maintain the business of the South Improvement Company against injury by competition, and to lower or raise the gross rates of transportation for such times and to such extent as might be necessary to overcome the competition." This reference to legality was gratuitous. Contrary to judicial decisions requiring common carriers to charge equal rates to all customers, Rockefeller secured substantial rebates for the Company; e.g., a 40-cent-per-barrel rebate on the regular 80-cent rate for oil shipped from Titusville, Pennsylvania to Cleveland, Ohio. Emboldened by his success, Rockefeller argued that the rival rail lines would destroy themselves competing for oil freight unless a single refining corporation allocated a settled proportion of oil shipments among them. All three rail lines were thus induced to rebate to the South Improvement Company $1.06 per barrel on the regular rate of $2.56 for oil shipped from Pennsylvania to New York by any *competitor* of the South Improvement Company!

Rockefeller wielded this railroad contract like a club. On the date it was signed, there were twenty-six rival refineries in Cleveland. Rockefeller threatened "to crush" any competitor which did not sell its refinery to his Standard Oil Company. Within three months, Ida Tarbell reports:

The entire independent oil interest of Cleveland collapsed. . . . Of the twenty-six refineries, at least twenty-one sold out. From a capacity of probably not over 1,500 barrels of crude a day the Standard Oil Company rose . . . to one of 10,000 barrels. By this maneuver it became master of over one-fifth of the refining capacity in the United States.

The most extraordinary aspect of Rockefeller's tactic was that the railroad contract had not yet gone into effect. It never did. It never could. Not only did it violate established law, but the day the rate discriminations became known, every oil producer in Pennsylvania refused to sell to the South Improvement Company. Shortly thereafter, the Pennsylvania legislature rescinded the charter of the South Improvement Company.

Although a committee of the United States Congress condemned the South Improvement Company as the "most gigantic and daring conspiracy a free country had ever seen," Rockefeller emerged unscathed and unchastened. In 1874, Rockefeller traded Standard Oil stock to purchase leading refineries in Philadelphia and Pittsburgh. Shortly thereafter he bought a major refinery in New York City. Fortified by new and far more surreptitious railroad rebates, Rockefeller applied the same business tactics nationally that he had first employed in Cleveland. Within five years, he controlled 95 percent of all refined oil shipments.

But he did so through a corporate form that permanently altered the course of American history. Effectively blocked by the law of every state from organizing any one corporation large enough to possess the assets of 95 percent of the nation's refineries, Rockefeller's legendary counsel, S.C.T. Dodd, devised the corporate trust. Under a trust, several legally separate corporations deposited a controlling interest of their stock with a common board of trustees in return for a contractual right to dividends. In effect, the trust was a transparent evasion of chartering restrictions on corporate size. The trustees of the Standard Oil Trust had exactly the same powers as the managers of the earlier Standard Oil Company. But the Trust had one great advantage over an illegally organized corporation: it was totally secret. Only five to ten years later were the legislatures of Pennsylvania, New York, and Ohio able to establish that "Standard was simply a revival of the South Improvement Company."

The dimensions of the Standard Oil Trust's success were not lost on the business community. In 1884, a Cotton Oil Trust was organized in the State of Arkansas. In 1887, three great trusts, the "Whiskey Trust," the "Sugar Trust," and the "Lead Trust" were created. By 1890, twenty-four trusts with a total capitalization of $376,000,000 had been formed.

The reaction in most states was furious. Railroad regulatory statutes were enacted by Illinois, Iowa, Wisconsin, and Minnesota between 1871 and 1874. After the U.S. Supreme Court affirmed the constitutionality of state railroad commission regulation in 1877, thirty other states and the federal government enacted laws affecting railroad operation by 1890.

Also by 1890 twenty-seven states and territories had enacted laws intended to destroy or prevent trusts or monopolies. Fifteen states had taken the further precaution of incorporating antitrust provisions in their constitutions. And in 1890, when Congress enacted the Sherman Antitrust Act, it became the law everywhere that "Every contract, combination, in the form of trust or otherwise, or conspiracy, in restraint of trade . . . is declared to be illegal."

The trusts were on the ropes. In 1890, the high court of New York ruled it was a violation of law for corporations to enter into the "Sugar Trust" and ordered that "partnership" disbanded. And in 1892, in the most important case of all, the Supreme Court of Ohio ruled that the Standard Oil Trust was "organized for a purpose contrary to the policy of our laws" and therefore "void."

Without exception, each of these actions was based not upon the new antitrust statutes but rather upon the common law of corporations. Trusts were unlawful because the charters of the constituent corporations gave them no power to enter one. As the Ohio Supreme Court held, "The act so done is ultra vires [beyond the powers] of the corporation and against the public policy. . . ."

Of the early trusts that were national in scope, only one, the Standard Oil Trust, survived. It did so in blatant defiance of the law. Besides its unlawful organization, its repeated violations of common law antitrust doctrines, its several conspiracies to violate the common and statutory laws of common carriers, John D. Rockefeller or his associates apparently lied in testimony before the United States Congress in 1872, the legislatures of Ohio and New York in 1880, and trial courts in both states. Repeatedly Standard bribed employees of its customers or rival corporations or the railroads to gather information about its competitors' business. In 1884, Standard was alleged to have bribed the Ohio legislature to elect H. B. Payne, the father of Standard's Treasurer, to the United States Senate. Between 1890 and 1892, six separate attempts were made to bribe Ohio Attorney General David K. Watson to desist from his antitrust action. For five years, Standard refused to comply with the 1892 Ohio Supreme Court ruling ordering its dissolution. And in 1898, when Ohio's Attorney General Monnett brought a contempt action to revoke its charter, Standard survived only by taking advantage of the most deliberately subversive corporate law ever enacted.

NEW JERSEY—"THE TRAITOR STATE"

In 1890, James B. Dill, a young New York attorney, took the ferry across the Hudson to persuade the Governor of New Jersey to transform the Garden State into a "Mecca for Corporations." Like many businessmen and lawyers of his day, Dill believed that the large corporation was "inevitable and good." He believed that government, rather than restricting corporations, should free them to engage in unrestrained competition in the marketplace. This "war for survival" would not only eliminate the least competent, but it would hone the methods of the survivors. As John D. Rockefeller would later analogize, "The growth of a large business is merely the survival of the fittest. . . . The American Beauty Rose can be produced in the splendor and fragrance which bring cheer to its beholder only by sacrificing the early buds which grow up all around it."

But Dill did not go to Trenton to promote the tenets of Social Darwinism. He went there to get rich. And New Jersey did not legalize the business trust because of philosophical convictions. It did so to raise tax revenues and also, as documents in the archives of the State of New Jersey indicate, because the Governor, the Secretary of State, and other leading politicians of the state were bribed.

Dill's proposal to Governor Abbett was simplicity itself: Enact a corporate law that will enable business to do business "just as business pleases." Charge a designated incorporation fee and an even more substantial annual "franchise" tax. But do not keep this "liberal" law a secret. Quite the contrary, argued Dill: allow me to form "The Corporation Trust Company of New Jersey" to advertise it; let me persuade corporations, both big and small, of the advantages of incorporating in New Jersey.

With New Jersey experiencing a severe fiscal crisis, Governor Abbett's enthusiasm was immediate. And when Dill explained that the Corporation Trust Company could turn a profit by handling incorporation paperwork, Abbett was only too happy to accept stock in the Trust Company and serve as a director for the duration of his term in office. So, later, were Secretary of State Henry Kelsey and Democratic State Committee Chairman Allen McDermott, who also agreed to serve as officers of the Trust Company while holding political office.

In 1891 New Jersey went into the chartermongering business. A statute was rushed through the legislature authorizing New Jersey corporations to buy and sell the stock or property of other corporations and to issue their own stock as payment. This "Holding Company" Act effectively legalized the trust organization by authorizing a single corporation to control the stock or assets of its competitors in the same fashion as a trust. Lest anyone misunderstand, in 1892 New Jersey repealed its antitrust law. In 1893, New Jersey garnered $434,000 in corporation fees. Three years later the first "reform" governor of New Jersey in thirty years appointed James B. Dill to chair a Revision Committee, and by 1896 New Jersey had completely revolutionized corporate law.

Broadly, the General Revision Act of 1896 had three basic themes, which, to this day, comprise the heart of all "modern" state corporation statutes.

First, unlimited corporate size and market concentration were permitted. The "Holding Company" provision was broadened to read:

Any corporation may purchase, hold, sell, assign, transfer, mortgage, pledge, or otherwise dispose of the shares . . . or any bonds, securities, or evidences of indebtedness created by any other corporation or corporations of this or any other state, and while owner of such stock may exercise all the rights, powers, and privileges of ownership, including the right to vote thereon.

In the 1896 Act, however, these breathtaking privileges were mere prelude. The fifty-year limitation on corporate life was removed. Corporations might be formed for any lawful purpose. They could carry on their business in any state or in any foreign country. New Jersey corporations could merge or consolidate at will and thereafter the consolidated corporation could sell, mortgage, lease, or franchise any property so obtained.

Second, by revising capitalization requirements, New Jersey made concentration downright easy. In 1896, New Jersey invented "stock watering." Since 1891, New Jersey corporations had been allowed to purchase the stock of other corporations by payment in their own stock. In 1896 they were given carte blanche to exaggerate or "water" the value of the acquired company, for "the judgment of directors as to the value of property purchased shall be conclusive." This meant putative monopolists could buy up competing corporations without paying a penny in cash while offering the owners of the acquired corporation quantities of stock too irresistible to refuse. Everyone profited but the public investor. He or she was then induced to pay cash for shares in a giant "sound" corporation, some of whose assets were imaginary. Since New Jersey did not require stock promoters to disclose the basis of purported assets, shareholders "became pawns," in Professor William Ezra Ripley's words, "in the great game of chance by reason of that mystery."

And third, New Jersey's 1896 revisions eviscerated shareholder control. The 1896 Act permitted stockholders to be classified, preferred and common, and unequal power given to them. Consequently, the organizers of a corporation could sell large quantities of nonvoting stock to the public while retaining all of the voting stock for themselves. But a New Jersey corporation did not have to go that far. It could distribute voting stock to everyone while simultaneously granting directors the right to amend bylaws without the consent of shareholders. Or, it could rely solely on the "proxy" device. Under the revised law, all shareholder meetings were required to be held in New Jersey. Since it was usually inconvenient for most shareholders to attend meetings there, shareholders were given the Hobson's choice of not voting or signing proxies designating management representatives to vote for them.

After the 1896 Revision Act, the largest corporations, quite literally, flocked to New Jersey. In the prior 16-year period 1880–1896, exactly 15 corporations with authorized capital of $20,000,000 or more had been chartered under New Jersey's General Corporation Laws. In the next seven years, 1897–1904, 104 were. In 1896, New Jersey granted 854 charters and gained $857,000 in franchise tax revenues; in 1906, 2,093 firms were chartered there, generating $3.2 million in tax revenues.

As early as 1900, economist G. H. Montague estimated that 95 percent of the nation's "major" corporations were chartered in New Jersey. For example, Standard Oil, which was on the verge of losing its charter in Ohio for repeated violations of the law, reincorporated in New Jersey in 1899. In 1901, the United States Steel Corporation, then the nation's largest company, was incorporated in New Jersey with a total capitalization of $1,370,000,000. In 1904, John Moody identified five other "Greater Industrial Trusts": the Amalgamated Copper Corporation, the American Smelting and Refining Company, the American Sugar Refining Company, the

Consolidated Tobacco Company, and the International Mercantile Marine Company. All five were incorporated in New Jersey.

These same years witnessed the greatest merger movement in American history. In a dizzying seven-year period, the corporate law of one state helped transform the United States economy from a reasonably competitive to an oligopolistic structure. Shaw Livermore calculated that 328 combinations, effected between 1888 and 1905, controlled roughly two-fifths of the manufacturing capital of the country as of 1904. Abraham Kaplan of the Brookings Institution similarly concluded that of 92 "major" trusts in the year 1904, 78 controlled 50 percent or more of the sales in their respective fields; 26 of the 78 controlled 80 percent or more.

New Jersey's corporate laws were bitterly resented. Yet while muckraking journalists accused "Jersey" of "trafficking in treason" and other states vehemently protested this subversion of their corporate laws, New Jersey's only concern, according to Lincoln Steffens, was "Does it pay?"

It did. By 1902, New Jersey was earning so much from corporation filing fees and franchise taxes that it was able to abolish all property taxes and still pay off its entire state debt. By 1905, it had a $2,940,918 surplus in its treasury and a governor who could brag:

Of the entire income of the government, not a penny was contributed directly by the people. . . . The state is caring for the blind, the feebleminded, and the insane, supporting our prisoners and reformatories, educating the younger generations, developing a magnificent road system, maintaining the state governments and courts of justice, all of which would be a burden upon the taxpayer except for our present fiscal policy.

But retaliation against the "traitor state" was impossible, for the United States Supreme Court had ruled in 1886 that a corporation was a "citizen" within the meaning of the privileges and immunities clause of the Constitution. This meant that a corporation chartered by New Jersey had the same right to do business in a second state as a corporation chartered by that state. New Jersey buttressed this constitutional shield with two "retaliatory statutes": the first refused to enforce the criminal or contractual laws of any other state against a New Jersey corporation; the second provided that when the laws of any other state taxed or penalized a New Jersey corporation doing business in that other state, New Jersey would impose the same taxes or penalties on the corporations of that other state doing business in New Jersey.

As it became evident that New Jersey's ploy would work, other states—anxious for some of New Jersey's lucrative franchise tax income—decided to switch rather than fight. First West Virginia, then Maine, Delaware, Maryland, and Kentucky entered the charter-mongering business. As corporations and their annual fees gravitated toward the states with the laxest laws, the balance of the states began weakening their laws to hold onto their tax base. A law review note complained, "For a state to be conscientious would be synonymous with cutting its own throat." Social Darwinism was stood on its head. "[T]he corporate laws of the states tend to drag down one another to the level of the lowest. Competition between the states produces a survival of the unfit, a truly anomalous situation." Great industrial states such as Massachusetts and New York gutted their laws to reduce the attractions of New Jersey. The denominator kept getting lower. The Committee on Uniform Incorporation Law concluded in 1904:

The present system seems to offer:

1. The maximum of protection for fraud;

2. The minimum of protection and convenience for honest dealing; and

3. The best opportunity for small states and territories to fill their coffers with the proceeds of taxing outsiders, and the best chances for their petty public officials to get a good income without doing any work.

By 1912, New Jersey had reshaped the corporate law of virtually every state in its own image:

- Forty-two states, by then, permitted the organization of corporations for "any lawful purpose."

- Twenty-four states issued perpetual charters, and in most of the rest charter renewal had become pro forma.

- Eighteen states permitted the merger and consolidation of corporations. Such combinations were specifically prohibited in only two states and limited in only seven.

- Forty states had abolished the requirement that capital stock must be paid for in money.

- Nine states declared the judgment of the board of directors as to the value of property for which stock is issued conclusive except in case of fraud.

Ironically, of all the states with so-called "liberal" incorporation laws, only New Jersey ever reformed. In 1913, shortly after New Jersey's Governor Woodrow Wilson had been elected President, Wilson proposed seven detailed provisions (known as "The Seven Sisters Acts") to outlaw the trust and the holding company. In his final annual message as Governor, Wilson explained:

The corporation laws of the state notoriously stand in need of alteration. They are manifestly inconsistent with the policy of the Federal Government and with the interests of the people in the all-important matter of monopoly, to which the attention of the nation is now so earnestly directed. The laws of New Jersey, as they stand, so far from checking monopoly actually encourage it. . . . These are matters which affect the honor and good faith of the state. We should act upon them at once and with clear purpose.

Within days, a bemused nation witnessed the strange spectacle of a state known as "The Mother of Trusts" prohibiting any corporation or combination of corporations from: acquiring a monopoly; conspiring to limit production or increase prices; preventing competition; fixing prices; buying stock in competing corporations with a view toward controlling them; discriminating in price save on the basis of quantity, quality, transportation, or other "valid" charges; or issuing stock for property unless the property was the full equivalent of the money value of the stock.

This penitence proved short-lived. By 1917, New Jersey had repealed most of the "Seven Sisters Acts." But reform did have one enduring effect. New Jersey's hegemony of the incorporation of giant companies was forever shattered. Any state that could elect Woodrow Wilson governor could never be fully trusted by big business again. Henceforth, the largest corporations would have to look elsewhere to find a more congenial home.

DELAWARE—OPERA BOUFFE

What began as tragedy in New Jersey was institutionalized as farce in Delaware. Following New Jersey's lead, Wilmington attorney Josiah A. Marvel, with the aid of a New York attorney and the financial editor of a New York newspaper, drafted and secured unanimous approval in 1899 for the predecessor of Delaware's present General Corporation Law. Marvel then formed the Corporation Service Company—upon whose board sat the most prominent citizens of the Diamond State, namely the leaders of Delaware's legislature—and began mailing out pamphlets to advertise the advantages of the new law as if it were a miraculous new patent medicine:

> The State of Delaware has just adopted the most favorable of existing general corporation laws. . . . The law is based upon that of the State of New Jersey and embraces all of the beneficial provisions and safeguards found in the laws of that State. It has, however, in many respects advanced far beyond New Jersey and made Delaware a far more attractive home for a business corporation. . . . It does not encourage reckless incorporations nor permit the existence of wildcat companies. But it furnishes at least expense, ample right to stockholders, and reduces restrictions upon corporate action to a minimum. . . . The original fee to be paid for incorporation is small,—about three-fourths of that in New Jersey, for instance. The annual tax is very small. In New Jersey, for instance, a corporation with a capital of $4,000,000 pays $3,000 annual tax. In Delaware, it pays but $1,500. . . . Stockholders and directors may hold their meetings wherever they please and need never meet in the State of Delaware (New Jersey stockholders *must* meet in that State). . . . The stock and transfer books (which in New Jersey corporations must be kept in the State) may be kept in or out of Delaware, in the discretion of the company. . . . The examination of the books by intermeddlers is made much more difficult under the Delaware laws than under the laws of any other state. . . . The liability of the stockholder is absolutely limited when the stock has once been issued for cash, property or services. . . .

What Marvel had done was to take New Jersey's revised corporation statute and systematically make it worse. In Marvel's haste to make Delaware's business code more attractive than New Jersey's, however, he had included provisions to permit stock watering which were patently unconstitutional under the Delaware

Constitution of 1897. But that hardly mattered. The legislature was so pleased with the prospect of reducing property taxes that it readily amended the constitution to conform to the corporate law.

Wall Street, however, resisted these inducements. In spite of obvious financial advantages, the New York bar for over a dozen years assiduously avoided tiny Delaware and its curious Josiah Marvel—he had taken to styling himself "Dr. Marvel"—for being too uncouth, too crass, and too eager. Besides, New Jersey was closer.

Then, in 1913, Wilson's reforms "ruined" New Jersey and Wall Street appreciated Delaware for the first time. Delaware's tininess, which previously had seemed so laughable, was now recognized as its greatest virtue. In a "pygmy" state, corporate franchise taxes would always matter. More importantly, tiny Delaware was predictable: its politics had always been conservative, always pro-business.

Eagerly, Delaware seized its opportunity. An 1899 law review article derisively described the attitude of the legislature in Dover: "Little Delaware . . . is determined to get her little tiny, sweet, round, baby hand into the grab-bag of sweet things before it is too late." Beginning in 1915, Delaware periodically revised its corporation law to adopt "suggestions" forwarded by the New York bar. In short order, Delaware replaced New Jersey as the leading charterer of the largest industrial corporations—a position it has held ever since.

Delaware, of course, retained the most attractive features of New Jersey's liberal law, most significantly those which permitted economic concentration to be preserved and enhanced. Indeed, by permitting "stock pyramiding," Delaware allowed financiers not only to hold control of a subsidiary corporation through a parent but to reduce their personal investment in the controlling stock to a trivial amount by selling off most of the parent's equity in nonvoting stock or bonds. This procedure could be repeated at several successive levels so that investors such as the Van Sweringen brothers were able to control billion-dollar combinations with a personal investment of less than one percent of the total equity value.

A further reason why Delaware became, in Professor's Dodd's

words, "the happy hunting ground for the corporate promoter" was the following provision in Delaware's 1899 Act:

The certification of incorporation may also contain any provision which the incorporators may choose to insert for the management of the business and for the conduct of the affairs of the corporation, and any provision creating, defining, limiting, and regulating the powers of the corporation, the directors and stockholders; provided, such provisions are not contrary to the laws of this State.

These sanguine little words literally turned corporate law inside out. The first hundred years of the corporation's history in the United States had established one rule above all else: The business corporation could only exercise powers explicitly provided or necessarily implied in its charter with the state. Delaware's "self-determination" provision allowed the corporation to be a lawmaker itself. The corporation could conduct business in any way it chose as long as the state did not explicitly prohibit it.

During the 1920s, the promoters and managers of Delaware corporations used this power of self-determination to assault the last vestiges of shareholder control. Shareholders were substantially disenfranchised through the proliferation of nonvoting preferred and common shares and almost as completely disbarred through the invention of "restricted," "limited," or "contingent" voting shares.

Next fell shareholders' dividend rights. With the classification of stock, the board of directors' "inherent" power to declare or not to declare dividends took on an unexpected meanin now "inherently" had the right to favor or prejudice particular classes of shareholders each quarter.

By amendments in 1927 and 1929, the doyens of the New York City bar and the Delaware Legislature went even further. "Blank stock" was created. This permitted financiers to organize a corporation with large blocks of authorized but unissued stock whose "voting powers, designations, preferences, . . . or rights" could be subsequently fixed by the board of directors. Similarly, "stock purchase options" could be issued at low prices to favored investors before the public offering of shares.

The cumulative effect of these financial devices was, in

the words of Adolf Berle, to accord management "the power of confiscation . . . by using them or a combination of them, appropriately, the profits of the enterprise and also in considerable measure the underlying assets may be shifted from one group of stockholders to another." By 1932, when Adolf Berle and Gardiner Means published *The Modern Corporation and Private Property*, their seminal study of the United States economy and corporate law, there had evolved a "corporate system" as far removed from the Jacksonian economy as a plutocracy is from a democratic state.

This transformation involved the concentration of economic power and the dispersion of stock ownership. The two hundred largest nonbanking corporations had combined assets of $81 billion, or 49.2 percent of the wealth held by over 300,000 nonbanking corporations. In the largest corporations, thousands, sometimes hundreds of thousands, of individuals owned shares with the result that in most of these firms no single individual held an important proportion of the total ownership. Correspondingly, stock dispersion and legal devices such as nonvoting stock and stock pyramiding had vested control of at least 177 of the largest 200 corporations in owners of a minority of the outstanding shares.

To be more specific, Berle and Means calculated that in 23 percent of the largest 200 corporations a minority shareholder or group possessed a large enough block to own "working control" of the corporation. That is, their 15 or 20 percent of voting shares could invariably attract sufficient support from the dispersed majority to form a 51 percent or greater faction. In 21 percent of these largest 200 corporations, control was the result of a legal device; while in 44 percent, a management group with trivial shareholdings maintained control through the machinations of the proxy system.

The foundation of this entire corporate system was the opera bouffe in Delaware. In 1932, for some 42,000 corporations, including more than one-third of the industrial corporations listed on the New York Stock Exchange, Delaware was "home." In one office alone of the Industrial Trust Building in Wilmington, 12,000 separate corporations claimed their existence; and in the lobby of that very same building, 12,000 separate corporations posted their names in identical picayune lettering in a determined attempt to comply with the General Corporation Law's requirement that a corporate sign be "displayed." Each day, six or 12 or sometimes several dozen annual shareholders meeting were held in the good offices of the corporation trust companies—for many corporations had amended their by-laws to require such Delaware meetings when they realized that Wilmington was so inconvenient a location that few shareholders would ever attend. And each day a handful of proxy holders for each corporation holding a meeting would arrive and solemnly call the shareholders to order. With strict regard to all statutory formalities, they would nominate and elect directors, and often also elect an office boy of the trust company to serve as the required resident agent. Then they would carefully total their proxies and five minutes later adjourn, management having successfully reelected itself.

There was only one legal fiction more empty than that of the annual shareholders meeting in Wilmington. And that was the role of the legislature in Dover. In return for an institutionalized bribe—corporate franchise taxes and related fees averaged 31 percent of Delaware's total state revenues from 1913–1934—the democratically elected legislature had totally abdicated its responsibilities as a lawmaker. Not once had the legislature questioned the propriety of a single revision forwarded by the New York bar. Typically, amendments were rushed through House and Senate committees in five minutes and enacted by the full General Assembly within days. The General Corporation Law became so reckless, so indifferent to shareholders' rights that federal district court judge Landis was moved to exclaim: "The State of Delaware would face indictment for licensing such corporations as the Pan Motor Company if I could summon a sovereign state into court."

DELAWARE FOREVER

By 1963, the other states had begun to catch up. After World War II, the corporate laws of over 30 states had been revised to make them more "competitive." Then, in the summer of 1963, Delaware's Secretary of State Elisha Dukes received the disturbing news that both New Jersey and Maryland intended to further amend their laws to "out-Delaware" Delaware. Dukes was even more disturbed to learn that new corporate filings had dropped 19 percent in the first six months of 1963. Corporation franchise taxes declined to a mere 7 percent of Delaware's total state revenues. The state's hegemony thus endangered, Dukes and later Governor Elbert Carvel treated these developments with the seriousness of a nation facing a foreign threat. Explained Governor Carvel, the problem of corporation revenue is too important to get involved in "wrangling" or "partisan political hassles."

After consultation with corporate service company officials and the Wilmington bar—which after World War II had supplanted Wall Street as the guardian of the General Corporation Law—the Governor asked the legislature to appropriate $25,000 to the Secretary of State to study and recommend revisions to Delaware's General Corporation Law. As described in Harry First's pathbreaking article in the *University of Pennsylvania Law Review*, the legislature responded accordingly—the preamble of their law of December 31, 1963 being perhaps the most remarkably candid document in the history of corporate law:

WHEREAS, the State of Delaware has a long and beneficial history as the domicile of nationally known corporations; and

WHEREAS, the favorable climate which the State of Delaware has traditionally provided for corporations has been a leading source of revenue for the State; and

WHEREAS, many States have enacted new corporation laws in recent years in an effort to compete with Delaware for corporate business; and

WHEREAS, there has been no comprehensive revision of the Delaware Corporation Law since its enactment in 1898 [sic]; and

WHEREAS, the General Assembly of the State of Delaware declares it to be the public policy of the State to maintain a favorable business climate and to encourage corporations to make Delaware their domicile . . .

Mindful of this resolution, Secretary of State Dukes appointed himself and nine others to a Delaware Corporation Law Revision Commission. Their mission: "to ascertain what other states have to attract corporations that we do not have" and then recommend amendments to the existing law.

To say that the Revision Committee was "pro-management" is to put it mildly. The chairman of the Commission was C. A. Southerland, who bracketed twelve years of service as Chief Justice of the Delaware Supreme Court with a somewhat more lucrative practice as senior partner and then of counsel to Delaware's largest corporate law firm, Potter, Anderson, and Corroon. S. Samuel Arsht, Henry Canby, Richard Corroon, and Daniel Herrmann were likewise senior partners in corporate law firms; indeed, they were widely regarded as the leaders of the Wilmington corporate bar. Alfred Jervis and David Jackman were the chief executives of two of the largest corporation service companies. Ms. Margaret Storey was head of the Corporation Department in the Secretary of State's office. Her full-time job was incorporating companies—as was Elisha Dukes' primary job as Secretary of State. The only exception was the tenth member of the Commission, Irving Morris, a plaintiff's lawyer, who handled a large percentage of shareholder derivative suits brought in Delaware.

The Commission then delegated its authority to a three-man drafting committee composed of corporate lawyers Arsht, Canby, and Corroon, whose firms represented such giant companies as Allis-Chalmers, General Motors, Ford Motor Company, Dupont, and Texaco. The drafting committee assumed "full responsibility" for the statute. Although the full Revision Commission had hired Professor Ernest F. Folk to serve as Reporter, the drafting committee felt free to reject Folk's recommendations and entirely excluded him from their deliberations. The committee, on the other hand, corresponded with the leading corporate law firms, including New York City's White & Case and Cravath, Swaine, and Moore; and directly with corporations such as General Foods and Shell Oil Co., among 125 others. Not only did these letters welcome suggestions, they also "publicized" what one member of the Revision Committee referred to as "the serious effort being made to attract corporations" to Delaware. This publicity proved effective. Even before the revised statute was written, U.S. Steel Corporation—citing the good business climate—relocated in "the little community of truck-farmers and clam diggers," a new client for Morris, Nichols, Arsht, and Tunnel.

Ultimately, the revisions to the Delaware General Corporation Law—the most influential business statute in the country, the closest thing we have to a national corporate law—were written in the law office of one S. Samuel Arsht.

As Richard Corroon put it, the Revision Commission expected "very little, if any, trouble in the Delaware General Assembly." And for good reason. It is difficult to imagine a less likely body to enact a national corporation law than the Delaware legislature. To this day the General Assembly serves as a part-time legislature meeting no more than 70 days a year, normally in half-day sessions. Legislators have no secretaries, no staff, and invariably supplement their $6,000 yearly salary with outside "full-time" jobs. "Simply stated," a commentator wrote of the 1967 Revision:

The Commission never expected the legislature to do anything with this law except pass it. One member of the Commission referred to the legislature as "just a bunch of farmers." Corroon did attend a caucus of Democratic senators and Canby did attend a caucus of Republican senators. But Corroon was out in fifteen minutes, Canby in three, and neither was asked any questions about the law.

The bill passed unanimously and became effective on July 3, 1967. The statute was an immediate financial success. According to the January 12, 1969 *New York Times*, "Delaware began chartering new companies at a record-breaking clip after it revised and liberalized its corporation laws to meet modern needs. Before the revisions were made in July, 1967, Delaware was signing up new corporations at an average of 300 a month. . . . [Delaware is now] chartering new corporations at a record rate of 800 a month. . . ." The article concluded with Secretary of State Duke's statement, "The franchise tax will bring the state about $21 million in the fiscal year ending June 30."

But that was just the beginning. By 1971 corporation franchise taxes and related corporate income represented $55.5 million out of $246 million in state revenue collections, approximately 23 percent of the total—the result of a stampede of the leading industrial corporations to the Diamond State. Of *Fortune* magazine's 1,000 largest industrial corporations, 134 reincorporated or incorporated for the first time in Delaware in the years 1967–1974. This meant that by late 1974, Delaware was "home" for 448 of the 1,000 largest corporations—including 52 of the largest 100, and 251 out of the largest 500. More impressive still, these 448 corporations accounted for over 52 percent of the sales of the largest 1,000 manufacturers.

A 1974 Report to the Governor of Delaware further highlighted the special relationship between Delaware and the largest corporations. Although Delaware had chartered 76,000 corporations by June, 1974, franchise tax revenues received from the largest 556 corporations equaled 64 percent of all franchise tax revenues; revenues received from the largest 950 corporations equaled nearly 80 percent of the total.

An examination of the 1967 Revisions explains in part why Delaware has remained the favorite of big business. Management power and perquisites were broadened as never before by such provisions as: section 242—only directors, not shareholders, may propose amendments to the corporate charter; sections 143 and 122(15)—plans for loans to officers, stock options, stock bonuses, and incentive compensation were authorized, but lacking procedures to avoid abuses or even disclose to shareholders the amounts involved; section 145—officers and directors could be indemnified for all court costs and settlements of criminal and civil cases without court or shareholder approval; and section 252—management was given the power to merge certain subsidiary corporations without a shareholder vote.

Yet the language of Delaware's statute alone cannot fully explain the state's success. Since 1967, several states, including Georgia, Maryland, New Jersey, Ohio, Pennsylvania, Tennessee, and Virginia, have replicated some or all of the key provisions of the Delaware statute. As the American Bar Association's *Model Business Corporation Act Annotated* documents, there is presently little difference between the revised Delaware General Corporation Law and the statutes employed by New York, Ohio, New Jersey, and Pennsylvania—the four runners-up in the large industrial incorporation business—or the American Bar Association's own Business Corporation Act which serves as a model for approximately 20 other states.

True, the speed with which Delaware adopted "technical" amendments in 1969, 1970, 1973, and 1974 may give corporate executives confidence that as soon as further "liberalizations" of corporate law are conceived, Delaware will be among the first states—if not the very first—to promulgate them. Nonetheless, Delaware's definitive advantage is not its statute alone, but rather the manner in which its judiciary interprets it. In the past 20 years, the Supreme Court of Delaware seems to have become just as committed to enhancing Delaware's "favorable business climate" as the Wilmington corporate bar.

Court decisions since 1957, for example, have established the following:

- Delaware grants incumbent management a nearly unlimited power to cause its corporation to repurchase its own shares to avoid a take-over by a rival group even when this prevents shareholders from effectively exercising their right to choose between competing management groups.

- The shareholders' historical appraisal right, or right to sell their shares back to the corporation before it consummates a merger which will substantially alter the character of the corporation, has been eliminated for all corporations if the merger is formally labeled a "sale of assets."

- Delaware has, in most instances, refused to protect the rights of minority shareholders in a subsidiary corporation, deferring instead to the "business judgment" of the executives of the parent corporation.

- Delaware has furthered the decline of the board of directors by refusing to hold directors responsible for knowing—or learning—about criminal price-fixing practices occurring in the corporation they supposedly manage.

These and similar decisions so outraged Professor William Cary, a former chairman of the Securities and Exchange Commission, that he published a case-by-case analysis of Delaware's judicial "deterioration of corporate standards" in the *Yale Law Journal* of March 1974. "Perhaps there is no public policy left in Delaware corporate law except the objective of raising revenue," Cary reasoned; "consciously or unconsciously, fiduciary standards and standards of fairness generally have been relaxed. In general, the judicial decisions can best be reconciled on the basis of a desire to foster incorporation in Delaware."

Not that the judiciary had much choice. In no state is an anti-management decision so likely to be reversed by the legislature. As a New York attorney once explained, "The Delaware legislature will do anything it can for management. If the Delaware Chancery Court handed down a decision unfavorable to management, the legislature would enact a statute that corrects the court's decion so that in the future in a similar situation, management will clearly win."

And in no state is the supreme court so dominated by members of the corporate bar. Three of the seven men who served as Justice or Chief Justice of the Delaware Supreme Court between 1951 and 1973 (Messrs. D. F. Wolcott, C. A. Southerland, and D. L. Herrmann) had previously been senior partners in corporate law firms. A fourth (J. M. Tunnell, Jr.) left the bench to join a corporate law firm. A fifth (C. L. Terry) was a leading supporter of the 1967 Revision Statute during his term as Governor.

All this led Professor Cary to the conclusion that the Supreme Court of Delaware lacked sufficient independence or impartiality to judge corporate litigation. Cary noted that the United States Supreme Court in *Ward v. Village of Monroeville, Ohio* had held that a petitioner was "entitled to a new trial and detached judge in the first instance," where he had been fined for a traffic violation before a mayor who also had responsibilities for revenue production. Almost one-half of the village income was derived from fines, forfeitures, costs, and fees imposed by the mayor's court.

By analogy, the State of Delaware derives a substantial portion, roughly one quarter, of its income from incorporation fees and franchise taxes; in the words of one of its Law Revision Commission members, "The Franchise Tax dollar is very important. . . . That is one of the reasons for the formation of this committee—to modernize and liberalize the Delaware Corporation Law." Thus both the courts and the legislature may be said to lack the neutrality and detachment "to hold the balance, nice, clear, and true," required in passing upon the complaints of the shareholders.

With the collapse of the Delaware judiciary, state corporate law has reached a terminal point. The entire function of state corporate law has been reduced to reflecting the preferences of the managers of the largest corporations. In 1972, Professor Ernest Folk, just five years after serving as Reporter for the 1967 Delaware Revision Statute, eulogized the end of state chartering:

State corporation law—both statutory and case law—has seen its day. Statutes have become so broad and sweeping that they let a corporation do just about anything it wants. A modicum of legal skill and common sense enables management to do its will, and to plan around—not to say evade— what few restrictions state law contains. State law does not and cannot exert any real controls. Corporation statutes and most judicial decisions largely tend to reflect the interests and orientation of management, or, to use another popular term, insiders.

In short, state law has abdicated its responsibility. As a result, so the argument must run, only federal law can handle the situation, and a massive infusion of federal legislation is needed. . . .

III

The Federal Chartering
Alternative

The freest government if it could exist would not long be accepted if the tendency of the laws was to create a rapid accumulation of property in a few hands and to render the great mass of the people dependent.

—Daniel Webster

LEGITIMACY LOST

THE BASIS OF all political power in the United States, our civics books tell us, is the consent of the governed. Lacking the authorization of our Constitution or our democratically elected legislators and executives, no political official may lawfully exercise power over a United States citizen. This ultimate accountability to the people is the cornerstone of the concept of "legitimacy" in a constitutional democracy. Thus, a President can legitimately command the armed services because the Constitution says he can. A majority of the Federal Power Commission can fix the wellhead price for interstate natural gas because legislation, passed by a duly elected Congress and signed by a duly elected Chief Executive, gives it this authority. On the other hand, a President can no longer impound monies that are congressionally appropriated, because Congress, overriding a presidential veto, has ruled that he may not.

Our largest corporations also exercise vast power—over workers, shareholders, customers, and other citizens. But with whose consent? And with what legitimacy? In a view as conventional the century before it was uttered as it was in the subsequent century, Henry Carter Adams explained the rationale of corporate franchise in his 1896 presidential address to the American Economic Association:

Corporations originally were regarded as agencies of the state. They were created for the purpose of enabling the public to realize some social or national end without involving the necessity of direct governmental administration. They were in reality arms of the state, and in order to secure efficient management, a local or private interest was created as a privilege or property of the corporation. A corporation, therefore, may be defined in the light of history as a body created by law for the purpose of attaining public ends through an appeal to private interests.

Corporations were therefore granted certain privileges—like limited liability, perpetual life, and the equal protection of the laws in return for their social utility. And they were accorded substantial freedom to act and contract because of the consensual nature of their relations: a consumer was free to choose and to buy or not.

Yet today this consensual cornerstone has crumbled. In a vast array of nonmarket impacts—chemicals, gases and particulates—there occurs compulsory consumption; a resident of El Paso, for example, cannot choose *not* to breathe the air polluted by the American Smelting and Refining Company's smokestacks. Also, in many transactions, consumers simply don't know what they are buying—either because corporations fail to disclose material information or because consumers lack the sensory ability to detect, for example, carcinogenic agents in their purchases. Finally, corporations have proven to have short-run profit horizons, exhibiting indifference to the effect of their abuses on future generations. The nineteen-year-old girl who contracts cancer because her mother consumed DES during pregnancy can hardly be described as entering into a consensual economic relationship.

This devolution can be traced to the breakdown of those controls which have historically legitimized corporate power. These controls were to insure that corporations efficiently and responsibly served the public purpose:

- *state chartering*, as described in detail in chapter II, has become a revenue game between states to see which could produce a more nominal corporation code in order to garner chartering business;

- *competition* may thrive in some small business and service sectors, but it is largely inoperative among the oligopolies that dominate the "planning economy";

- *remedial law*—to compel companies to pollute less or disclose more—is difficult to obtain because big business can wield political power to avoid legislation it opposes or endlessly delay enforcement actions;

- *federal regulation* often involves agencies with people coming from or going to regulated firms, collaborating with business rather than regulating it at arm's length;

- *labor unions* certainly contest management over their wages but even Professor Galbraith, who coined the term a couple of decades ago, agrees that they have failed to be a "countervailing power" to management authority generally;

- *shareholders*, so diffused and divorced from genuine corporate control, are far more likely to sell out their shares rather than throw out venal or inept management;

- *the board of directors*, like all cuckolds, is often the last to know when its dominant partner—management—has done something illicit.

These breakdowns have contributed to the high level of individual irresponsibility now so apparent in many companies, as foreign and domestic business bribes indicate. Individual accountability has failed in the collective entity called the corporation since, in Professor Christopher Stone's words, "We have arranged things so that people who call the shots do not have to bear the full risks." In the old days when a butcher sold you bad meat from an animal he had bought, raised, slaughtered, and prepared, the customer at least knew whom to blame. When a bridge collapses, so, usually, does the reputation of its engineer. But who exactly is to blame when a large corporation produces a dangerous drug, engages in political bribery, or tries to overthrow foreign governments?

Pinpointing authority and illegality in large companies is as futile as discerning exactly who ordered an FBI black bag job or a CIA "destabilization" attempt. The corporate entity diffuses roles and decisions, discourages individual accountability, and hence encourages individual irresponsibility. Indeed, even when we do know whom to blame, we are not much better off. Of the business executives convicted of Watergate campaign finance offenses, the overwhelming majority are still ensconced in their executive suites.

With the decline of corporate law, of economic competition, and of individual responsibility, the large American corporation has escaped from its orbit of intended restraint. In so doing, it has gained power but lost legitimacy. As law professor Abram Chayes has written, "the modern business corporation [has] emerged as the first successful institutional claimant of significant unregulated power since the nation-state established its title in the sixteenth and seventeenth centuries." Yet "there is in a democracy no place for the exercise of irresponsible power," concluded Walton Hamilton in discussing a series of Supreme Court antitrust decisions. "Where it exists it must be broken up or directed to the public good."

A HISTORY OF FEDERAL CHARTERING

A federal role in corporate enterprise has occasionally won federal endorsement. The government was a minority stockholder in the First and Second Banks of the United States. Nationally chartered banks were created by an Act of Congress in 1864. In 1904–5, the American government acquired all the shares of the Panama Railroad Company. World War I stimulated a wide and rapid extension of the use of the government-owned corporation, such as the incorporation and takeover of the United States Shipping Board Emergency Fleet. The 1922 China Trade Act specifically permits federal charters for firms trading with China. In 1924 the federally run Inland Waterways Corporation was formed. In the 1930s the Tennessee Valley Authority, a government authority, performed a function private capital would not perform. During the Depression, numerous government-owned corporations arose. Also, government-business partnerships like Comsat, Amtrak, and the National Corporation for Housing Partnerships are examples of direct involvement by the federal government in the running of business corporations.

Thus, there is little doubt today that the federal government can charter business corporations.* But aside from these periodic and often inadequate efforts to meet short-run exigencies, the federal government has refused to charter large corporations across-the-board. Not that it has lacked the opportunity to do so.

The idea that the federal government could charter corporations first arose during the Articles of Confederation, when in 1781 the Confederation granted a national charter to the Bank of North America. During the Constitutional Convention in 1787 James Madison twice proposed that the Constitution expressly empower Congress "To grant charters of corporation in cases where the public good may require them and the authority of a single state may be incompetent." Although no formal vote on it was ever taken, the proposal was rejected by some delegates as unnecessary and by others as leading to monopolies which could dominate the federal government. Thomas Jefferson repeated this anxiety in his arguments with Alexander Hamilton over a United States bank. Such a bank would overawe the states, said Jefferson, permitting vast consolidations of economic power to dominate our economic life. Jefferson lost the battle when Congress and President Washington approved the Bank of the United States in 1791. Eventually Jefferson lost the war as well, since great economic consolidations *did* come to dominate our economy, albeit via state and not federal incorporation.

A century later, in the 1880s, the public became concerned about the economic and political power of the huge trusts. Some reformers called for a form of federal licensing of corporations in order to control their excesses. Instead, the 1890 Sherman Antitrust Act was passed, looking to competition rather than regulation

* Although once hotly disputed, there is today no serious question that a federal chartering law would be constitutional under the commerce clause and the enabling provision of the necessary and proper clause. "The determinative test of exercise of power by Congress is simply whether the activity sought to be regulated is 'commerce which concerns more than one state' and has a real and substantial relation to the national interest," said the Supreme Court in 1964. This decision traced its rationale back to the seminal 1942 case of *Wickard v. Filburn*. There the Supreme Court ruled that the federal government could regulate so local an activity as corn grown by a farmer for his own consumption if it could demonstrate this "affected" interstate commerce.

to restrain the trusts. But this law failed to control the trust and monopoly problem, as Chapter VII elaborates. By 1899 William Jennings Bryan went on record as favoring a federal license whenever a corporation wanted to conduct interstate business. Two years later President Theodore Roosevelt had his own idea. In his first message to Congress in 1901, he said, "The first essential in determining how to deal with the great industrial combinations is knowledge of the facts—publicity. . . . The Government should have the right to inspect and examine the workings of the great corporations engaged in interstate commerce." This view was embodied in his proposal for a Bureau of Corporations, which was created by Congress and became part of the Department of Commerce in 1903.

The Bureau's purpose was exposure of the "bad" trusts. It collected information and conducted investigations into corporate abuses, reporting its findings to the President, who could then make them public. But this scheme conflicted with antitrust principles by accepting the fact of corporate consolidations; and it had no formal connection to antitrust enforcement by the Justice Department. The *New York Times* charged that the "legislation accomplished nothing. . . . It does not bust the trusts. . . . It will appease the public clamor against trusts and it will do the trusts and combinations no harm. That is to say, it will fool the people, and that is the purpose of the Republican Congress." Roosevelt himself referred to the Bureau's work as "tentative," "advisory," and "experimental."

Again opponents of monopolies looked elsewhere for salvation, and again federal chartering became a candidate. This time, however, support for the approach seemed overwhelming. Between 1903 and 1914, Presidents Roosevelt, Taft, and Wilson all voiced support for a federal incorporation or licensing scheme in their annual messages to Congress. President Taft had his attorney general, George Wickersham, draft a federal licensing bill and propose it to Congress in 1910.

In 1908 the *Wall Street Journal* supported a federal licensing bill, saying "why should not the Federal Government . . . embody this underlying principle in a statement of control under which the development of corporations may in general proceed?"

That same year three officials of National Association of Manufacturers were even more blunt. "Federal incorporation, if not a national necessity, would prove to be at least a national blessing. . . . [It would] remove from the business of the country those corporations which are controlled either by criminals or visionary enthusiasts, and protect one corporation from the oppression and rapacity of another." Variants of a federal corporate law were endorsed by the 1904 Democratic Platform, the 1908 Republican Platform, and the 1912 Democratic Platform. Twenty different bills were introduced in one or both Houses of Congress between 1903 and 1914. Scholars and politicians favored it as a logical way of promoting the public interest.

Despite this array of support, the Clayton and Federal Trade Commission Acts of 1914 became law instead of federal chartering. Support for the latter never coalesced at any one time. Taft had changed his mind about it by 1912, and the Senate Interstate Commerce Committee, after holding lengthy hearings on federal incorporation in 1913, concluded in the final committee report that it was "neither necessary nor desirable at this time." Improving marginally the antitrust laws, and creating a successor agency to the Bureau of Corporations, the FTC, attracted the most support when the moment of political judgment arrived.

Between 1915 and 1932, eight Congressional bills were introduced relating to federal incorporation or licensing. During the Depression of the early 1930s, however, the National Industrial Recovery Act was passed. In certain respects, Franklin Roosevelt saw the NRA as a form of federalization of corporations, providing "a rigorous licensing power in order to meet rare cases of noncooperation and abuse." There was brief talk during this time by both labor and management of replacing the NRA codes by federal chartering of the large companies and trade associations. Instead, the government opted for the Securities Acts of 1933 and 1934, requiring full and accurate disclosure of material facts in a public offering and regulating the practices of the national exchanges, and for other New Deal regulatory schemes—the Federal Communications Commission in 1934, the Public Utility Holding Company Act of 1935, and the Civil Aeronautics Board in 1938.

Nevertheless, the late Thirties witnessed the most sustained drive for federal licensing to date. Senator Joseph O'Mahoney, a populist Senator from Wyoming, energetically and repeatedly promoted the idea of "National Charters for National Business." By emphasizing that "a corporation has no rights; it has only privileges," he sought to return to the days when charters policed as well as permitted. In 1938 his Subcommittee of Federal Licensing of Corporations held four volumes of hearings on S.3072, a bill which he and Senator William Borah co-sponsored. Senator O'Mahoney later made it clear that the important choice was between a federal and a state role in the control of the corporation's powers. His proposal, more farreaching than its predecessors, provided for the following:

- corporations whose gross assets (including those of subsidiaries) exceeded one hundred thousand dollars were required to obtain a federal license to engage in interstate business;

- detailed information on the financial affairs of the corporation, including dealings with foreign firms, had to be periodically supplied to the FTC;

- diversification "incidental to the business in which it is authorized to engage," as well as ownership of the stock in other companies, was forbidden (but this rule was prospective only, leaving existing relationships unchanged);

- any corporation in violation of the antitrust laws, or one which discriminated by sex, employed child labor, or refused to bargain collectively, could lose its federal license and hence its right to do interstate business;

- penalties ranged from nominal fines for a thirty-day period during a violation of the license, to one percent of the book value of the capital stock or assets per month, to actual revocation of the license following hearings by the FTC and an action instituted by the Attorney General in any district court.

Although the bill went nowhere—the war effort derailed any momentum built up by the hearings and O'Mahoney's Temporary National Economic Committee (TNEC)—O'Mahoney remained firm in his belief in such legislation. In a statement to the TNEC at its closing session on March 11, 1941, he said:

It is idle to think that huge collective institutions which carry on our modern business can continue to operate without more definite responsibility toward all the people of the Nation than they now have. To do this it will be necessary, in my judgment, to have a national charter system for all national corporations. . . . One thing is certain: We cannot hope to stop the process of concentration if we are willing to continue to allow the States to create the agencies through and by which the concentration has been brought about.

Thus, whenever federal chartering was considered a vehicle of corporate law reform, an alternative remedy became public policy. The outrage against the trusts in the 1880s institutionalized itself in the 1887 Interstate Commerce Commission and the 1890 Sherman Act. The turn-of-the-century merger wave and depression of 1903 culminated in the Bureau of Corporations, which evolved into the 1914 Federal Trade Commission enforcing the Clayton Act. The Depression led to the creation of securities laws, industry codes, and additional regulatory agencies.

But as Chapter I indicated, these remedies have failed to contain the excessive power and costs of corporate power. For such structural problems we need the structural reform of federal chartering, not merely some tinkering alterations.

Today the case for federal chartering becomes compelling for two basic reasons. First, to control national and multinational corporations requires national authority. *State* chartering is a costly anachronism—as logical as the state printing of money or passports. If a criminal crosses state borders, the *Federal* Bureau of Investigation is called in; if a commodity or service travels interstate, so, too, should the jurisdiction of the *federal* government—over the structure of corporate governance. Other than a few corporate lawyers and public officials in Deleware, who would not be embarrassed to defend the proposition that only a state, and not the federal government, can charter GM and ITT? The choice, ultimately, is between federal chartering and Delaware chartering.

And second, our current economic and ecological crises and corporate crime wave underscore the failure of the old corporate law system. Industrial structure and management power have either allowed or exacerbated structural "stagflation" throughout the 1970s—a condition of both high unemployment and inflation. And corporate officials, it now appears, routinely violate the law and attribute their behavior to custom or competitive pressures.

The problem is ultimately one of power: how can we limit unaccountable power and how can we ensure that those who do exercise managerial power are the best managers feasible? The following four chapters on corporate governance, corporate disclosure, corporate monopoly, and an Employee Bill of Rights—the four substantive sections of our federal chartering proposal—each elaborate how the largest 700 corporations can begin to be both more democratic and more efficient.

The Content of Federal Chartering

IV

Who Rules
the Corporation?

Who selected these businessmen, if not to rule over us, at least to exercise vast authority, and to whom are they responsible? The answer to the first question is quite clearly: they selected themselves. The answer to the second is, at least, nebulous.

—Dean Edward S. Mason

ALL MODERN state corporation statutes describe a common image of corporate governance, an image pyramidal in form. At the base of the pyramid are the shareholders or owners of the corporation. Their ownership gives them the right to elect representatives to direct the corporation and to approve fundamental corporate actions such as mergers or bylaw amendments. The intermediate level is held by the board of directors, who are required by a provision common to nearly every state corporation law "to manage the business and affairs of the corporation." On behalf of the shareholders, the directors are expected to select and dismiss corporate officers; to approve important financial decisions; to distribute profits; and to see that accurate periodic reports are forwarded to the shareholders. Finally, at the apex of the pyramid are the corporate officers. In the eyes of the law, the officers are the employees of the shareholder owners. Their authority is limited to those responsibilities which the directors delegate to them.

In reality, this legal image is virtually a myth. In nearly every large American business corporation, there exists a management autocracy. One man—variously titled the President, or the Chairman of the Board, or the Chief Executive Officer—or a small co-terie of men rule the corporation. Far from being chosen by the directors to run the corporation, this chief executive or executive clique chooses the board of directors and, with the acquiescence of the board, controls the corporation.

In its most consolidated form, corporate autocracy assumes the character of a corporation like ITT. Here is the ninth largest industrial corporation in the United States; with annual sales over $11 billion; 200,000 shareholders; over 400,000 employees; operations in 90 separate nations; administered through some 265 subsidiary corporations. Yet for over a decade ITT management has been constructed around a single domineering executive, Mr. Harold S. Geneen. Journalist Anthony Sampson glimpsed the nature of Geneen's leadership when he described the monthly four-day meeting through which ITT's multinational operations were coordinated:

One hundred and twenty people are assembled in the big fourth-floor room . . . taken up with a huge horseshoe table, covered in green baize, with blue swivel armchairs and a name in front of each chair, with a bottle of mineral water and a volume of statistics. In the chairs sit the top men of ITT from all over Europe, like diplomats at a conference: in the middle are the senior vice presidents. Among them, swiveling and rocking to and fro in his armchair, surveying the faces and gazing at the statistics, is an owlish figure behind a label saying Harold S. Geneen.

A low voice, from one of the comptrollers, intones the salient facts about each batch of figures; and as the voice talks, a small, sharp arrow appears on the screen, alongside the relevant figure. Some of the figures have brackets round them, indicating a loss, and there the arrow lingers specially long (it seems almost like an extension of Geneen's finger). From time to time, Geneen's voice, also very low, interposes with a question. Why has a target not been reached, why is an inventory figure too high? The chief executive officer justifies himself tensely and briefly: "We're already looking into that, Mr. Geneen." Geneen nods or swivels around or utters some mild reproof. The arrow moves on to the next incriminating figure.

The meetings, whether in Brussels or New York, are the central ordeal of the ITT discipline, the test that its men are attuned to the openness of the system. As Geneen explained to me, it is not enough for him to see the figures; he must see the expression of the man that presents them, and how he presents them. The words "I want no surprises" are always there, in the background. If there *is* a surprise, the reaction is immediate; a task force will be immediately appointed, perhaps two or three task forces unaware of each other, to find out the reason, to supply a solution. For a newly joined manager—and especially from a company newly acquired by ITT—the ordeal can be terrifying. . . .

A basic defect with corporate autocracy, at ITT and elsewhere, is its inefficiency. As corporate operations have grown more complex and technologies more sophisticated, checks upon senior management have all but disappeared. The result has often been irrational decisions, hurried decisions, decisions based upon inadequate factual analysis or executive self-favoritism. Surveying a decade that had seen the wreck of the Penn Central, cost overrun catastrophes at both Lockheed and Douglas Aircraft, the slow, resistible decline of A & P, and a host of conglomerate stock collapses, J. Irwin Miller, president of Cummings Engine, concluded, "I think we've just gone through a decade of rather surprisingly bad decisions by businessmen worldwide. Some of them so bad that nobody would have guessed it."

Recessionary economic conditions since 1970 have further dramatized the deteriorating quality of American business management. In 1975 alone, W.T. Grant, once the third largest variety store in the United States, filed for voluntary bankruptcy after amassing debts of $1.8 billion, largely the result of overexpansion during the nine-year presidency of Louis Lustenberger. In California, the co-founders of the Daylin retailing empire resigned after filing for bankruptcy—they too tried to become too big too fast. Chrysler, for years the nation's fourth largest industrial company, lost over $300 million in 1974 and 1975 as a result of chairman Lynn Townsend's earlier decisions to bypass the small-car market just as the nation headed into the soaring fuel costs associated with the "energy crisis." In October, Townsend abruptly resigned. At RCA, Robert Sarnoff was fired. Since the corporation's 1971 $490 million write-off for its ill-planned lurch into the mainframe computer business, Sarnoff's leadership had become increasingly erratic—culminating in $65 million of losses in its electronics manufacturing in the first eight months of 1975 and slippage of the NBC network to third in television ratings. At three other corporations there was not time to change leaders. The Chicago, Rock Island

and Pacific Railroad, Bowman Instruments, and Good Hope Industries, a little known $250 million petroleum firm, all sought judicially supervised reorganization. Teetering on the brink were three leading airlines, TWA, Eastern, and Pan Am—each victims, among other problems, of over-ordering costly jumbo jets and an inability to sell them in the glutted airbus market. More fortunate were the giant Gulf and Royal Dutch–Shell Oil Corporations, which quietly absorbed a $1 billion loss on an inoperable prototype nuclear power plan developed by their joint venture, General Atomic Company. The reactor, however, was only one of several "Edsels" in the nuclear field last year. In late 1975, Westinghouse reneged on contracts to supply uranium to more than 20 utilities because the market price per pound had risen to roughly $20 to $30 above Westinghouse's fixed-price contracts. If held liable for the price difference, the corporation will lose as much as $1.9 billion. Even more astonishing was the judgment of the Pacific Gas and Electric Company. Shortly before inaugurating operations of its largest nuclear power plant, the firm discovered that the plant had been constructed within two miles of a major geological fault; it may have to be refortified if not scuttled.

1975 was also a year of reckoning for a dozen major conglomerates. For the billion-dollar apparel retailer Genesco, the past 36 months, sermonized *Business Week*, "have been bedlam." Overextended by a pell-mell acquisition binge in the 1960s, the firm sold off nearly 200 retail outlets but still finished in the red. U.S. Industries was criticized by one of its own managers for expanding "into too many businesses it knew nothing about"; costly infighting last year resulted in the stock selling for less than a third of its liquidation value. At the $2.5 billion Rapid American company, synergy worked in reverse with nearly all of its acquisitions showing lower profits or bigger losses in the years since they were acquired. Singer Company, Consolidated Foods, General Foods, Ryder Systems, and Mattel—historically all single-industry companies which had lost heavily by expanding into unrelated fields—placed ailing subsidiaries on the block. The "de-conglomeratization" of $4.7 billion Rockwell International was particularly striking. As the economy turned down in the early 1970s, President Robert Anderson persisted in an acquisition program that added 23 new companies in eight years lest the company "stagnate." Then when debt costs cut profits by 35 percent, he suddenly put 12 companies up for sale and slashed research and development funding. Even ITT, long the largest and most successful conglomerate, suffered a decline. The company stumbled so obviously on currency speculation and three major acquisitions—Hartford Fire Insurance, Levitt, and Avis—that *Fortune* magazine ran a two-part article all but accusing Harold Geneen of mismanagement. "There has patently been a loss of self-confidence at ITT, and it is the product of more than one misadventure."

The common theme of these many instances of mismanagement is a failure to restrain the power of senior executives. A corporate chief executive's decisions to expand, merge, or even violate the law can often be made without accountability to outside scrutiny. There is, for example, the detailed disclosures of the recent bribery cases. Not only do these reports suggest how widespread corporate foreign and domestic criminality has become; they also provide a unique study in the pathology of American corporate management.

At Gulf Corporation, three successive chief executive officers were able to pay out over $12.6 million in foreign and domestic bribes over a 15-year period without the knowledge of "outside" or non-employee directors on the board. To do so, chairman William K. Whiteford transferred an Assistant Comptroller to a Bahamian subsidy in 1959 to launder Gulf monies and hide transactions "off-the-books." Whiteford also hired Claude Wild to serve as Gulf's Washington lobbyist, and empowered Wild personally or through 19 other executives to make illegal political contributions to politicians ranging from such national figures as Senator Lyndon Johnson, Senator Hugh Scott, Senator Henry Jackson, and Congressman Wilbur Mills to such local figures as utility commissioners in Pennsylvania. Although the actions of Whiteford and his successors as chairmen were found by the McCloy Committee to be "shot through with illegality," these executives were able to involve as many as forty Gulf executives in fraudulent accounting or delivery of pay-offs, and banish at least one squeamish vice president—all without public disclosure or effective internal challenge.

At Northrop, chairman Thomas V. Jones and vice president

James Allen were able to create and fund the Economic and Development Corporation, a separate Swiss company, and pay $750,000 to Dr. Hubert Weisbrod, a Swiss attorney, to stimulate West German jet sales without the knowledge of the board or, apparently, other senior executives.

At 3M, chairman Bert Cross and finances vice president Irwin Hansen ordered the company insurance department to pay out $509,000 for imaginary insurance and the bookkeeper to fraudulently record the payments as a "necessary and proper" business expense for tax purposes. Although the transactions lacked required documentation, they were approved by both departments and later "verified" by Haskins and Sells, the outside auditor.

Ashland Oil Corporation's chief executive officer, Orwin E. Atkins, involved at least eight executives in illegally generating and distributing $801,165 in domestic political contributions, also without question. Not only was the board not informed until the Special Prosecutor's Office and Internal Revenue Service compelled Atkins to dribble out details of the misappropriation of funds, but Ernst and Ernst, Ashland's accountants, did not effectively investigate any of half a dozen separate accounts it discovered that suggested Ashland's illegal course of action.

The Legal Basis of Management Power

The legal basis for such a consolidation of power in the hands of the corporation's chief executive is the proxy election. Annually the shareholders of each publicly held corporation are given the opportunity of either attending a meeting to nominate and elect directors or returning proxy cards to management or its challengers signing over their right to vote. Few shareholders personally attend meetings. Sylvan Silver, a Reuters correspondent who covers over 100 Wilmington annual meetings each year, described representative 1974 meetings in an interview: At Cities Service Company, the 77th largest industrial corporation with some 135,000 shareholders, 25 shareholders actually attended the meeting; El Paso Natural Gas with 125,000 shareholders had 50 shareholders; at Coca Cola, the 69th largest corporation with 70,000 shareholders, 25 shareholders attended the annual meeting; at Bristol Meyers with 60,000 share-holders a like 25 shareholders appeared. Even "Campaign GM," the most publicized shareholder challenge of the past two decades, attracted no more than 3,000 of General Motors' 1,400,000 share-holders, or roughly two-tenths of one percent.

Thus, corporate directors are almost invariably chosen by written proxies. Yet management so totally dominates the proxy machinery that corporate elections have come to resemble the So-viet Union's euphemistic "Communist ballot"—that is, a ballot which lists only one slate of candidates. Although federal and state laws require the annual performance of an elaborate series of rituals pretending there is "corporate democracy," in 1973, 99.7 percent of the directorial elections in our largest corporations were uncon-tested.

Of the 6,744 corporations required to file data with the Securi-ties and Exchange Commission, incumbent management retained control in at least 6,734 companies, or 99.9 percent. In the 500 largest industrial corporations—corporations which account for some 66 percent of the sales of all industrial corporations in the United States—no incumbent management was even challenged in 1973. One-sided as these results are, they are entirely typical for the largest business corporations. During the 18 years for which data are available, 1956–73, management has won 99.9 percent of all proxy solicitations in 10 out of 18 years.

THE BEST DEMOCRACY MONEY CAN BUY

The key to management's hegemony is money. Effectively, only incumbent management can nominate directors—because it has a nearly unlimited power to use corporate funds to win board elections while opponents must prepare separate proxies and cam-paign literature entirely at their own expense.

There is first management's power to print and post written communications to shareholders. In a typical proxy contest, man-agement will "follow up" its initial proxy solicitation with a bom-bardment of five to ten subsequent mailings. As attorneys Edward Aranow and Herb Einhorn explain in their treatise, *Proxy Contests for Corporate Control:*

Perhaps the most important aspect of the follow-up letter is its role in the all-important efforts of a soliciting group to secure the *latest-dated* proxy from a stockholder. It is characteristic of every proxy contest that a large number of stockholders will sign and return proxies to one faction and then change their minds and want to have their stock used for the opposing faction.

The techniques of the Northern States Power Company in 1973 are illustrative. At that time, Northern States Power Company voluntarily employed cumulative voting, which meant that only 7.2 percent of outstanding shares was necessary to elect one director to Northern's 14-person board. Troubled by Northern's record on environmental and consumer issues, a broadly based coalition of public interest groups called the Citizens' Advocate for Public Utility Responsibility (CAPUR) nominated Ms. Alpha Snaby, a former Minnesota state legislator, to run for director. These groups then successfully solicited the votes of over 14 percent of all shareholders, or more than twice the votes necessary to elect her to the board.

Northern States then bought back the election. By soliciting proxies a second, and then a third time, the Power Company was able to persuade (or confuse) the shareholders of 71 percent of the 2.8 million shares cast for Ms. Snaby to change their votes.

Larger, more experienced corporations are usually less heavy-handed. Typically, they will begin a proxy campaign with a series of "build-up" letters preliminary to the first proxy solicitation. In Campaign GM, General Motors elevated this strategy to a new plateau by encasing the Project on Corporate Responsibility's single 100-word proxy solicitation within a 21-page booklet specifically rebutting each of the Project's charges. The Project, of course, could never afford to respond to GM's campaign. The postage costs of soliciting GM's 1,400,000 shareholders alone would have exceeded $100,000. The cost of printing a document comparable to GM's 21-page booklet, mailing it out, accompanied by a proxy statement, a proxy card, and a stamped return envelope to each shareholder might have run as high as $500,000.

Nor is it likely that the Project or any other outside shareholder could match GM's ability to hire "professional" proxy solicitors such as Georgeson & Company, which can deploy up to 100 solicitors throughout the country to personally contact share-holders, give them a campaign speech, and urge them to return their proxies. By daily tabulation of returned proxies, professional solicitors are able to identify on a day-by-day basis the largest blocks of stock outstanding which have yet to return a favorable vote.

Management's "army" in a proxy contest will also include at-torneys to prepare necessary documents for the SEC and distract the opposition with costly litigation; accountants and statisticians to prepare the most self-serving financial analysis allowable; and public relations advisors to prepare advertisements for trade jour-nals and the financial section of major newspapers. In the past 25 years there have been no more than a dozen instances in which in-surgents have been able to match management expenses in a major proxy fight. Over the past decade, only the MGM proxy contest of 1967 has seen insurgents match management expenses in a large corporation's proxy contest for control.

A second advantage—and one that no outsider can match—is management's ability to use corporate personnel on its own behalf. Clerical help and clerical facilities including printing presses, pho-tocopying machines, and addressing machines are invariably em-ployed. Salespersons skilled in talking to customers are frequently assigned to the telephones to answer inquiries and to supplement the professional proxy solicitors by making direct calls to share-holders. Moreover, senior executives can be assigned to telephone particularly important shareholders who may be impressed by the personal call of a top executive.

State corporations law has done nothing to correct this in-equality of corporate resources. Although leading cases in Dela-ware and New York have engaged in much gnashing of teeth about limiting management expenditures to: (a) proxy contests involving a "policy" issue, (b) expenditures necessary to inform shareholders about the "policy" issue, and/or (c) "reasonable" expenses—no deci-sion since 1907 in either jurisdiction has denied management the power to expend corporate funds or use corporate personnel ex-actly as management chooses. Even such seemingly "unreasonable" expenditures as public relations counsel, "entertainments," chartered airlines, limousines, and the indirect cost to the corporation of using officers and employees on behalf of an incumbent director slate have survived judicial scrutiny. By contrast, state courts have firmly established the rule that insurgents, unlike management, are not entitled to reimbursement of any campaign expenses as a matter of right. Challengers must defray all their own expenses, with the single slim hope of later being reimbursed *if* they are successful and the stockholders approve.

MANAGEMENT CONTROL OF INFORMATION

Management's grip on corporate power is tightened by its authority to print and distribute annual, quarterly, and other reports to shareholders. Besides the formal proxy statement, these reports usually embody the only detailed information shareholders receive about their corporation.

Neither state nor federal law places any meaningful restrictions on the amount of money management may spend reporting to shareholders. SEC Proxy Rules *do* require certification of financial statements. The report, however, "may be in any form deemed suitable by the management" and is not subject to the same standards of truthfulness that the text of a proxy solicitation is subjected to. Consequently, though every word of an insurgent shareholder's communications with other shareholders may be challenged if it is arguably "false or misleading," most management reports are subject to no textual regulation whatever.

Unfortunately, management reports are frequently "false and misleading." They are often written in an upbeat public relations jargon which emphasizes "positive" aspects of the past business year while rationalizing or ignoring management mistakes, financial losses, corporate or executive criminal violations, or civil actions successfully prosecuted against the corporation. Frequently, as much as half of the text of an annual report is represented by oversized charts, colored illustrations, and kindred public relations gimmickry.

There is often little difference between the text of a failing corporation's annual report and a healthy corporation's report. For example, although subsequent congressional testimony made clear that Lockheed would have gone bankrupt unless it received an emergency loan guarantee from the federal government, Lockheed's 1969 annual report managed to ignore the prominent debate in Congress over whether the federal government should "bail out" the firm. Instead shareholders read the following:

> It is disappointing to have to record a net loss for the year. Yet setbacks like this are singularly possible in an industry so dependent upon government policy and the ebb and flow of domestic and international developments.
>
> We have experienced them before and in each case have emerged stronger than ever. We are confident this will be so again. We say this not out of easy optimism but from the knowledge that we have many broadly based defense and commercial programs with high business potential and that we are expending much technical effort to meet the nation's future needs.

The report then spent six pages suggesting that Lockheed's financial difficulties were primarily the result of contractual misunderstandings with the federal government. It strongly suggested that the federal government would compromise in these disputes. It was only *after* the Senate voted an Emergency Loan Guarantee by the razor-thin margin of 49–48 in August 1971 that Lockheed reported to its shareholders that without this congressional subsidy the corporation would have collapsed.

A similar lack of veracity appeared in the 1973 Annual Report of the Franklin New York Corporation, whose principal subsidiary was the Franklin National Bank, the largest state bank ever to fail in the United States. Just a few months before the Comptroller declared the Franklin National Bank insolvent, the corporation's management reported to its shareholders that "In 1973 Franklin crossed an important threshold so that it is now in a position to move forward in establishing itself as a major worldwide financial institution and a leading money center banking operation." Nowhere in the report was any mention made of the foreign currency speculation or improvident real estate loans which four months later caused the bank's demise. This was a serious omission, for the preponderance of financial loss caused by Franklin's collapse was absorbed by the shareholder-readers of this report, not the management or the public relations firm which wrote it. These shareholder-readers were given absolutely no warning of what was coming, no opportunity to exert their prerogative to change management or to vote a more timely dissolution.

Nor can insurgent shareholders obtain much additional information from their own corporation when they prepare for a proxy challenge. They lack the legal tools to gain access to live interviews with corporate executives, board meetings, or memoranda which could document internal debate, management error, derogations of law, sloppy execution of policy, or even the content of management's policy formulations.

All of which is a bizarre commentary on the Securities and Exchange Commission. The federal security laws emphasize disclosure. The Commission has claimed that its Proxy Rules "represent an effective contribution to corporate democracy" because disclosure enables individual investors to exercise some measure of control over the management of their corporation. Although the Securities and Exchange Act of 1934 authorizes the SEC to require annual and quarterly reports, including the authority to prescribe "the items or details to be shown in the balance sheet and the earnings statement . . . ," shareholders can not compel their corporation to give a product line or division accounting so as to uncover unprofitable operations. Specific management mistakes may thus be submerged in consolidated financial reports. Shareholders may wish to know whether executives are using expense accounts improperly or are being indemnified for certain civil or criminal liabilities. They cannot find out. They may wish to read minutes of the meetings of corporate directors—whom they elect—or reports of decisions by executives respecting corporate property—which shareholders own. Under federal securities laws, they have no legal rights to do so.

Under state statutory law, shareholders theoretically have broad rights to examine corporate records. State statutes typically authorize inspection of shareholder lists—without which a shareholder could not even begin a proxy solicitation—and "other books and records." But this access is circumscribed by legal requirements of "good faith," "proper purpose," and minimum share ownership, as well as ample opportunities for management to delay compliance with legitimate shareholder demands by forcing expensive court tests.

Almost invariably shareholders prevail in court battles to secure a shareholder list, for, as a leading Pennsylvania decision put it, ". . . the right to examine the stockholders' list is a basic privilege of every stockholder of a corporation and should be given the widest recognition as fundamental to corporate democracy." But the courts are reluctant to enforce shareholder demands for other information. Doctrinally, this has been rationalized as deterring excessive "stockholder agitation." The Supreme Court of Minnesota rather melodramatically explained why in the leading case of *State Ex rel. Pillsbury v. Honeywell:*

> In terms of the corporate norm, inspection is merely the act of the concerned owner checking on what is in part his property. In the context of the large firm, inspection can be more akin to a weapon in corporate warfare. The effectiveness of the weapon is considerable: "considering the huge size of many modern corporations and the necessarily complicated nature of their bookkeeping, it is plain that to permit thousands of shareholders to roam at will through their records will render impossible not only any attempt to keep their records efficiently, but the proper carrying on of their business." . . . Because the power to inspect may be the power to destroy, it is important that only those with a bona fide interest in the corporation enjoy the power. . . .

Alarming as the specter of "thousands of shareholders roaming at will" through once efficient corporations may be, it can only be conjured up by courts so cunning as to overlook their inherent judicial power to restrict any shareholder access to corporate data to reasonable numbers of shareholders at reasonable times and reasonable places. Yet phantom or not, this rationale has been employed in recent decisions to deny one A&P shareholder access to the minutes of board meetings and information relevant to store closings; to deny Ralston Purina shareholders access to monthly profit analyses employed by management; and to deny shareholders of Gulf Sulphur Corporation information concerning a firm with which Gulf proposed to merge.

MANAGEMENT CONTROL OF THE LAW

Management power is further entrenched by three significant legal advantages.

First, in approximately 90 percent of all large industrial corporations, cumulative voting is not required. In these corporations, a minority of shareholders—even a minority as substantial as 49.9 percent—may be precluded from electing even one director to the board.

Under cumulative voting, each shareholder is entitled to votes equal to the number of his or her shares multiplied by the number of directors to be elected. The shareholder may cast all his or her votes for a single candidate or distribute them among two or more candidates as he or she sees fit. Cumulative voting, therefore, helps to protect the *financial* interest of minority shareholders by assuring them voice on the board of directors. And it protects the *political* interest of minority shareholders. For without cumulative voting, the tendency of large industrial corporations to perpetuate one-party rule is powerfully enhanced. As Professor Charles M. Williams demonstrated after analyzing proxy contests for the years 1943–1948, corporations with cumulative voting were more than twice as likely to have proxy contests as those without.

Because of these benefits, cumulative voting has enjoyed considerable popularity. From 1870, when Illinois became the first state to require cumulative voting, until 1955, 23 states had established absolute requirements for cumulative voting. Additionally, federal law requires cumulative voting for over 5,000 banks subject to the Federal Banking Act of 1933 (although the intent of this law has often been frustrated by bank holding company structures); and the Securities and Exchange Commission has consistently required cumulative voting for corporations subject to the Public Utility Holding Act of 1935 and corporations undergoing reorganization under Chapter X of the Bankruptcy Act. As an attorney snapped in 1950 in frustration at Wisconsin's refusal to enact cumulative voting, "Cumulative voting is so obviously in accord with our basic political philosophy of group representation and the party system that it is difficult to understand the legislature's repeated rejection of it, except in terms of a response to the pressure of corporate management's interest."

Unfortunately, "the pressure of corporate management's interest" often does prevail in state corporation law. Between 1955 and 1972, five states dropped mandatory cumulative voting. In 1973, Michigan changed from mandatory to permissive cumulative voting; in 1974 both California and Ohio considered—but did not enact—similar legislation. Today, in Delaware, as well as 32 other states, cumulative voting is not required. True, in most of these states, cumulative voting is permitted. In practice, however, permissive cumulative voting offers little but an illusory right. Studies by Professor Williams in 1951 and the Conference Board in 1973 indicate that only about 15 percent of the corporations in states with permissive cumulative voting have provided for this right.

And even in those few corporations which voluntarily institute cumulative voting, most states provide ample devices to subvert it. Although cumulative voting aims to prevent a simple majority from maintaining absolute corporate control, Delaware permits a simple majority to amend the corporate charter to repeal cumulative voting. And Delaware and some 42 other jurisdictions allow the "classification" of the board of directors. This device reduces to one third or one half the number of directors required to stand for election anually and thus increases the minimum vote necessary to elect a director.

Management's second legal edge is its power to issue nonvoting stock or classes of stock with unequal voting rights. For example, prior to December 1, 1955, there were three classes of stock in Ford Motor Company: common, Class A, and Class B. Only the Class B shares (4.94 percent of total equity), all of which were owned by Ford family interests, were entitled to vote.

Only Illinois and a few other states forbid the issuance of classes or series of stock without voting rights. But the refusal of both the New York Stock Exchange and the American Stock Exchange to list corporations with nonvoting stock has substantially reduced the number of corporations which may totally eviscerate shareholder suffrage, although neither exchange actively enforces equal voting rights.

The third statutory device for impairing shareholder suffrage rights is a provision common to the law of Delaware and apparently every other jurisdiction requiring the submission of proxy materials only to *shareholders of record*. This innocent sounding requirement effectively disenfranchises approximately 50 percent of the beneficial owners of corporate stock in the largest industrial corporations. For approximately 50 percent of the stock in the 1,800 companies traded on the New York Stock Exchange is held by mutual funds, life insurance or property and casualty insurance companies, private pension funds (usually administered through commercial bank trust departments), state and local pension funds, foundations, university endowment funds or other institutional investors. The result is a mockery of shareholder democracy: *Approximately 50 percent of the votes in our largest industrial corporations are cast by financial intermediaries—not the real owners.*

These institutional shareholders provide virtually no check to corporate management. Most financial institutions, according to the SEC's 1971 *Institutional Investor Study*, follow what is known as "The Wall Street Rule": An investment in a business corporation is considered an investment in that corporation's management; if the financial institution ceases to like what management is doing, the institution sells the stock. By examining the voting practices of 215 large institutions between January 1, 1967 and September 30, 1969, the SEC determined that approximately 30 percent of these institutions *always* voted for management (in elections other than votes for directors). For the remaining institutions, both voting against management and abstention were found "to be a relatively infrequent phenomenon." For example, in only 26 instances did any of the 215 institutions vote against an acquisition favored by management, "a miniscule fraction of such transactions."

The SEC conducted its study before the proliferation of shareholder proposals directed at social issues and precipitated by Campaign GM. In the past five years, some financial institutions have established formal procedures to consider shareholder public policy or ethical proposals. According to newsletters published by the Council on Economic Priorities and the Investor Responsibility Research Center, a small number of church-related funds, foundations, and universities have supported shareholder proposals respecting disclosure of political contributions; withdrawal from

South Africa, Rhodesia, or Namibia; opposition to military production; or review of corporate safety, environment, occupational discrimination, or community programs. Since most institutional shares are voted by banks, insurance companies, and mutual funds, and these financial institutions have shown only a negligibly greater willingness to oppose management, the overall pattern of institutional voting has changed little in the past five years.

MANAGEMENT CONTROL OF OTHER FUNDAMENTAL
DECISION-MAKING

Historically, shareholders controlled the business corporation not only through the election of directors but also through shareholders' power to initiate and vote upon all fundamental changes in the character of the corporation. Management's ability to initiate change was carefully circumscribed by requiring two-thirds or three-fourths affirmative votes for charter amendments, bylaw changes, mergers, sales of assets, stock issuance, recapitalization, or dissolution and was further limited by shareholder appraisal and preemptive rights.

Under Delaware's General Corporation Law, shareholders have lost nearly all power to initiate corporate change. Only the board of directors may propose charter amendments, a merger, or a sale of assets. The SEC Proxy Rules complement Delaware's corporation law by denying shareholders opportunity to communicate opposition to management proposals or to suggest modifications in management's formal proxy proposals.

This rout has been substantially replicated in all other leading chartering states. Indeed, the trend of recent revisions to state corporation law has been to attempt to deny the shareholder any vote at all! Modern corporate draftsmen invariably write short, purely formal certificates of incorporation and then place most of a corporation's actual governing rules in its bylaws, which the certificate establishes can be revised by the corporation's directors without any shareholder vote. For example, when ITT reincorporated in Delaware in 1967, it did so by creating a Delaware corporation called the "DeLitt Corporation" and by then merging ITT, previously a Maryland corporation, into DeLitt. The certificate of incorporation of DeLitt was only 1½ pages long. It reads in toto:

CERTIFICATE OF INCORPORATION
OF
DELITT CORPORATION

Article 1

The name of the corporation is Delitt Corporation (hereinafter called the "Corporation"). The name and mailing address of its incorporators are as follows:

NAME	MAILING ADDRESS
John J. Navin	320 Park Avenue, New York, N.Y. 10022
William J. Donovan	320 Park Avenue, New York, N.Y. 10022
DeForest Billyou	320 Park Avenue, New York, N.Y. 10022

Article 2

The address of the registered office of the Corporation in the State of Delaware is No. 100 West Tenth Street, in the City of Wilmington, County of New Castle. The name of its registered agent at such address is The Corporation Trust Company.

Article 3

The purpose of the Corporation is to engage in any lawful act or activity for which corporations may be organized under the General Corporation Law of Delaware.

Article 4

The total number of shares of stock which the Corporation has authority to issue is 100 shares of capital stock of the par value of $100 per share.

Article 5

Whenever the vote of stockholders at a meeting thereof is required or permitted to be taken for or in connection with any corporate action by any provision of the General Corporation Law of Delaware, the meeting and vote of stockholders may be dispensed with if the holders of stock having not less than the minimum percentage of the vote required by statute for the proposed corporate action shall consent in writing to such corporate action being taken, provided that prompt notice must be given to all stockholders of the taking of such corporate action without a meeting and by less than unanimous written consent.

Article 6

In furtherance and not in limitation of the powers conferred by law, the Board of Directors is expressly authorized:

(a) To make, alter, amend or repeal the By-Laws of the Corporation.

(b) To direct and determine the use and disposition of any annual net profits or net assets in excess of capital; to set apart out of any of the funds of the Corporation available for dividends a reserve or reserves for any proper purpose; and to abolish any such reserve in the manner in which it was created.

(c) To establish bonus, profit-sharing, stock option, retirement or other types of incentive or compensation plans for the employees (including officers and directors) of the Corporation and to fix the amount of the profits to be distributed or shared and to determine the persons to participate in any such plans and the amounts of their respective participations.

(d) From time to time to determine whether and to what extent, and at what time and places and under what conditions and regulations, the accounts and books of the Corporation (other than the stock ledger), or any of them, shall be open to the inspection of the stockholders; and no stockholder shall have any right to inspect any account or book or document of the Corporation, except as conferred by statute or authorized by the Board of Directors or by a resolution of the stockholders.

(e) To authorize, and cause to be executed, mortgages and liens upon the real and personal property of the Corporation.

Article 7

The corporation reserves the right to amend, alter, change or repeal any provision contained in this Certificate of Incorporation, in the manner now or hereafter prescribed by statute, and all rights conferred upon stockholders herein are granted subject to this reservation.

The key sentence is contained in Article 6: "In furtherance and not in limitation of the powers conferred by law, the Board of Directors is expressly authorized: (a) To make, alter, amend or repeal the By-Laws of the corporation. . . ." What ITT tried to do, as so many other giant Delaware corporations have tried to do, was to totally shut shareholders out of the governing process except in those rare instances in which the Delaware General Corporation Law explicitly requires a shareholder vote—which is not very often.

True, technically, section 251(c) grants shareholders a vote on management merger proposals. But this, in fact, is a mere snare for the dim-witted. Only a small minority of corporate fusions actually trigger this shareholder vote. The overwhelming majority employ one of three conventional loopholes (discussed in the Sources).

Similarly, section 271 limits shareholder suffrage in a sale, lease, or exchange of assets to transactions involving "all or substantially all" of a corporation's property and assets. Since most large industrial corporations are highly diversified, this provision effectively insures their shareholders will never vote. For example, General Motors could sell an automobile division such as Pontiac or Cadillac and not require a vote. It could liquidate hundred-million-dollar plants which manufacture refrigerators, diesel engines, and trucks or auction off all of its Detroit real estate and relocate in the Peoples Republic of China, and shareholders would have no choice in the matter. Only if GM sold *all* assets used to manufacture "automotive products" (about 75 percent of the corporation) would a sale of assets require a shareholder vote.

Moreover, section 271 is the only Delaware statute concerning corporate divisions. A Delaware corporation may create and fund new subsidiary corporations, regardless of size; liquidate these subsidiaries or comparable divisions and distribute assets to shareholders; or spin-off new corporations altogether without any shareholder vote. As business corporations have evolved these new forms, Delaware and other principal chartering states have deliberately not kept pace. Corporate executives have not hesitated to take advantage of this laxity. In the past three years many Delaware corporations have "gone private" and bought up minority shareholdings at bargain prices during a depressed stock market. This will allow favored shareholders or the firm itself to reap the profits when the company's stock price rises. Other senior managements have used the merger provisions to prevent take-over bids—which can benefit all shareholders—by requiring super-majorities, such as 75 or 90 percent, to consent to any consolidation or sale of the companies assets.

Whither/Wither the Board of Directors?

But does not the board of directors with its sweeping statutory mandate "to manage the business and affairs of every corporation" provide an internal check on the power of corporate executives? No. Long ago the grandiloquent words of the statutes ceased to have any operative meaning. "Directors," William O. Douglas complained in 1934, "do not direct." "[T]here is one thing all boards have in common, regardless of their legal position," Peter Drucker has written. *"They do not function."* In Robert Townsend's tart analysis, "[M]ost big companies have turned their boards of directors into nonboards. . . . In the years that I've spent on various boards I've never head a single suggestion from a director (made as a director *at* a board meeting) that produced any result at all."

Recently these views were corroborated by Professor Myles Mace of the Harvard Business School, the nation's leading authority on the performance of boards of directors. In *Directors—Myth and Reality*, Mace summarized the results of hundreds of interviews with corporate officers and directors.

Directors do not establish the basic objectives, corporate strategies or broad policies of large and medium-sized corporations, Mace found. Management creates the policies. The board has a right of veto but rarely exercises it. As one executive said, "Nine hundred and ninety-nine times out of a thousand, the board goes along with management. . . ." Or another, "I can't think of a single time when the board has failed to support a proposed policy of management or failed to endorse the recommendation of management."

The board does not select the president or other chief executive officers. "What is perhaps the most common definition of a function of the board of directors—namely, to select the president—was found to be the greatest myth," reported Mace. "The board of directors in most companies, except in a crisis, does not select the president. The president usually chooses the man who succeeds him to that position, and the board complies with the legal amenities in endorsing and voting his election." A corporate president agreed: "The former company president tapped me to be president, and I assure you that I will select my successor when the time comes." Even seeming exceptions such as RCA's 1975 ouster of Robert Sarnoff frequently turn out to be at the instigation of senior operating executives rather than an aroused board.

The board's role as disciplinarian of the corporation is more apparent than real. As the business-supported Conference Board conceded, "One of the most glaring deficiencies attributed to the corporate board . . . is its failure to monitor and evaluate the performance of the chief executive in a concrete way." To cite a specific example, decisions on executive compensation are made by the president—with perfunctory board approval in most situations. In the vast majority of corporations, Professor Mace found, the compensation committee, and the board which approves the recommendations of the compensation committee, "are not decision-making bodies."

Directors do not even ask discerning questions. It is considered "discourteous," a breach of "corporate manners" for directors to "challenge" the president or other corporate officers. This can be a very expensive form of decorum, as the Penn Central's shareholders painfully discovered. At the time of its collapse in June 1970, Penn Central was the largest railroad in the country and the sixth largest industrial corporation overall. Within a two-year period, shareholders witnessed the decline of their shares from $86.50 to $2.75.

Why? "The board was definitely responsible for the trouble," recounted outside director E. Clayton Gengras. "They took their fees and they didn't do anything. Over a period of years, people just sat there. That poor man from the University of Pennsylvania [University President Gaylord P. Harnwell], he never opened his mouth. They didn't know the factual picture and they didn't try to find out." As the Penn Central rushed towards its monumental crack-up, the board routinely approved every proposal forwarded by management. Although Penn Central was desperate for capital, the directors paid out nearly $100 million in dividends. The board never saw a capital expenditures budget. It never understood the inaccuracies published in Penn Central's annual reports. Just six hours before the corporation filed its bankruptcy petition, the board routinely approved new contracts for eight corporate executives, apparently unaware even then of the dimensions of the Penn Central's crisis. "All of this raises the serious question as to whether giant corporations affecting the everyday lives of our population . . . should continue to be governed in the traditional fashion or whether a new system of corporate directorships should be devised," concluded the House Banking and Currency Committee.

Yet boards will continue to be dysfunctional as long as they remain the creature of the corporate chief executive. For it is the chief executive who, like the family owner-manager in a small corporation, selects new members of the board. And it is the chief executive who de-selects existing board members when nominations for the board are necessary for annual shareholders' meetings.

Our own survey of the boards of the 200 largest industrial corporations found that the average board had a total of 14.49 directors, including 7.93 "outsiders" (that is, directors who were not employees of the corporation) and 6.56 insiders (or employee directors). Some 69 percent of the outside directors were fellow corporate executives; 6 percent were investment bankers; 7 percent were lawyers. Only 2 percent were women; a lesser percentage were black. Hence over 90 percent of the directors of our largest corporations either worked for the corporate chief executive or were fellow corporate executives, corporate bankers, or corporate lawyers.

Most "outside" directors appear to be chosen because of their status. "Presidents and chairmen of large and respected companies," one corporate president observed, "enjoy the prestige of serving on similar large and respected company boards. They are identified with their peers. They find the experience socially satisfying. Outside directorships provide a few more lines in their *Who's Who,* and it is a little bit like being knighted to say 'I'm a director of General Motors, or General Electric, or AT&T.' " Frequently, the chief executive chooses his friends, or individuals known to be "sympathetic" or "congenial," to be directors. "You certainly don't want anyone on your board who even slightly might be a challenge on a question of your tenure, so you pick personal friends with prestige titles and names," a corporate president explained. Another executive agreed: "What would you do if you were president? You control the company and you control the board. You want to perpetuate this control. . . . You sure as hell are not going to ask Ralph Nader. . . ."

At its worst, the outside director system degenerates into a private club, as the president of a west coast company explained:

You've got to remember that the outside directors of large national and regional companies are members of a sort of club. To be considered for admission you must have the title as president or chairman of a respectable and respected organization. This is what some young people call the Establishment. But these are the people you do business with, travel around with, serve on community projects with—and it has to be a group the members of which get along together. Regionally each area has its elite. Sometimes many will in fact be members of the same golf or social club. Here in Los Angeles you will find a great number of directors with membership in the Los Angeles Country Club; in Cleveland the same is true of the Union Club—each city has its hard core members of the club group.

Exceptions to this pattern become news events. In reporting on General Motors' 1971 annual shareholders' meeting, the *Wall Street Journal* noted that, "The meeting's dramatic highlight was an impassioned and unprecedented speech by the Rev. Leon Sullivan, GM's recently appointed Negro director, supporting the Episcopal Church's efforts to get the company out of South Africa. It was the first time that a GM director had ever spoken against management at an annual meeting." Now Rev. Sullivan is an unusual outside director, being General Motors' first black director and only "public interest" director. But what makes Leon Sullivan most extraordinary is that he was the first director in *any* major American corporation to come out publicly against his own corporation when its operations tended to support apartheid.

Yet as lethargic as outside directors usually are, employee directors tend to be even less effective. The typical vice president/inside-director is in a very precarious position at a board meeting. Unwilling to say anything in disagreement with his boss, he usually sits quietly and waits until he is called upon to speak. Disagreements with other corporate executives are invariably resolved out of the board room. The effect is to present outsiders with a "united front": to make the corporate chief executive's decisions seem inevitable.

So staffed, board meetings in most large industrial corporations have become formalized into a monthly or bimonthly ritual, usually lasting about one to three hours. Much of this time is consumed by perhaps a 30-minute to an hour review of operations for the last period (month or quarter) by the president or vice president of finance. This is followed by board approvals of capital appropriations and of the actions of the executive committee taken since the last meeting. The meeting often concludes after senior executives have described a new research development or a major operations program. Usually the entire meeting—which is closed to shareholders—is choreographed by the corporate chief executive. He chooses which officers shall speak. He writes the agenda. When he wants to be asked about a particular issue, he plants the relevant question.

The impossibility of so infrequent or so circumscribed meetings of the board enabling directors to effectively "manage" their corporation was sardonically illustrated by the congressional testimony of H. O. Havemeyer, a corporate chieftain of an earlier day:

Q. As a member of that board, what else have you done?
A. *Oh, I have convened and talked.*
Q. You have convened and talked?
A. *And adjourned.*
Q. Well, you have convened and talked?
A. *And adjounred.*
Q. Well, what have you talked about?
A. *Statistics.*

This testimony was given in 1887 when outside directors were typically the "tools" or "dummies" of the controlling corporate president or bank. A popular gag on Wall Street was that the role of an outside director was to receive his five-dollar gold piece at the start of each meeting and then obediently fall asleep. Directorial lassitude is not so obvious today. Yet considering that the size and complexity of corporate enterprise has significantly increased since 1887 while the frequency and length of directors' meetings has not, it is a fair assumption that the outsiders who obediently nod through ceremonial board meetings today are little better informed than their brethren who slept before them.

Certainly directors' sources of information remain as much subject to management control today as they did 90 years ago. After resigning from TWA's board, former United States Supreme Court Justice Arthur Goldberg had this complaint: "What the typical board of directors gets is a recommendation which seems monolithic. . . . It's not like a court, where a judge can order a brief from both sides." Recently the *quantity* of preparatory information available to outside directors has significantly increased. Yet the thickened reports and whirlwind plant tours are still only what the corporate chief executive wants outsiders to see. "In many corporations," found Professor Melvin Eisenberg, "the executives go so far as to wholly deny the board—supposedly entrusted with supreme power over the corporation—access to certain categories of information." For instance, a 1971 survey found that only 17 percent of 474 industrial firms sent manufacturing data to directors prior to board meetings, only 21 percent sent marketing data, and 11 percent sent no data at all.

And outside directors have little personal incentive to doubt management. A 1973 survey of 378 manufacturing corporations with assets of $50 million or more showed that outside directors received median annual fees of approximately $5,900, while inside directors generally are not paid at all. On top of the $100,000 + incomes typically earned by outside directors, who are corporate chief executives or vice presidents, leading investment bankers, or law firm partners, such annual retainers or meeting fees seem like peanuts. The result is counterproductive. Outside directors rationalize not doing very much by the fact they are not paid very much.

How, then, can one reconcile the grand imperative, "The business and affairs of every corporation . . . shall be managed by or under the direction of . . . a board of directors" with the reality of this "non decision-making body"? The fashionable response is that the board is a legal fiction. Management control has overwhelmed the rule of law.

This widely held view is only half right. Management has deposed the board of directors—but it has done so under color of law. No rule within the modern corporation statutes prohibits management from nominating and serving as directors. Corporation law has abrogated directional independence by omission. Moreover, even if the statutes provided structural safeguards to maintain the independence of the board, these could not undo the effect of two provisions found in most state corporation laws.

The first provision is exemplified by a Delaware Corporation Law section which provides that a director shall "be fully protected in relying in good faith upon . . . reports made to the corporation by any of its officers." The meaning of this provision is very simple. Directors have no duty to know. "Unless something occurs to put them on suspicion that something is wrong, directors are entitled to rely on the honesty and integrity of [management]," held the leading case of *Graham v. Allis-Chalmers Manufacturing Company*. Directors are not required to "put into effect a system of watchfulness." They need not anticipate problems nor verify the accuracy of reports upon which they rely.

A second provision of the Delaware General Corporation Law accomplishes the same result by allowing the board to *formally* delegate responsibility for most corporate business to a committee dominated by inside directors. Our survey of the 200 largest industrial corporations indicates that approximately two-thirds of the corporations had withdrawn directorial powers from the full board—typically a majority of whose members were outsiders—to an executive committee at least half of whose members were insiders.

A much smaller number of corporations accomplish a comparable result by delegating authority to an insider-dominated finance committee. In our survey of the 200 largest industrial corporations, we found that 16 corporations had delegated authority to a finance committee, half or more of whose members were insiders.

Examples of the delegation of the board's authority to either an insider-dominated executive or finance committee have been well described by attorney John A. McMullen:

At IBM—four directors, all top level officers of the corporation, control the all-important executive and finance committees; in addition, three of them are members of the powerful Corporate Office. At GM, four or five men, all inside directors of the company, dominate the executive and finance committees of the board as well as the administration committee comprised of key officers and directors. . . . DuPont's executive committee consists of the company's chairman of the board, president, and six senior vice presidents. Each of these men is entirely relieved of day-to-day functional responsibilities; each operates jointly with his fellow committee members to set overall corporate policy, and acts only as an advisor to the operating department from which he originally derived his skills, training, and experience.

Yet, whether or not the board formally resolves to delegate operational authority to an executive committee between board meetings, the actuality is that employee directors or other senior executives invariably exercise the powers of initiation. It does not matter whether key corporate decisions are initiated by a single corporate autocrat or a board committee or a committee operating out of the office of the president. Senior executives call the shots. This is what Berle and Means meant by their insightful descriptions of "management control." This is why state corporation law is moribund. Not only is it written by corporate management's representatives, it is also hopelessly inaccurate. In appreciating the law of corporate governance, one rule above all others must be followed: *Concentrate on the omissions.* Where state law does not require directors to be, corporate executives inevitably are.

The Limitations of Shareholder Litigation

STATE LAW: THE NON-DUTY OF CARE

The erosion of shareholder authority within the corporation would be less serious if shareholders were able to oppose the abuses of corporate management in court. In theory, civil litigation remains the shareholder's ultimate check. The problem is that, except for certain limited claims under the federal securities laws, it rarely works. Long ago judicial doctrines reduced the state shareholder action to a trivial value.

Earliest was the judicial rejection of the principle of *ultra vires* action. In its classical form, the doctrine of *ultra vires* envisioned the corporate charter as a contract between the state, corporate management, and the shareholders. Corporations were prohibited from performing certain acts, not because they were illegal but because neither the state nor the shareholders had agreed to them. Shareholders could enjoin corporate officers and directors from engaging in actions "beyond their powers." Accordingly, in a leading 1867 case, a single shareholder blocked a railroad from extending its railway to a more distant point than that specified in the charter because that was not the enterprise he had bargained for.

With the rise of the corporate enabling acts, the principle of *ultra vires* declined. Shareholder limitations were overridden through court discoveries of "implied" or "auxiliary" powers. In the 1896 case of *Jacksonville M. P. Ry. & Nav. Co. v. Hopper*, for example, the United States Supreme Court held that the Florida railway company might engage in leasing and running a resort hotel, on the curious logic that "to maintain cheap hotels or eating houses . . . would not be so plainly an act outside the powers of a railway company as to compel a court to sustain the defense of ultra vires. . . ." By 1931, *Fletcher's Cyclopedia of Corporations* could proclaim, "the theory that a corporation can do no acts beyond its authority [has been] discarded by a majority of the courts in the country."

Paralleling the decline of *ultra vires* has been the universal refusal of state courts to hold corporate directors or officers liable for negligence. Because they are vested with great power over other people's property, the law has always nominally required, in the language of the present New York statute, that "Directors and officers shall discharge the duties of their respective positions in good faith and with that degree of diligence, care, and skill which ordinarily prudent men would exercise under similar circumstances in like positions."

In practice, the typical judicial or statutory formulation of the duty of care is too vague to require much of anything. As Yale Law School's Professor Joseph Bishop concluded after an extensive review of the case law:

The search for cases in which directors of industrial corporations have been held liable . . . for negligence uncomplicated by self-dealing is a search for a very small number of needles in a very large haystack. Few are the cases in which the stockholders do not allege conflict of interest, still fewer those among them which achieve even such partial success as denial of the defendant's motion to dismiss the complaint.

In all, Professor Bishop was able to find only four recent cases in which a state court held that a shareholder had alleged a good cause of action for negligence uncomplicated by self-dealing. In only one of these cases did a state court rule on the merits that a corporate officer was liable for negligence. And in that case, the word "negligence" had been used as a euphemism for dishonesty.

This result is primarily the fault of statutory draftsmen. They have refused to identify *how* a corporate officer meets his duty of care. They have never identified what specific actions he must perform; what specific responsibilities are his. In the absence of a clear standard from the legislature, state courts have refused to guess.

At most, state courts will hold corporate directors or executives liable for conduct involving obvious self-enrichment such as fraud, misapplication of funds, diversion of corporate business opportunities, or causing the corporation to make excessive payment for the purchase of their property. Yet even in these types of cases, where the actions of corporate officers amount to simple and obvious theft, the procedural rules of state corporation law have been skewed to discourage shareholder suits.

The most onerous bars to shareholder litigation are the so-called "security for expenses" provisions enacted by New York, New Jersey, Pennsylvania, Michigan, California, and 13 other states. These provisions require a complaining shareholder owning less than a stated amount of stock—typically 5 percent of the stock or shares worth less than $50,000—to "give security for the reasonable expenses, including attorney's fees, which may be incurred" by both the corporation and the parties defendant in a shareholder action. Since the cost of defendants' legal fees may amount to hundreds of thousands of dollars, the security for expense provision, when enforced, presents a formidable barrier to shareholder action.

The rules respecting attorneys' fees pose a second procedural pitfall for shareholder actions. Nearly every jurisdiction provides that only shareholders whose suits are successful may be reimbursed by the corporation for attorneys' fees. This rule seeks to discourage attorneys from bringing nonmeritorious suits. Several states, however, further provide that attorneys' fees may be awarded only if a substantial monetary benefit is conferred upon the corporation. As a practical matter, this standard precludes shareholder litigation in all cases except those of overreaching where a monetary benefit—the amount taken—is readily apparent.

In all other cases it is normally cheaper to sell the stock than to compel the corporation to obey the law.

FEDERAL SECURITIES LAW: "TAKING OVER THE UNIVERSE GRADUALLY"?

To some extent, federal securities law—and federal court decisions—have compensated for the atrophy of state shareholder protection.

In 1968, the influential Second Circuit Court of Appeals handed down its celebrated *S.E.C. v. Texas Gulf Sulphur* decision which revolutionized the case law interpreting Rule 10b-5 under the 1934 Securities and Exchange Act. Rule 10b-5 provides that it is unlawful for any person to employ a fraudulent scheme, to make any untrue statement, or to fail to state a pertinent fact when purchasing or selling a security. *Texas Gulf* substantially broadened this antifraud rule by holding that corporate directors, officers, and employees violated 10b-5 when they purchased company stock knowing of a huge mineral strike before this fact was generally known or communicated to the public.

A federal district court, also in 1968, ruled in *Escott v. Bar Chris*—a decision some commentators initially believed would have even greater effect on directorial behavior than *Texas Gulf*. In *Bar Chris* security holders asserted that a bowling alley construction company that had sold them convertible debentures had filed a registration statement prior to the sale of the bonds which contained false statements and omissions. After concluding that the registration statement did, indeed, contain numerous inaccuracies, the district court stunned Wall Street by holding all nine directors who signed the prospectus—including two new to the board—liable. In summing up their liability, the court seemed to move far toward creating a federal duty of care, at least with respect to registration statements:

Section 11 imposes liability in the first instance upon a director, no matter how new he is. He is presumed to know his responsibility when he becomes a director. He can escape liability only by using that reasonable care to investigate the facts which a prudent man would employ in the management of his own property. In my opinion, a prudent man would not act in an important matter without any knowledge of the relevant facts, in sole reliance upon representations of persons who are comparative strangers and upon general information which does not purport to cover the particular case. To say that such minimal conduct measures up to the statutory standard would, to all intents and purposes, absolve new directors from responsibility merely because they are new. This is not a sensible construction of section 11, when one bears in mind its fundamental purpose of requiring full and truthful disclosure for the protection of investors.

The cumulative result of these and other federal securities law decisions led the *Wall Street Journal* to exclaim in early 1973, "[D]irectors of corporations now face more perils than Pauline ever did!" In a similar vein, Harvard Law School's securities expert, Professor Louis Loss, observed in 1969 that "the great Rule 10b-5," which had emerged as the principal basis of liability under the federal securities laws, "seems to be taking over the universe gradually."

In retrospect, both views seem overstated. The basic reason the securities laws will neither "take over the universe" nor seriously "imperil outside directors" is that they are restricted to a discrete set of securities transactions. Although present securities laws do require corporate officers to file with the SEC accurate periodic financial reports and securities registration statements, not make false and misleading statements in proxies, nor defraud outsiders in connection with their own securities purchases or sales, the securities laws do not, emphasized the Supreme Court in 1971, reach transactions which otherwise involve "internal corporate mismanagement."

And in late 1973, the Second Circuit Court of Appeals held in *Lanza v. Drexel* that only corporate officers who recklessly or deliberately defrauded shareholders could be held liable for money damages under Rule 10b-5. In refusing to follow the reasoning of the district court in the *Escott v. Bar Chris* case, the appeals court made plain that an outside director who was "merely negligent" in his participation in a fraudulent securities transaction had little to fear.

The consequence of *Lanza* and similar recent decisions has been to leave federal securities law in a crazy quilt pattern. The federal securities laws, for example, will not reach a deliberate though not self-enriching decision of corporate executives to engage in an unprofitable line of business unless there has been an accompanying failure of disclosure. Nor will they reach decisions which *do* enrich corporate officers unless they involve security transactions. Liability seems so haphazard and fortuitous that former SEC Chairman William Cary was moved to complain:

There is no justification for a *federal* law disciplining or holding a tippee liable for misusing inside information concerning management decisions but not monitoring the misconduct of management itself. . . . It is absurd that a corporate transaction, clearly unfair though perhaps not fraudulent, should be subject to attack in the federal courts only upon the ground that it has not been disclosed to shareholders rather than because of its inherent inequity.

NULLIFY THE JUDGMENT: INDEMNIFICATION INSURANCE

Not only is it difficult for shareholders to successfully sue their companies, but even successful judgments often can be nullified. Seventeen states today permit corporations to purchase indemnification insurance for their directors and officers against, in the words of a typical policy, any "wrongful act [committed] . . . in their capacities as directors or officers." A 1974 survey of the Fortune 500 list found that 80 percent of these companies carried indemnification insurance. A similar sample of corporations listed on the New York Stock Exchange found that 76.1 percent carried such insurance. Since indemnification insurance was virtually unknown as recently as a dozen years ago, and most insurance policies were purchased within the past five to seven years, it is a fair assumption that nearly every large industrial corporation permitted by state law will carry indemnification insurance within a short time.*

* One reason for the enormous leap in the number of corporations carrying indemnification insurance has been the scare tactics employed by the insurance companies. The general tenor of their approach is illustrated by an advertisement on page six of the *Wall Street Journal*, March 21, 1968, featuring a composite photograph of a board of directors presided over by a stuffed duck and the explanatory text, "As a corporate officer or director, you may be a sitting duck for a shareholder or third party liability suit." A similar ad appears on page nine of the same issue wherein a sullen looking stockholder announces that he "might just sue every company director reading this newspaper," and reminds the presumably panicking directors that he is just one of "24 million potential enemies."

There is, to be sure, a persuasive case for indemnifying corporate directors against the costs of nonmeritorious legal claims. If innocent directors had to settle such suits because they lacked the resources to hire competent attorneys, responsible men and women would be discouraged from becoming directors. But current indemnity statutes are not limited to the purpose of protecting innocent officers from the costs of nonmeritorious suits. They also protect guilty officers from accountability for their wrongs and reduce incentives for lawful conduct.

Delaware's statute exemplifies this overbreadth. It allows a corporation

> to purchase and maintain insurance on behalf of any person who is or was a director, officer, employee or agent of the corporation . . . against any liability asserted against him and incurred by him in any such capacity, or arising out of his status as such, whether or not the corporation would have the power to indemnify him against any such liability under the provisions of this section.

As written, this provision permits the corporation to insulate its officers from *all* potential liabilities. Officers may be insured against any negligence, self-dealing, looting the corporation or embezzlement, all conflicts of interest, and deliberate statutory violations. They may be reimbursed for violations of federal safety, civil rights, environmental, tax, or antitrust laws. They may even be insured against the same judgments in derivative actions that an earlier provision of the same statute provided a corporation could not indemnify directly.

Delaware defends such insurance as a form of compensation, arguing that the corporation could make a larger compensation arrangement with the executive and let him pay for the insurance himself. But the question is not how much officers' compensation should be, but rather whether wrongful acts *should* be indemnified at all. Why should an executive of a drug company be indemnified for the costs of a criminal fine if he is convicted of allowing a harmful drug to injure several thousand people when the same act as a private individual would send him to jail? An untenable double standard has been created. The more powerful an executive becomes, the less likely he is to pay for an abuse of power.

Conflicts of Interests

In almost every primary economic relation of the industrial corporation—to competing corporations, to banks, to suppliers, to distributors, to investors—the law now permits (in many instances, encourages) the most blatant division of loyalties.

Most threatening is the anticompetitive practice of *interlocking directorates*. A philosophic cornerstone of American business is that vigorous competition will enable firms to have comparable access to capital, supplies, distributors, and markets, and thus an equal chance to succeed or fail on the merits. But if competing corporations place directors on each other's boards, there is opportunity to conspire on price or territory. If corporate officers sit on the boards of their banks or suppliers or distributors, there arises the obvious temptation to obtain preferential treatment based on favor and friendship. Then the race is not to the swift, but to the well-connected. Louis Brandeis saw the problem early in this century:

The practice of interlocking directorates is the root of many evils. It offends laws human and divine. Applied to rival corporations, it tends to the suppression of competition and to violation of the Sherman law. Applied to corporations which deal with each other, it tends to disloyalty and to violation of the fundamental law that no man can serve two masters. In either event it leads to inefficiency; for it removes incentive and destroys soundness of judgment. It is undemocratic, for it rejects the platform: "A fair field and no favors"—substituting the pull of privilege for the push of manhood.

With Brandeis as a major proponent, Congress in 1914 enacted the Clayton Act, section 8 of which expressly forbids any person from serving on the boards of two or more competing corporations. Until recently, however, section 8 had not been enforced. Through 1952, some 38 years after the enactment of the Clayton Act, the Department of Justice had not litigated a single case to a decision by a court. Through December 1975, the Department had instituted a total of 15 cases. The Federal Trade Commission, which has concurrent enforcement responsibilities, had filed only 13 complaints under section 8 of the Clayton Act through January 1965. Only one of these complaints resulted in a cease and desist order; the remainder were dismissed when the directors involved discontinued the prohibited relationship. As Chairman Emanuel Celler's House Antitrust Subcommittee concluded in 1965 after a lengthy study of interlocks among competitors: enforcement had been neither "prompt nor vigorous."*

Shortly after Celler's study was released, economist Peter Dooley calculated that there were a total of 4,007 directorships held by the directors of the 200 largest nonfinancial corporations and the 50 largest financial corporations. "While most of these directors sat on a single board, 562 sat on two or more boards: Five men held six directorships each. In all, 1,404 directorships were held by multiple directors." Two hundred and thirty-three of the 250 corporations had at least one director who sat on the board of at least one other of the largest corporations. Most significantly, fully 297 interlocks involved companies which were competitors. "While illegal under the Clayton Act," observed Professor Dooley, "the law has not been effectively enforced, so that the institution of interlocking directorates continues to provide a vehicle for restricting competition. . . ."

Our own more recent survey of the boards of directors of the 50 largest industrial corporations identified eight apparent instances of illegal interlocks. John T. Connor, for example, is both a director of General Motors and Chairman of Allied Chemical, though Allied Chemical produces seat belts, shoulder harnesses, and airbags, all of which GM either presently manufactures or potentially could. Dean McGee is a director of General Electric and Chairman of Kerr-McGee, though both sell nuclear fuels. Henry S. Wingate is a director of both U.S. Steel and International Nickel Company of Canada, both of which mine nickel, iron ore, and other competing metals.

Even beyond inadequate enforcement of its provisions, section 8 only forbids interlocks among competitive corporations. Interlocks among corporations which provide services, supplies,

* In the past three years the Federal Trade Commission has begun to enforce the Act, bringing three major actions, the most important of which required seven directors common to the boards of 12 competing oil and gas corporations to resign. More recently the Justice Department awoke from its long slumber and brought an action in 1975 against the Bank of America holding company and certain insurance companies which allegedly competed in providing designated services.

funding, or distribution for each other equally violate the fundamental law that no man can serve two masters. They are also far more numerous. In 1974, the Center for Science in the Public Interest analyzed interlocking directorates and advisory committee connections of the eighteen largest United States oil corporations. They found 460 interlocking connections in all, including 132 interlocks with banks, 31 interlocks with insurance companies, 12 interlocks with utilities, 15 interlocks with transportation corporations, and 224 interlocks with manufacturing and distribution corporations. Oil company ties with banks (which supply capital), insurance companies (which provide an underwriting service), distribution companies (which distribute oil company products), and utilities, transportation, and manufacturing corporations (which purchase oil products) inevitably diminish the arm's length atmosphere in which effective competition thrives.

Such clubbishness, however, is typical of this nation's largest corporations. Our survey of the 50 largest industrial corporations and 10 largest commercial banks found that the 50 largest industrialists had 54 interlocks with the 10 leading commercial banks and 24 interlocks among themselves. Our survey also established that it has become a common practice for the leading commercial banks to bring together competitors on their boards of directors. For example, on its board Chase Manhattan unites directors from competing companies in four industries: industrial chemicals (Allied Chemical, Celanese, and Commercial Solvents Corporation); drugs (Pfizer and Squibb); paper goods (Celanese and International Paper); and oil (Exxon, Royal Dutch Petroleum, and Standard Oil of Indiana). Continental Illinois brings together leading agricultural equipment producers Caterpillar Tractor and International Harvester; food producers Esmark and Kraftco; and railroads Chicago-Milwaukee and Illinois Central.

When interlocks are viewed on a city-by-city basis, it becomes clear that there are substantial social costs as well—as in the case of Minneapolis-St. Paul. In January 1971, Richard Gibson, a methodical staff reporter for the *Minneapolis Star*, described the social structure of a major industrial city by examining the boards of the 20 or so leading Twin City industrial corporations and eight leading banks. What he found was a tight little net or what he called swapping: Burlington Northern placed its executive on the board of General Mills, and General Mills reciprocated by placing an executive on the board of Burlington Northern. Honeywell, Pillsbury, 3M, and Dayton Hudson just placed executives everywhere, as did the leading banks.

But Gibson went beyond the statistics and examined the personalities involved. He found that the boards of the 30 leading corporations in a major metropolitan area of some two million people were dominated by 19 men. Eight served on three or more boards; five men served on four boards; six served on five boards or more. Crucially, these were the men that served as chairman or led the key committees. All but one of these men, Professor Walter Heller, was a corporate executive. Fourteen of the 19 were corporate chief executives. Examined in social terms, the economy of Minneapolis looks like an oligarchy.

Certainly no one would argue that all interlocks, whether among competitors, in financing, supply, or distribution relations, direct or indirect, lead to collusive behavior. But it is unnecessary that any interlock occur. There are sufficient directors available so that each board may be staffed by disinterested persons. The costs of interlocks—favoritism, joint price or output actions, discouragement of entrepreneurs—must be weighed against what are at best negligible advantages.

Conflict of interests can also occur when large industrial corporations invite their investment banker or outside counsel to serve on their boards. For the investment banker, especially, this creates a stark division of loyalty. In addition to underwriting security offerings and related corporate financial services, he typically does investment counseling, employs brokers, and administers mutual funds. He is just as likely to perceive his primary obligation to run to his investment clients as to the shareholders of the corporation he directs. As one top executive explained, "As soon as you have an investment banker [on the board], you put yourself in a position where one group of shareholders might be favored at the expense of other shareholders."

A worse situation occurs when the investment banker is favored at the expense of *all* shareholders. J. M. Juran and J. Louden, authors of the American Management Association's study, *The Corporate Director*, cited instances where investment bankers have been guilty of guiding the company into a poor acquisition to create a need for selling securities. Investment banker-directors have insisted on being involved—for a fee—when the corporation seeks to borrow money from an insurance company or other lender. And when a corporation has an investment banker on its board, it becomes very difficult to transact business with other investment bankers. "Having a senior partner of an investment banking firm on our board is notice to the world that we are his captive client," said one corporate president. "Of course this is the main reason investment bankers want to be on so many boards. They think of board membership as a very good way of assuring that the business of the company goes only to them. It's a sort of Operation Stakeout. It tags the company as belonging to one particular firm."

A similar division of loyalties occurs when corporate counsel serves on the board. Attorneys have a financial interest to increase the corporation's law bills, rather than economize for its shareholders. This inability of lawyer-directors to give disinterested counsel has led some law firms to discourage partners from serving on clients' boards. For example, New York City's Debevoise, Plimpton, Lyons and Gates will not permit a partner to go on a board without the approval of the firm as a whole. Skadden, Arps, Slate, Meagher and Flom, also of New York, flatly prohibits partners from becoming directors "except in extenuating cases." Nonetheless, an exhaustive 1971–72 study of some 12,000 companies, which filed information statements with the SEC, found that approximately one in six employs an attorney from the company's outside counsel as a director.

Aggravating the costs to shareholders of these structural conflicts of interest is the tolerance by modern corporate law of self-enriching executive conduct. As early as an 1846 Supreme Court opinion, the rule was well established that any contract between an interested director and his corporation was voidable at the mere insistence of the corporation or any of its shareholders regardless of the fairness or unfairness of the transaction. Professor Harold Marsh explained why:

Under this rule it mattered not the slightest that there was a majority of so-called disinterested directors who approved the contract. The courts stated that the corporation was entitled to the unprejudiced judgment and advice of all of its directors and therefore it did no good to say that the interested director did not participate in the making of the contract on behalf of the corporation. . . .

By 1880, this principle "appeared to be impregnable. . . . It was stated in ringing terms by virtually every decided case, with arguments which seemed irrefutable, and it was sanctioned by age." One scholar termed this the "fundamental law of morals and of human nature" and identified its Biblical origin: "No man can serve two masters." "Fraud is too cunning and evasive," reasoned a New Jersey court, "for courts to establish a rule that invites its presence."

Today this principle is dead. The Delaware General Corporation Law not only tolerates interested conduct by corporate officers and directors; it has made self-dealing the norm.

Under current Delaware law, the chief executive of a corporation and other senior corporate executives may serve on the board of directors or compensation committee which: (1) sets executive salaries; (2) sells or purchases property from corporate executives; (3) loans money—on a secured or unsecured basis; with or without interest—to corporate executives; and (4) establishes pension plans, profit sharing plans, stock bonuses, retirement, benefit, incentive, and compensation plans (including "phantom stock"—a risk-free, cost-free stock option plan), trusts; health insurance; or deferred income plans for such corporate officers or their dependents.

Not only may corporate officers engage in such self-dealing but shareholders under Delaware law are nearly powerless to minimize the amount of corporate largess top executives pay themselves. Any contract or transaction between the corporation and an interested executive is permissible as long as it is "fair." But, in Delaware, fairness is presumed. Professor Ernest Folk, the leading commentator of Delaware's General Corporation Law, explains that "Given Delaware's presumption of sound business judgment with respect to board decisions, the courts will try to determine whether the decision can be attributed to any rational business purpose, and if so, there will be no judicial preemption of the decision."

There seem to be few practical limits to this doctrine. For example, if a corporate chief executive were so graceless as to embezzle $500,000, there is little question that even in Delaware he would be required to return the money and would be subject to criminal prosecution. Yet if that same corporate executive raised his salary $500,000 and received the approval of a board of directors he selected, there is equally little question that a Delaware court would term this "fair"—so long as the chief executive could point to similar salary increases in his industry or received the $500,000 through an "incentive bonus" or profit participation plan.

In the absence of judicial limitations, excessive remuneration has become the norm. In 1974 the executive compensation (salary, bonus, deferred income, and directors' fees) of the highest paid executive at the 50 largest industrial corporations was approximately $400,000—or about as much in one year as many of their employees earn in a lifetime and two and one-half times the average executive compensation of $145,000 earned by the highest paid executive at the 50 largest industrial corporations in 1963.

Contrary to the conventional wisdom, top executive salaries do not generally decrease in response to a decline in corporate sales or profits. In the recessionary years 1970–1973, Professor Wilbur Lewellen, a leading authority on executive compensation, found that the "mean" salary for the top executive at 50 large manufacturing corporations increased steadily from $251,867 in 1970, to $287,759 in 1971, $323,802 in 1972, and $389,277 in 1973.

But salary, bonus, and deferred income are only the most obvious benefits appropriated by corporate chieftains. Equally important is ownership income. Nearly every large industrial corporation offers its top executives stock options. These options allow executives to buy shares of stock in their corporation at a fixed price at any time or at specified times—often with the help of company-secured low interest loans or interest-free loans—and subsequently sell them.

From the shareholder's point of view, the result is a classic case of "heads we lose, tails you win." Over time, executives are able to build up a substantial fortune in corporate stock without personal risk. The more they do so, the more they dilute the value of other stockholders' shares.

We examined the stock holdings of the highest paid executives at the 50 largest industrial corporations to get some indication of the extent of executive stock holdings. From the start, we eliminated from consideration the seven highest paid chief executives whose stock holdings were either largely inherited or largely "founder's shares": Henry Ford II (Ford Motors), Robert Sarnoff (RCA), Brooks McCormick (International Harvester), Willard Rockwell (Rockwell International), Armand Hammer (Occidental Petroleum), Sanford McDonnell (McDonnell Douglas) and J. P. Grace (W. P. Grace). The 43 remaining chief executives were "employee" executives. Yet each owned an average of $1,566,009 of his corporation's stock, according to the most recent proxy statements filed with the SEC and the closing stock prices of October 1, 1975.*

This crude figure illustrates three points. First, primarily at shareholder expense, the top executives of our largest corporations can, and often do, build up million-dollar fortunes in corporate stock on top of their substantial cash and deferred compensation. Second, the income of top executives is significantly increased each year by dividends from their corporate stock. Using our 43 top executives as an example again, each received an average of $60,382 in dividend income in 1974 above and beyond a $400,000 salary. Third, each top executive will further be enriched by increases in the price of the stock. Professor Lewellen has determined that a similar list of chief executives at the fifty largest industrial corporations (after deleting "extreme values" such as inherited or founder's stockholdings) averaged $220,087 per year in capital gains income for the four years 1960–63.

---

* This figure is admittedly a very crude approximation of ownership income. On the one hand, it does not distinguish the shares the executives purchase with their own money from those the company gave them through stock options, stock bonuses, or loan arrangements. On the other hand, it understates the amount of ownership income of these executives by making no allowance for the fact that corporate chief executives frequently sell stock they own in their own corporation and put their money in other investments.

Additionally, pension or retirement benefits have swollen. McKinsey and Company's 1975 Executive Compensation Survey found that all but one of 577 major U.S. corporations studied had a pension or profit-sharing retirement plan to pay former executives a fixed income each year after they retire. Almost half of the companies provide either a thrift or savings plan or a profit-sharing plan in addition to the pension plan. Our own survey found that the 21 chief executives of the 50 largest corporations who disclosed their estimated annual retirement benefits anticipated an income of $133,910 per year after they retire. And corporate executives also enjoy other benefits such as life and medical insurance; free medical service; educational grants for their children; indemnification insurance; company apartments; country club membership; luncheon or dinner club membership; chauffeur-driven cars; free legal and tax counseling; personal financial counseling; expense accounts; and other amenities. This myriad of stock bonus, insurance, and benefit programs increases the income of corporate chiefs by approximately 50–75 percent above their $400,000 direct remuneration to an actual income of approximately $600,000 to $700,000 per year.

Yet if excessive remuneration were a conflict of interest confined to the corporate chief executive, it would seem small once it was divided by the total number of shares in most large industrial corporations. What makes the executive compensation conflict truly expensive is that the corporate chief executive not only sets his own salary but also determines the remuneration of other executives all the way down the line. It is clearly in the corporate chief executive's personal interest to seek the greatest possible rewards for his subordinates as well as himself. For a corporate chief who can "deliver" high salaries increases the personal loyalty of his subordinates. And the higher his subordinates' income, the higher the chief executive's income must be.

A good illustration of this is General Electric, where in 1974 Reginald Jones, the chairman, received a compensation of $501,200. Walter Dance, Jack Parker, and Herman Weiss, the next three highest paid executives, received $400,750; $400,500; and $400,000, respectively. The next 107 highest paid officers averaged direct compensation of $121,240. Aggregate figures for "executive groups" at the other 50 largest industrial corporations were approximately the same. In the average corporation, the 31 or so officers ranked immediately below the five highest paid executives received an average of $99,256 in direct remuneration, which would equal approximately $150,000 imputing the present value of stock bonus programs, retirement benefits, insurance, and other perquisites.

A compensation system is obviously askew when a private business corporation must pay a chief executive compensation and benefits of over $600,000 when this is 15 times the $40,000 or so the United States government must pay its highest ranking general, regulator, or Senator. Or when it must pay its next 20–100 senior executives an average of $150,000 each when the federal government expends a maximum of $38,000 per year to hire its highest ranking civil servants, and California, this nation's largest state, pays its governor $49,000.

This is not to deny that the entrepreneur or corporate founder who, at substantial risk, introduces a new or better good or service should not be given a substantial incentive to make an unusual personal contribution to society. But we are concerned here with the administrators of large industrial corporations who, at minimal personal risk, serve as the bureaucrats of private industry. These individuals receive their staggeringly large salaries and stock options by rising through executive ranks—in exactly the same way that government's civil servants rise through civil service ranks—and by then exploiting the laxity of state corporate laws that their predecessors helped write.

Remedies

REVAMPING THE BOARD

The modern corporation is akin to a political state in which all powers are held by a single clique. The senior executives of a large firm are essentially not accountable to any other officials within the firm. These are precisely the circumstances that, in a democratic political state, require a separation of powers into different branches of authority. As James Madison explained in the *Federalist No. 47*:

The accumulation of all powers, legislative, executive, and judiciary, in the same hands, whether of one, a few or many, and whether hereditary, self-appointed, or elective, may justly be pronounced the very definition of tyranny. Were the federal constitution, therefore, really chargeable with this accumulation of power, or with a mixture of powers, having a dangerous tendency to such an accumulation, no further arguments would be necessary to inspire a universal reprobation of the system.

A similar concern over the unaccountability of business executives historically led to the elevation of a board of directors to review and check the actions of operating management. As a practical matter, if corporate governance is to be reformed, it must begin by returning the board to this historical role. The board should serve as an internal auditor of the corporation, responsible for constraining executive management from violations of law and breach of trust. Like a rival branch of government, the board's function must be defined as separate from operating management. Rather than pretending directors can "manage" the corporation, the board's role as disciplinarian should be clearly described. Specifically, the board of directors should:

- establish and monitor procedures that assure that operating executives are informed of and obey applicable federal, state, and local laws;

- approve or veto all important executive management business proposals such as corporate by-laws, mergers, or dividend decisions;

- hire and dismiss the chief executive officer and be able to disapprove the hiring and firing of the principal executives of the corporation; and

- report to the public and the shareholders how well the corporation has obeyed the law and protected the shareholders' investment.

It is not enough, however, to specify what the board should do. State corporations statutes have long provided that "the business and affairs of a corporation shall be managed by a board of directors," yet it has been over a century since the boards of the largest corporations have actually performed this role. To reform the corporation, a federal chartering law must also specify the manner in which the board performs its primary duties.

First, to insure that the corporation obeys federal and state laws, the board should designate executives responsible for compliance with these laws and require periodic signed reports describing the effectiveness of compliance procedures. Mechanisms to administer spot checks on compliance with the principal statutes should be created. Similar mechanisms can insure that corporate "whistle blowers" and nonemployee sources may communicate to the board—in private and without fear of retaliation—knowledge of violations of law.

Second, the board should actively review important executive business proposals to determine their full compliance with law, to preclude conflicts of interest, and to assure that executive decisions are rational and informed of all foreseeable risks and costs. But even though the board's responsibility here is limited to approval or veto of executive initiatives, it should proceed in as well-informed a manner as practicable. To demonstrate rational business judgment, the directorate should require management "to prove its case." It should review the studies upon which management relied to make a decision, require management to justify its decision in terms of costs or rebutting dissenting views, and, when necessary, request that outside experts provide an independent business analysis.

Only with respect to two types of business decisions should the board exceed this limited review role. The determination of salary, expense, and benefit schedules inherently possesses such obvious conflicts of interest for executives that only the board should make these decisions. And since the relocation of principal manufacturing facilities tends to have a greater effect on local communities than any other type of business decision, the board should require management to prepare a "community impact statement." This public report would be similar to the environmental impact statements presently required by the National Environmental Policy Act. It would require the corporation to state the purpose of a relocation decision; to compare feasible alternative means; to quantify the costs to the local community; and to consider methods to mitigate these costs. Although it would not prevent a corporation from making a profit-maximizing decision, it would require the corporation to minimize the costs of relocation decisions to local communities.

To accomplish this restructuring of the board requires the institutionalization of a new profession: the full-time "professional" director. Corporate scholar frequently identify William O. Douglas' 1940 proposal for "salaried, professional experts [who] would bring a new responsibility and authority to directorates and a new safety to stockholders" as the origin of the professional director idea. More recently, corporations including Westinghouse and Texas Instruments have established slots on their boards to be filled by full-time directors. Individuals such as Harvard Business School's Myles Mace and former Federal Reserve Board chairman William McChesney Martin consider their own thoroughgoing approach to boardroom responsibilities to be that of a "professional" director.

To succeed, professional directors must put in the substantial time necessary to get the job done. One cannot monitor the performance of Chrysler's or Gulf's management at a once-a-month meeting; those firms' activities are too sweeping and complicated for such ritual oversight. The obvious minimum here is an adequate salary to attract competent persons to work as full-time directors and to maintain the independence of the board from executive management.

The board must also be sufficiently staffed. A few board members alone cannot oversee the activities of thousands of executives. To be able to appraise operating management, the board needs a trim group of attorneys, economists, and labor and consumer advisors who can analyze complex business proposals, investigate complaints, spot-check accountability, and frame pertinent inquiries.

The board also needs timely access to relevant corporate data. To insure this, the board should be empowered to nominate the corporate financial auditor, select the corporation's counsel, compel the forwarding and preservation of corporate records, require all corporate executives or representatives to answer fully all board questions respecting corporate operations, and dismiss any executive or representative who fails to do so.

This proposed redesign for corporate democracy attempts to make executive management accountable to the law and shareholders without diminishing its operating efficiency. Like a judiciary within the corporation, the board has ultimate powers to judge and sanction. Like a legislature, it oversees executive activity. Yet executive management substantially retains its powers to initiate and administer business operations. The chief executive officer retains control over the organization of the executive hierarchy and the allocation of the corporate budget. The directors are given ultimate control over a narrow jurisdiction: Does the corporation obey the law, avoid exploiting consumers or communities, and protect the shareholders' investment? The executive contingent retains general authority for all corporate operations.

No doubt there will be objections that this structure is too expensive or that it will disturb the "harmony" of executive management. But it is unclear that there would be any increased cost in adopting an effective board. The true cost to the corporation could only be determined by comparing the expense of a fully paid and staffed board with the savings resulting from the elimination of conflicts of interest and corporate waste. In addition, if this should result in a slightly increased corporate expense, the appropriateness must be assessed within a broader social context: should federal and state governments or the corporations themselves bear the primary expense of keeping corporations honest? In our view, this cost should be placed on the corporations as far as reasonably possible.

It is true that an effective board will reduce the "harmony" of executive management in the sense that the power of the chief executive or senior executives will be subject to knowledgeable review. But a board which monitors rather than rubber-stamps management is exactly what is necessary to diminish the unfettered authority of the corporate chief executive or ruling clique. The autocratic power these individuals presently possess has proven unacceptably dangerous: it has led to recurring violations of law, conflicts of interest, productive inefficiency, and pervasive harm to consumers, workers, and the community environment. Under normal circumstances there should be a healthy friction between operating executives and the board to assure that the wisest possible use is made of corporate resources. When corporate executives are breaking the law, there should be no "harmony" whatsoever.

ELECTION OF THE BOARD

Restructuring the board is hardly likely to succeed if boards remain as homogeneously white, male, and narrowly oriented as they are today. Dissatisfaction with current selection of directors is so intense that analysts of corporate governance, including Harvard Law School's Abram Chayes, Yale political scientist Robert Dahl, and University of Southern California Law School Professor Christopher Stone, have each separately urged that the starting point of corporate reform should be to change the way in which the board is elected.

Professor Chayes, echoing John Locke's principle that no authority is legitimate except that granted "the consent of the governed," argues that employees and other groups substantially affected by corporate operations should have a say in its governance:

> Shareholder democracy, so-called, is misconceived because the shareholders are not the governed of the corporations whose consent must be sought. . . . Their interests are protected if financial information is made available, fraud and overreaching are prevented, and a market is maintained in which their shares may be sold. A priori, there is no reason for them to have any voice, direct or representational, in [corporate decision making]. They are no more affected than nonshareholding neighbors by these decisions. . . .
>
> A more spacious conception of 'membership,' and one closer to the facts of corporate life, would include all those having a relation of sufficient intimacy with the corporation or subject to its powers in a sufficiently specialized way. Their rightful share in decisions and the exercise of corporate power would be exercised through an institutional arrangement appropriately designed to represent the interests of a constituency of members having a significant common relation to the corporation and its power.

Professor Dahl holds a similar view: "[W]hy should people who own shares be given the privileges of citizenship in the government of the firm when citizenship is denied to other people who also make vital contributions to the firm?" he asks rhetorically. "The people I have in mind are, of course, employees and customers, without whom the firm could not exist, and the general public, without whose support for (or acquiescence in) the myriad protections and services of the state the firm would instantly disappear. . . ." Yet Dahl finds proposals for interest group representation less desirable than those for worker self-management. He also suggests consideration of codetermination statutes such as those enacted by West Germany and ten other European and South American countries under which shareholders and employees separately elect designated portions of the board.

From a different perspective, Professor Stone has recommended that a federal agency appoint "general public directors" to serve on the boards of all the largest industrial and financial firms. In certain extreme cases such as where a corporation repeatedly violates the law, Stone recommends that the federal courts appoint "special public directors" to prevent further delinquency.

There are substantial problems with each of these proposals. It seems impossible to design a general "interest group" formula which will assure that all affected constituencies of large industrial corporations will be represented and that all constituencies will be given appropriate weight. Even if such a formula could be designed, however, there is the danger that consumer or community or minority or franchisee representatives would become only special pleaders for their constituents and otherwise lack the loyalty or interest to direct generally. This defect has emerged in West Germany under codetermination. Labor representatives apparently are indifferent to most problems of corporate management that do not directly affect labor. They seem as deferential to operating executive management as present American directors are. Alternatively, federally appointed public directors might be frozen out of critical decision-making by a majority of "privately" elected directors, or the appointing agency itself might be biased.

Nonetheless, the essence of the Chayes-Dahl-Stone argument is well taken. The boards of directors of most major corporations are, as CBS's Dan Rather criticized the original Nixon cabinet, too much like "twelve grey-haired guys named George." The quiescence of the board has resulted in important public and, for that matter, shareholder concerns being ignored.

An important answer is structural. The homogeneity of the board can only be ended by giving to each director, in addition to a general duty to see that the corporation is profitably administered, a separate oversight responsibility, a separate expertise, and a separate constituency so that each important public concern would be guaranteed at least one informed representative on the board. There might be nine corporate directors, each of whom is elected to a board position with one of the following oversight responsibilities:

1. Employee welfare
2. Consumer protection
3. Environmental protection and community relations
4. Shareholder rights
5. Compliance with law
6. Finances
7. Purchasing and marketing
8. Management efficiency
9. Planning and research

By requiring each director to balance responsibility for representing a particular social concern against responsibility for the overall health of the enterprise, the problem of isolated "public" directors would be avoided. No individual director is likely to be "frozen out" of collegial decision-making because all directors would be of the same character. Each director would spend the greater part of his or her time developing expertise in a different area; each director would have a motivation to insist that a different aspect of a business decision be considered. Yet each would simultaneously be responsible for participating in all board decisions, as directors now are. So the specialized area of each director would supplement but not supplant the director's general duties.

Although not a symmetrical analogy, the most successful precedent for dividing the representative responsibilities and constituencies is, of course, the Constitution of the United States. There, too, a basic question was one of motivation: How to design a political administration which would retain an equal respect for the rights of all of its citizens. Only by arranging "ambition . . . to counteract ambition" did the Federalists believe such respect would endure. By granting the President, the two houses of Congress, and the judiciary different geographic constituencies, different terms, and different duties, the various factions of the nation's citizens were most likely to be insured some representation within the government. "Hence a double security arises to the rights of the people. The different governments will control each other, at the same time that each will be controlled by itself," explained Madison in *Federalist No. 51*.

In recent years, some business corporations have also perceived the advantages of creating constituent voices within the structure of the firm. Reverend Leon Sullivan, the only black director on General Motors' board, has made plain that he considers it his special responsibility to advance the interests of GM's black employees and dealers. His representation, among other things, has led to an increase in the number of blacks being trained to be GM executives. Gillette's Vice President for Product Integrity, Robert Giovacchini, is said to perform a similar role. Although not a member of the board, Mr. Giovacchini has been given the authority to recall any Gillette product, quash any advertising claim, or order any packaging change he feels is necessary to protect the company's consumers.

Only by institutionalizing the duties and power that individuals like Reverend Sullivan and Robert Giovacchini hold can responsible corporate government be brought to each large firm.

For in most giant corporations, no specific executive official or board member is responsible for protecting the interests of employees, consumers, the environment, or local communities. No one outside of senior management reviews the most important business decisions to assure their compliance with law, financial integrity, efficiency, or long-term corporate goals. Because these concerns become everybody's general interest, they become nobody's particular interest—and often go unattended.

To maintain the independence of the board from the operating management it reviews also requires that each federally chartered corporation shall be directed by a purely "outside" board. No executive, attorney, representative, or agent of a corporation should be allowed to serve simultaneously as a director of that same corporation. Directorial and executive loyalty should be furthered by an absolute prohibition of interlocks. No director, executive, general counsel, or company agent should be allowed to serve more than one corporation subject to the Federal Corporate Chartering Act.

Several objections may be raised. First, how can we be sure that completely outside boards will be competent? As elaborated subsequently, corporate campaign rules will be redesigned to emphasize qualifications. This will allow shareholder voters to make rational decisions based on information clearly presented to them. It is also a fair assumption that shareholders, given an actual choice and role in corporate governance, will want to elect the men and women most likely to safeguard their investments.

A second objection is that once all interlocks are proscribed and a full-time outside board required, there will not be enough qualified directors to staff all major firms. This complaint springs from that corporate mentality which, accustomed to 60-year-old white male bankers and businessmen as directors, makes the norm a virtue. In fact, if we loosen the reins on our imagination, America has a large, rich, and diverse pool of possible directorial talent from academics and public administrators and community leaders to corporate and public interest lawyers.

But directors should be limited to four two-year terms so that boards do not become stale. And no director should be allowed to serve on more than one board at any one time. Although simultaneous service on two or three boards might allow key directors to "pollinize" directorates by comparing their different experiences, this would reduce their loyalty to any one board, jeopardize their ability to fully perform their new directorial responsibilities, and undermine the goal of opening up major boardrooms to as varied a new membership as is reasonable.

The shareholder electoral process should be made more democratic as well. Any shareholder or allied shareholder group which owns .1 percent of the common voting stock in the corporation or comprises 100 or more individuals and does not include a present executive of the corporation, nor act for a present executive, may nominate up to three persons to serve as directors. This will exclude executive management from the nomination process. It also increases the likelihood of a diverse board by preventing any one or two sources from proposing all nominees. To prevent frivolous use of the nominating power, this proposal establishes a minimum shareownership condition.

Six weeks prior to the shareholders' meeting to elect directors, each shareholder should receive a ballot and a written statement on which each candidate for the board sets forth his or her qualifications to hold office and purposes for seeking office. All campaign costs would be borne by the corporation. These strict campaign and funding rules will assure that all nominees will have an equal opportunity to be judged by the shareholders. By preventing directorates from being bought, these provisions will require board elections to be conducted solely on the merit of the candidates.

Only the actual or "beneficial" owners of stock should be eligible to vote. Financial intermediaries shall be required to "pass through" voting rights in approximately the same manner that present New York and American Stock Exchange rules require broker-dealers to "pass through" proxies and corporate reports to shareholders owning stock in street name accounts. Already a number of major firms, including Sears, Roebuck, General Motors, McDonnell Douglas, and United States Steel, "pass through" voting rights to hundreds of thousands of employees holding stock in joint pension funds.

Finally, additional provisions will require cumulative voting and forbid "staggered" board elections. Thus any shareholder faction capable of jointly voting approximately 10 percent of the total number of shares cast may elect a director.

A NEW ROLE FOR SHAREHOLDERS

The difficulty with this proposal is the one that troubled Juvenal two millennia ago: *Quis custodiet ipsos custodes,* or, Who shall watch the watchmen? Without a full-time body to discipline the board, it would be so easy for the board of directors and executive management to become friends. Active vigilance could become routinized into an uncritical partnership. The same board theoretically elected to protect shareholder equity and internalize law might instead become management's lobbyist.

Relying on shareholders to discipline directors may strike many as a dubious approach. Historically, the record of shareholder participation in corporate governance has been an abysmal one. The monumental indifference of most shareholders is worse than that of sheep; sheep at least have some sense of what manner of ram they follow. But taken together, the earlier proposals—an outside, full-time board, nominated by rival shareholder groups and voted on by beneficial owners—will increase involvement by shareholders. And cumulative voting insures that an aroused minority of shareholders—even one as small as 9 or 10 percent of all shareholders—shall have the opportunity to elect at least one member of the board.

But that alone is hardly sufficient. At a corporation the size of General Motors, an aggregation of 10 percent of all voting stock might require the allied action of over 200,000 invididuals—which probably could occur no more than once in a generation. To keep directors responsive to law and legitimate public concerns requires surer and more immediate mechanisms. In a word, it requires arming the victims of corporate abuses with the powers to swiftly respond to them. For only those employees, consumers, racial or sex minorities, and local communities harmed by corporate depradations can be depended upon to speedily complain. By allowing any victim to become a shareholder and by permitting any shareholder to have an effective voice, there will be the greatest likelihood of continuing scrutiny of the corporation's directorate. Shareholder involvement can be further enhanced by the disclosures discussed in the next chapter, by the opportunity to attend periodically scheduled directors' meetings to ask questions or present grievances, and by reform of the shareholder derivative action so that any investor who identifies a corporate violation of law may bring lawsuit without risk of financial loss.

For the purpose of motivating the board to perform its intended role, however, it is appropriate to inject shareholders further into corporate governance wherever they have a financial or other incentive to perform effectively.

Six weeks before a vote on any fundamental transaction—which can be defined as executive proposals involving the purchase, sale, lease, merger, consolidation, financing, refinancing, dissolution, or liquidation of assets equal to, say, 10 percent of the corporation's total assets or over $100 million, or the authorization of corporate securities in any amount—the board should forward a written statement to the shareholders explaining the transaction, the vote by which the transaction was approved by the board, the reasons why members of the board approved the transaction, the reasons why other members opposed it, and the foreseeable costs and risks of implementing the proposal. This provision would provide for shareholder votes on all business decisions above a certain minimum size, however named. By requiring directors to publicly elaborate their reasoning—reasoning which may be judged not only during this vote but also during subsequent board elections or mismanagement suits—there would be a powerful incentive for directors to police themselves.

A complementary provision should allow any shareholder or allied shareholder group holding stock equal to a minimum of one percent of all outstanding stock to simultaneously publish a dissenting view or, at any time, to propose amendments to the corporate charter or bylaws.

AFFECTED COMMUNITIES

Shareholders are not the only ones with an incentive to review decisions of corporate management; nor, as Professors Chayes and Dahl argue, are shareholders the only persons who should be accorded corporate voting rights. The increasing use by American corporations of technologies and materials that pose direct and serious threats to the health of communities surrounding their plants requires the creation of a new form of corporate voting right. When a federally chartered corporation engages, for example, in production or distribution of nuclear fuels or the emission of toxic air, water, or solid waste pollutants, citizens whose health is endangered should not be left, at best, with receiving money damages after a time-consuming trial to compensate them for damaged property, impaired health, or even death.

Instead, upon finding of a public health hazard by three members of the board of directors or 3 percent of the shareholders, a corporate referendum should be held in the political jurisdiction affected by the health hazard. The referendum would be drafted by the unit triggering it—either the three board members or a designate of the shareholders. The affected citizens by majority vote will then decide whether the hazardous practice shall be allowed to continue. This form of direct democracy has obvious parallels to the initiative and referendum procedures familiar to many states—except that the election will be paid for by a business corporation and will not necessarily occur at a regular election.

What would happen to the local community if it voted to close a dangerous plant? Three answers seem reasonable. First, the board of directors should have the opportunity to modify the local plant to reduce the health hazard. If the board chooses to do so, it should be allowed to submit its modification plan as a subsequent referendum for community approval. Second, if the corporation chooses to leave after the vote, it should be required to immediately repay the local community for all damages to its health and property by the outlawed activity. This valuation proceeding should occur in federal district court. If the corporation chooses to leave before the referendum vote, it should additionally be required to pay its local employees salaries for a reasonable interim period. Third, the referendum voting procedure should be flexible. Local communities should be given the opportunity to vote upon an initiative calling for the corporation to remedy a specific health hazard by a designated date as an alternative to one calling for immediate closing of a plant. Similarly, the board should be given the opportunity to submit a plan of modification simultaneously with the initial referendum vote.

This type of election procedure is necessary to give enduring meaning to the democratic concept of "consent of the governed." To be sure, this proposal goes beyond the traditional assumption that the only affected or relevant constituents of the corporation are the shareholders. But no longer can we accept the Faustian bargain that the continued toleration of corporate destruction of local health and property is the cost to the public of doing business. In an equitable system of governance, the perpetrators should answer to their victims.

V

Corporate Secrecy vs.

Corporate Disclosure

There is not a crime, there is not a dodge, there is not a swindle, there is not a vice which does not live by secrecy.

—Joseph Pulitzer

O N TELEVISION our major companies enthuse about their candor—as Exxon puts it, "We want you to know" —but the truth behind the image is that they are tighter than clams. Secrecy often seems the first rule of corporate bureaucracies, whether they are dealing with citizens, Congress, or the regulatory agencies.

To a Nader study group, for example, DuPont refused to disclose information about minority employment, even though required to supply such data to the Equal Employment Opportunity Commission, and refused to provide information as mundane as the company telephone book or its membership in trade associations. During Senator Estes Kefauver's investigation of the prescirption drug industry in the early 1960s, subpoenas required copies of all patent licensing agreements then in effect from the major drug firms. By a curious coincidence, all of the companies eventually filed copies of their U.S. agreements only. In 1968, the Senate Small Business Subcommittee on Monopoly asked General Motors for cost and profit data by product lines and operating divisions. Senator Gaylord Nelson, chairman of the Subcommittee, later remarked: "We did not subpoena the information, we merely asked for it politely. GM politely declined. GM did not then and does not now think the public has a right to know how the Automotive Group is doing, separately, much less the Chevrolet Division." In late 1974 the Joint Economic Committee issued subpoenas to the 17 largest retail food chains seeking information on their sales, costs, and net profits by major departments such as meat, grocery, and produce. Almost without exception the companies provided only sales figures, stating that they maintained no financial records showing profits or losses on these operations. In 1971 the Federal Communications Commission (FCC) announced it was abandoning its scheduled investigation into Bell Telephone because it lacked adequate budget and staff to examine the world's largest private corporation. The subsequent uproar in the Congress and the press helped change the agency's mind. But it has still not used its subpoena power in this inquiry. By mid-1973 the FCC trial staff reported that the "Bell System reaction in the period prior to February of this year can fairly be described as a classic case of foot dragging which threatened to thwart and abort the investigation."

Rather than the federal government challenging such secrecy, it often endorses nondisclosure. The key to this corporate secrecy is the Office of Management and Budget (OMB) and its rule of confidentiality. Under the 1942 Federal Reports Act, which aimed to cut down on the duplication of federal forms, the Budget Office was empowered to determine "whether or not the collection [of data] by any federal agency is necessary for the proper performance of the functions of such agency or for any other proper purpose." A business organization, now known as the Business Advisory Council on Federal Reports, was designated shortly thereafter the OMB's quasi-governmental advisor on questionnaires sent to ten or more firms. The Council's present membership includes representatives of the American Retail Federation, the U.S. Chamber of Commerce, the National Association of Manufacturers, Alcoa, Chrysler, Eastman Kodak, Western Electric, and other large enterprises. Although the Federal Reports Act clearly directed OMB to see that information collected by any federal agency shall "be tabulated in a manner to maximize the usefulness of the information to other federal agencies and the public," the Business Advisory Council persuaded the Budget Office to adopt a policy of "confidentiality." From the start, OMB-approved questionnaires asked "Does your agency pledge confidentiality?" To emphasize the importance of this question, agencies were then informed in the language of Standard Form No. 83 that "If the nature and extent of confidentiality to be accorded individual returns is not clear from the form or transmittal letter, this should be explained in the Supporting Statement."

Agencies seeking OMB clearance for surveys, consequently, have promised confidentiality *98 percent* of the time according to the OMB's own Statistical Policy Division. The remaining 2 percent involve mass collections of data by such agencies as the Social Security Administration or the Veterans Administration where confidentiality is irrelevant since the information is clearly designed for aggregate presentation. Thus, for all practical purposes, no business data collected under OMB's supervision identify individual companies or the contents of individual submissions. Data are only disclosed, if at all, in general figures.

OMB's dismal record eventually provoked Congress to tack on to the 1974 Alaska Pipeline Act a provision that the General Accounting Office (GAO), rather than OMB, supervise information requests by the independent regulatory agencies. Yet, within weeks, intensive corporate lobbying persuaded GAO to adopt OMB's standard question: "Does your agency pledge confidentiality?"

Today this policy of confidentiality extends far beyond the OMB and the GAO. With the single exception of the Securities and Exchange Commission (SEC), discussed subsequently, it is pervasive throughout the government.

The International Trade Commission, for example, for years has been securing annual reports from chemical firms on their production, sales, and prices charged for specific chemicals. Yet it refuses to release any of this information on a company basis, even to federal antitrust agencies or investigatory committees of Congress.

The Bureau of Mines has responsibility for scientific, technological, and economic research in the minerals industries. In response to an inquiry from the Corporate Accountability Research Group, the Director of the Bureau of Mines stated:

All quantitative data collected on a voluntary cooperation basis by this Bureau are collected on forms with a banner pledging to maintain the individual confidentiality of such data except for use of defense agencies or the Congress upon a proper request. Aggregate figures may be released to the public providing at least three separate operations comprise such aggregate.

The Bureau of the Census utilizes both the mandatory method and voluntary cooperation in its collection of data. But irrespective of method used, all individual company data are confidential. According to the Director of the Census Bureau, "All Census reports whether voluntary or mandatory are afforded confidential treatment. It is not necessary for individual companies to request confidential treatment since the confidentiality applies to all reports."

In the late 1950s the Federal Trade Commission filed suit to obtain copies of these reports—not from Census, but from certain firms in the paper industry. The Commission acted under its statutory authority to investigate unfair business conduct and practices. In 1961, the U.S. Supreme Court agreed with the FTC that such reports were not immune from legal process. An agitated business lobby then successfully pressured Congress to pass legislation which nullified the Supreme Court decision. The Census of Manufacturers forms now carry the warning legend "PENALTY FOR FAILURE TO REPORT," but add a softening note:

NOTICE: Response to this inquiry is required by law. By the same law, your report to the Census Bureau is confidential. It may be seen only by sworn Census employees and may be used only for statistical purposes. The law also provides that copies retained in your files are immune from legal process.

Congress has recently followed this same policy in the two-year extension of life for the Council on Wage and Price Stability. In early congressional deliberations, some members proposed that the Council contain real teeth—the authority to roll back undue price increases as well as subpoena powers to secure essential information. The result: the Council only has subpoena powers and it cannot publicly release any information secured. Specifically excluded from disclosure is "product line or other category information relating to an individual firm." Furthermore, copies of "periodic reports obtained by the Council" and retained in the reporting company's files are "immune from legal process," principally meaning requests under the Freedom of Information Act.

Why end such corporate secrecy? Because knowledge is essential to democracy, more corporate disclosure can educate, and even mobilize, communities about the hidden tolls local companies impose—such as pollution, discrimination or underpayment of taxes. Increased corporate disclosure can also nourish both traditional and "ethical" investors. What investor would not want to know early about potential pollution and employment discrimination problems, of the sort that are leading to large damage actions against offending companies?* And a small but growing community of ethical investors want to know more about their companies' social performance before investing. It can cost $250,000 for remedial training and custodial care over the lifetime of one child born retarded as a result of chemical poisoning—a cost invariably passed on to society through government subsidies, insurance, or private charity. If some investors seek to allocate their resources in order to minimize this kind of damage, they deserve encouragement.

More corporate disclosure will also help to loosen the tight embrace between government and business, which flourishes, like most embraces, in darkness. Giant corporations can more easily manipulate agencies into a data dependence if their mutual relations are not on the public record. Both at the state and at the federal level, argues economist Willard Mueller, governments are often "so woefully uniformed of corporate affairs that even honest and well intentioned men cannot effectively execute public policy." Mueller has described the current extent of corporate secrecy as an "intolerable situation."

* Such information can also educate the investor community about the general quality of management. As the Council on Economic Priorities discovered in its study of paper mills, the firms that invested the most in pollution control equipment were also the best managed. The two are not mutually exclusive but positively correlated. Foresight in one area reflects general foresight.

The need for more adequate disclosure of corporate financial affairs grows as American corporations grow in size and complexity. Our economic intelligence about many aspects of business organization is worse today than it was around 1900, when Roosevelt made his plea for opening to public view the "mammoth" corporations of his day.

Without adequate public reports from the largest corporations, federal antitrust, environmental, occupational safety, racial and sex discrimination, lobbying, and bribery violations cannot be effectively prevented. The enforcement divisions of the federal government are seriously understaffed; most individual litigants are priced out of the judicial process by the high costs of discovering evidence. By contrast, the Securities and Exchange Commission, which requires comprehensive disclosure of corporate financial operations, and the U.S. Commission on Civil Rights, which is empowered to publicize instances of racial discrimination, are among the most successful federal agencies. Both illustrate Felix Frankfurter's judgment that fraud or criminal conduct has a "shrinking quality" when exposed to public view. The routine disclosure of what will undoubtedly embarrass a company and damage good will—a managerial work force 99 percent white male or an advertising campaign lacking any scientific support—should tend to discourage its occurrence. The glare of the public spotlight may make corporate executives sweaty, but it can cleanse them as well.

Giant corporations offer varying rationales to shield themselves from such outside inquiries. Often they invoke the exigencies of the free enterprise system, which would supposedly be impaired if additional disclosure is compelled. Yet how can this view be reconciled with Adam Smith's notion that the success of competition depends on the knowledge of consumers and competitors? As the Federal Trade Commission noted in advancing its Line of Business Reporting Program,

Information plays a critical role in the efficient working of a free enterprise economy. Generally speaking the greater the amount of information which is possessed by all the groups which are interested in a given market, the more efficient the market will work. Other things being equal, then, society stands to reap benefits from the dissemination.

Invocations of the corporate version of free enterprise are frequently joined with impassioned pleas for privacy for the corporate "person" from the prying eyes of the public and competitors. Perhaps not since the antitrust laws were applied to labor unions rather than business firms at the turn of the century has such a beneficial concept—there competition; here privacy—been so misdirected. Chief Justice Marshall's definition of a corporation in 1819 as "an artificial being, invisible, intangible, and existing only in contemplation of law" still best expresses the idea that corporations are not endowed by their creator with any inalienable rights. In the words of a Supreme Court decision written many years later in 1906, since corporations are creatures of the state, "full and accurate information as to their operations should be made public at responsible levels." That sentiment, rather than any anthropomorphic attribution of individual rights to corporations, should govern relations between government, citizens, and the corporation.

Finally, a common rejoinder by corporations to increased social and financial disclosure is the legal doctrine of "trade secrecy." This amorphous doctrine has become to big business what executive privilege was to former President Richard Nixon: An all-purpose excuse for declining any information request. If knowledge, as Francis Bacon put it, is power, this is a classic abuse of power. For the actual trade secrecy privilege is quite narrow. Corporations have succeeded in broad use of the doctrine largely on the assumption that neither the government nor private persons would possess the time or the resources to challenge them in court.

In Chief Justice Warren Burger's view, there is one, and only one, general rationale for this doctrine: the encouragement of invention. If corporations did not have the ability to prevent their employees or competitors from appropriating the firm's most profitable ideas, the corporation would have little incentive to research and apply new technologies or sales techniques. Since the trade secrecy doctrine conflicts with the copyright and patent clause of the Constitution, which grants authors and inventors "for limited times the exclusive right to their respective writings and discoveries," the Supreme Court has long limited application of this and similar privileges.

The balance of this chapter explains what specific corporate data, in our view, the public most needs to know. But first it is necessary to describe how this data will be disseminated.

Current SEC regulations require each publicly held corporation to prepare two different annual financial reports. The logic of this scheme is somewhat reminiscent of the quarrels that set off the Egg War in *Gulliver's Travels.* For one annual report is bright and glossy, skimpy on useful information, and frequently crammed with the most outrageous distortions (as was illustrated in the previous chapter). A copy of this report is mailed to every shareholder. The second annual report, known as "the 10-K form," is far more informative, printed on plain buff paper, usually in eye-straining small print. This report can generally be obtained by visiting the SEC's public reference rooms in Chicago, Los Angeles, New York, or Washington, D.C., or addressing a special request to the corporation.

Instead, there should be one annual report equally available to shareholders, the SEC, and other interested persons—one not riddled with the exaggerations, omissions, and downright lies that current annual reports to shareholders frequently contain. To ensure this, its contents should be subject to the same high standards of truthful disclosure currently required of proxy solicitations, and it should not be as inconvenient to obtain as the 10-K. Not only should reports be disseminated to all shareholders, but copies should also be distributed to each depository library throughout the country and available at every office or plant (above a minimum size) of each federally chartered corporation.

Yet reforming the annual report alone will not ensure that all relevant corporate data will be easily available to all interested persons. Some corporations' mandatory disclosures will understandably be too expensive to include in a widely circulated annual report. Therefore, a residual mechanism called the *Corporation Register* should be established and published by the SEC. The *Register* would serve as the repository of information too voluminous to include in the corporation's annual report.

This dissemination process will ensure that citizens, investors, consumers, competitors, and employees will have access to the kind of data they need to make intelligent political and economic decisions. Exactly what kind of information are we talking about? The categories of key information—divided into social impact disclosure and financial disclosure—follow.

Social Impact Disclosure

POLLUTION

Almost overnight pollution became an issue of widespread public concern after the first Earth Day in 1970. Given the extent and costs of water pollution, it is not difficult to understand why. Each day the U.S. uses over 330 billion gallons of the liquid. Yet an estimated one-third of the nation's streams and all its major rivers are polluted. Vast bodies, such as Lake Erie, have neared ecological crisis from the stagnation of industrial effluents. The health hazard caused by Reserve Mining Company's asbestos-laden discharges into Lake Superior, threatening the residents of Duluth and other lakeshore communities, has been well reported. Possibly as serious is the discharge of cancer-producing polychlorinated biphenyls (PCBs) by two General Electric capacitor plants on the Hudson River. Property damage can be severe, as illustrated by the greater than $10 million damages done to the commercial fishing and recreational industries of Escambia Bay, Florida, between 1962 and 1973, where waste discharges from Monsanto, American Cyanimid, and other chemical producers were so dense that fish were described as having fins burnt off by pollution.

Most toxic water pollution is caused by business corporations. Some of this pollution, such as heavy metals, finds its way into drinking water systems as well. But the public is virtually unable to pinpoint corporate responsibility for pollution of our waterways. What little is known stems from operation of the Federal Water Pollution Control Act Amendments of 1972. These amendments established the National Pollution Discharge Elimination System (NPDES), which requires all plants discharging pollutants into a waterway to obtain a permit. Those plants which discharge either more than 500,000 gallons of water a day or designated toxic pollutants are directed to establish a monitoring system and publicly report certain data at least once a year. By contrast, those firms which discharge water directly into a municipal sewer system are not required to obtain an NPDES permit, but instead must meet specified pretreatment requirements.

By March 1975, approximately 90 percent of the 3,000 major industrial sources of water pollution had been issued permits. But little effort has been made to inform the public of excessive wastewater discharges or failures to meet compliance schedules. For a concerned citizen to determine whether a neighboring corporate plant is violating the Water Pollution Control Act, for example, he or she would have to travel to a State Water Quality Authority or an EPA regional office. There the data on file may be meaningless if the corporation has successfully sought confidentiality concerning its production levels.

The Federal Corporate Chartering Act should remove any mystery about the responsibility for toxic water pollution. Either in annual or quarterly reports to shareholders, or if length requires in aggregate figures in shareholder reports and in specific detail in the *Corporation Register*, each federally chartered corporation should disclose:

- the name and address of each plant discharge subject to an NPDES permit, what wastes are discharged, whether a monitoring program is required, and the relevant deadlines of any compliance schedule;
- the names of each plant discharge subject to pretreatment requirements for discharge into municipal facilities, what wastes are discharged, whether there is a monitoring program, and the relevant deadlines of any pretreatment compliance schedule;
- each instance in which an NPDES permit or a pretreatment limitation was exceeded, specifying the date, pollutants involved, cause, percentage of limitation exceeded, and steps taken to prevent recurrence; and
- the status of each lawsuit involving allegations of water pollution brought against the corporation by government or private litigants.

Air pollution also poses threats to our health and economic well being. It is hardly a new problem. An English royal decree in

1300 banned use of low grade coal for heating because it created choking smoke and soot. One Londoner who violated the decree paid for it with his life. By the 19th century the poet Shelley complained, "Hell is much a city like London, a populous and smokey city."

Today Shelley would more likely condemn Pittsburgh, where the air was so thick from steel factory soot in November 1975 that it was impossible to see more than 50 feet ahead in some parts of the Monongahela Valley. Still the Pennsylvanians were grateful that the bilious clouds were not as poisonous as those that killed 20 persons in nearby Donora in 1948 and sickened nearly half of the area's 13,000 residents. Or perhaps the poet would describe Elkton, Maryland, where noxious fumes from the Galaxy Chemical Company plant caused lymphatic cancer rates to soar 100 times above normal before the plant was sold in December 1975; or Hopewell, Virginia—until recently "Chemical Capital of the South"—where air and water emissions have conspired to cause a modern version of the black plague known as "Kepone poisoning," after the insecticide which is its source. Although still early in the probable latency period of the disease, over 70 local residents already exhibit tremors, weight loss, sterility, and brain and liver damage.

The respiratory death and injury toll from pollution is apparently dwarfed by cancer caused by pollution. The National Cancer Institute, now studying the links between pollution and cancer, estimates that up to 90 percent of all human cancers are environmentally caused—which includes chemicals released into the environment. By using computers to analyze death certificates over a 20-year period, the study has found high mortality rates from bladder cancer in areas of heavy auto production; high levels of bladder, lung, and liver cancer in areas of heavy chemical industry activity; and high rates of lung cancer near copper and lead smelters. Salem County, New Jersey, for example, across the Delaware River from a giant petrochemical complex in Wilmington, had the highest bladder cancer rate in the nation. Yet since cancer-causing agents have long latency periods, our society may have only begun to detect the extent of cancer caused by the industrial expansion and technological development of the past two decades.

Often the link between the newer technologies and deadly carcinogens seems esoteric. Scientists at the University of California, Harvard, University of Michigan, and the National Center for Atmospheric Research have recently demonstrated that chlorofluorocarbons emitted by aerosol spray cans may deplete the earth's ozone layer by as much as 16 percent within 25 years, thereby causing 100,000 additional cases of skin cancer annually. Yet corporations have frequently been able to successfully argue that suspected carcinogens, like suspected criminals, should be presumed innocent until proven guilty. Or that theoretical health fears should not be allowed to jeopardize existing jobs or plants. These arguments seem particularly tenuous in light of recent Environmental Protection Agency studies which demonstrated that although 15,710 lost their jobs over the past five years as a result of antipollution laws, 1.1 million persons found employment in the burgeoning pollution abatement industry. Where industrial air pollution will cause an estimated $23 billion in health and property damage in 1977, adding abatement gear worth $3.9 billion would reduce total damage to $13 billion.

Efforts to control air pollution center on the Clean Air Act Amendments of 1970. Under the Act, the Environmental Protection Agency is required to set national primary (health related) and secondary (welfare related, i.e., animals, vegetation, materials, and aesthetics) ambient air standards. Standards have been issued by EPA to date for the six major components of air pollution: sulfur oxides, particulate matter, nitrogen oxides, carbon monoxide, photochemical oxidants, and hydrocarbons.

States have primary enforcement responsibilities under the Act, subject to EPA supervision. They are required to submit implementation plans in order to meet the ambient air standards. Among the requirements state plans must meet are emission limitations for stationary sources, timetables for compliance, and monitoring and reporting of emissions. Emission reports are made public by statute.

While the Clean Air Act Amendments commendably attempt to include a large measure of disclosure, little information actually has reached the public. As with the Water Act, much information is collected and reported to EPA or the administering states, but not in a form easily understandable. Furthermore, almost no effort has been made by anyone, state or federal, to communicate this data to the public.

Federally chartered corporations would have to publicly disclose:

- the name and address of each plant subject to the Federal Clean Air Act Amendments of 1970;
- the names of plants currently subject to compliance schedules and when each stage of compliance has been or will be met;
- each instance in which an applicable air pollution limitation was exceeded, specifying date, duration, type of pollutant, percentage of limitation exceeded, and steps taken to prevent recurrence;
- the status of each suit brought against the corporation by government or private litigants involving air pollution.

Most of this information is already collected by corporations under existing law. Its disclosure is entirely consistent with the policy of the National Environmental Protection Act, which enjoins the federal government as a "continuing policy . . . to use all practicable means and measures" to protect environmental values. Pursuant to this Act, the Securities and Exchange Commission recently proposed new regulations which if adopted will require all publicly held corporations to disclose failures to comply with applicable environmental laws in shareholder reports and securities registration statements. But the SEC—at first refusing to act and then compelled to do so after a lawsuit brought by the Natural Resources Defense Council—has taken a far narrower approach than the solutions proposed above. In the SEC's view, the value of corporate shares is only likely to be affected by noncompliance with environmental laws which might indicate (1) extensive corporate costs or liabilities, (2) poor management, or (3) a future change in the public relations and regulatory framework in which a company operates.

But corporate law should do more than merely protect shareholders. Particularly in the areas of air and water pollution, the primary emphasis should be on disclosing information to the victims of environmental contamination which will give them the factual and legal means to terminate these dangerous violations of law.

OCCUPATIONAL SAFETY AND HEALTH

The lack of job safety in the American workplace is well documented. According to the *President's Report on Occupational Safety and Health*, workplace hazards claim 100,000 deaths each year; approximately 400,000 employees are disabled annually; in 1973, there were some six million job related injuries; over 2.6 million employees living in 1973 had been permanently disabled. As former Secretary of the Interior Stewart Udall has stated, "Of all the environments inhabited by Americans, the places where 80 million of us work and spend half our waking hours are among the most lethal."

Unlike the sweltering sweatshops and boiling vats of an earlier day, the causes of this annual slaughter are often invisible. The National Institute of Occupational Safety and Health (NIOSH) estimates that there are over 25,000 toxic substances currently present in American workplaces. An additional 500–600 toxic substances are introduced each year. Many of these substances are the unintended—or unknown—byproducts of new technologies or materials such as those employed in the plastics boom of the 1950s. The result, after long latency periods, is an increasing number of carcinogenic and other health disasters.

Last year the B. F. Goodrich Chemical Company informed the National Institute of Occupational Safety and Health that three employees in its Louisville, Kentucky, polyvinyl chloride production plant had died of angiosarcoma, a rare form of liver cancer. Through June 1975, 27 cases of the disease have been linked to occupational contact with vinyl chloride. Since some 4.6 million people live within five miles of plants that produce the chemical, L. William Lloyd of NIOSH predicts vinyl chloride is destined to become "the occupational disease of the century."

In another case, the Allied Chemical and Dow Chemical Companies reported high levels of lung and lymphatic cancer among workers handling inorganic arsenic, a chemical used in the production of ceramics, glass, and certain medicines. Rubber workers, routinely exposed to multiple cancer-causing substances, are dying of cancer of the stomach, cancer of the prostate, and of leukemia at rates ranging from 50–300 percent greater than the general population. About 50 percent of the 6,000 persons who mine uranium underground are expected to die of lung cancer as a result of exposure to that ore.

Nor do occupational carcinogens obediently remain within the factory gates. Asbestos fibers for example, pose a distinct take-home risk. Explains Dr. Joseph K. Wagoner, head of field studies at NIOSH: "the wives, children and relatives of many asbestos workers have died of mesothelioma and others will do so also as a result of the practice of asbestos carried into the home on worker's clothes or in some other manner." Already x-rays of the families of asbestos workers have revealed excessive rates of the lung abnormalities common to the workers themselves.

Recognizing the enormity of the problem of worker health and safety, Congress in 1970 enacted the Williams-Steiger Occupational Health and Safety Act ". . . to assure every man and woman in the Nation safe and healthful working conditions and to preserve our human resources. . . ." This Act—popularly known as OSHA—established the Occupational Safety and Health Administration within the Department of Labor to issue and enforce health and safety standards. It also required the Department of Health, Education and Welfare, through NIOSH, to develop criteria and recommend standards "which [assure] that no employee will suffer material impairment of health or functional capacity even if such employee has regular exposure to the hazard dealt with by such standard for the period of his working life." Today the Act covers more than 63 million employees.

A cursory reading of the statute seems to support President Nixon's assertion that "the bill represents in its culmination the American system at its best." Unfortunately, the reality behind OSHA's language evokes little praise.

Since the effective date of the Act, NIOSH has produced only 26 "criteria documents" with standard recommendations. On the basis of these materials, OSHA has produced only three standards: vinyl chloride, asbestos, and certain carcinogens. Although projects are underway, the agency has yet to issue standards for arsenic, coke oven emissions, lead, beryllium, ammonia, or sulfur dioxide.

Simply put, American factories and workplaces are creating new toxic substances at a faster rate than OSHA is condemning old ones. NIOSH officials concede that criteria documents need to be developed for "at least" one to two thousand more toxic substances. Yet its 1975 fiscal year budget for occupational cancer was only $2.1 million. Equally as troubling is inadequate enforcement of existing standards. With fewer than 800 inspectors to monitor over four million establishments, the average employer sees an OSHA inspector the equivalent of once every 66 years. After three years, only two firms have been convicted of criminal violations. The average fine received for a violation has been $25.

John Hynan, of OSHA's solicitor's office, sees no cause for concern in these statistics. "So long as workers have a general awareness of their rights under the law, and employers know that they're liable for civil penalties, then we're doing our job. Congress didn't intend that everyone be inspected." But private enforcement of the Act is generally impossible. Employers are required to file a report with the OSHA Area Director within 48 hours of each accident or health hazard that results in one or more fatalities or hospitalization of five employees or more. In addition they must maintain three reporting forms: a log of all injuries and illnesses, a supplemental report detailing additional information, and a yearly summary profiling the total number of injuries and illnesses in broad categories. Yet only the last form—which is of minimal value in bringing a civil action—is available to the employee.

Increased disclosure will not activate OSHA overnight nor make the workplace danger-free. But it would tell the worker and public just what is being handled, breathed, stepped in, and leaked each day, which, in turn, could lead business and government to take occupational safety and health more seriously.

Each federally chartered corporation should be required to determine each toxic substance present in each domestic workplace in any detectable quantity. This list should include substances in raw materials, intermediate phases, and finished products as well as byproducts and contaminants. It should be posted in the facility and published in the *Corporation Register*. All three OSHA logs should also be available for employee inspection. In addition, all reports filed with OSHA area directors should be prominently posted. Shareholder reports or the *Corporation Register* (depending on the number of pages involved) should disclose on a plant-by-plant basis all workplace-related deaths, disabling injuries, and government or civil litigation.

Comprehensive knowledge about the health or safety of their workplaces should help alert employees to seek adequate protection (or at least hazardous duty pay) during collective bargaining. The listing of toxic substances in the workplace would also greatly facilitate government and business control of such material. During the mercury contamination crisis of 1970, the Federal Water Quality Administration sought to discover all sources of mercury. They assembled emergency teams working in a crisis atmosphere and were aided by massive publicity, but it still took six months to develop a comprehensive list of these sources. Earlier listing of this substance in federally chartered corporations would have enabled discovery in those firms within days.

Finally, a complete inventory of toxic substances is essential for the protection of the public. There is no certain way to keep some toxic materials from leaking into the air and water. While major sources of pollutants and some hazardous pollutants are governed by the air and water pollution laws, many more toxic substances are not. Availability of toxic substance data to endangered local communities will help permit city and state governments to develop appropriate control and remedial legislation. Information, again, can lead to action.

EMPLOYMENT DISCRIMINATION

Discrimination against racial minorities and women remains a hallmark of Corporate America. While some progress has been made, minorities and women continue to be last hired (that is, if hired at all), first fired, offered the least attractive jobs, and lowest paid.

The median income for a black male fulltime worker in 1972 was $7,300 or 69 percent of the $10,590 paid a white male fully employed. The Equal Employment Opportunity Commission in 1974 found that 25 percent of the firms which employ more than 100 workers employ *no* black employees. The comparative unemployment rate for blacks—typically double that of whites—also testifies to employment discrimination. So does the fact that 44 percent of all white male workers hold white collar jobs while only 18 percent of nonwhite males do. As for women, the median income of a fulltime female employee is only 59 percent of a fulltime male worker. A 1969 study found that 96 percent of all jobs in the private sector paying over $15,000 were held by white males. As Marion Kellogg, one of only 15 women among 2,500 senior executives who direct the country's major corporations, puts it, "So you're looking for top-level women executives. Have you got a microscope?"

The federal government's efforts to combat employment discrimination began with the creation of the Equal Employment Opportunity Commission (EEOC) in 1964. Later, a first cousin, the Office of Federal Contract Compliance (OFCC), was established to enforce Executive Order No. 11246, which proscribes employment discrimination by federal contractors. The EEOC requires employers of more than 100 employees to file both a consolidated report for their overall operations and separate establishment reports for each establishment with more than 25 employees.

The basic Form EEO-1 breaks down all employment into nine categories: officials and managers, professionals, technicians, sales workers, office and clerical, craftsmen (skilled), operatives (semiskilled), laborers (unskilled) and service workers. It further requires listing the number of workers in each of these categories by sex and race. The EEOC does release aggregate summaries of this information containing nationwide totals and aggregate figures broken down by industry. But it is required by statute to keep confidential all EEO-1 information concerning specific employers.

Since being granted enforcement powers in 1972, the Equal Employment Opportunity Commission has been able to secure back pay, promotions, and conciliation agreements worth $284 million to workers. In two celebrated cases, American Telephone and Telegraph agreed to consent orders worth $117 million to its employees and nine steel corporations agreed to a $31 million back pay settlement for 46,000 employees. But the EEOC's efforts have been seriously handicapped by a cumbersome statutory structure, with the result that EEOC had a backlog of over 100,000 complaints by March 1975; the median period for resolution of an EEOC charge was 32 months.

The Rube Goldberg structure of the statute also discourages private enforcement. Under the Act, a victim of discrimination may not bring suit directly but only after the EEOC has determined not to proceed with the case or issued a right to sue notice. Private litigants are further handicapped by the difficulties in obtaining evidence. For example, in 1971 both McDonnell-Douglas and the Pentagon refused to disclose the number of blacks hired by McDonnell, contending that this was a "trade secret."

Congress should remove the "confidentiality" attached to the EEOC forms so that full enforcement of the Act will be possible. And Congress should go further. The basic EEO-1 form provides only the briefest definitions of its nine job categories, permitting management considerable leeway to make imaginative use of these classifications. Montgomery Ward & Co., for instance, classifies anyone as an official or manager who supervises two or more employees. At Sears and J. C. Penny, employees need supervise only three fellow employees to qualify for a managerial classification. Besides directing EEOC to tighten job classification definitions, Congress should require public disclosure of income breakdowns by race and sex. The EEO-4 form already requires that such information be collected from state and local governments.

Each federally chartered corporation should disclose its aggregate and plant-by-plant job category and income figures by race and sex. It should also disclose the details of all private or government suits brought against the company alleging employment discrimination that result in conciliation agreements, consent decrees, or litigation awards, and any affirmative action plan required by the federal government. Since corporations are already required to collect most of this information for payroll, tax, and EEOC purposes, there should be little additional expense involved.

CORPORATE ADVERTISING

How, even the credulous may ask, can corporations get away with it? How is it possible for so many companies to so persistently pollute the public's water and air or offend its sense of justice with so little effective response? There is no single answer, but an important contributing cause has been corporate manipulation of public and official opinion through mass media advertisements and governmental lobbying.

No other nation's citizens are bombarded by quite so intensive an advertising barrage as the United States. U.S. advertisers paid for 50 percent more advertising than all other nations in the noncommunist world combined in 1972. Total mass media expenditures in 1976 will equal $31 billion, or over $140 per person.

Such advertising could be serving important economic purposes. In Adam Smith's model, for example, it could enhance "consumer sovereignty" by informing buyers of the existence of competing products, as well as their quality, costs, and benefits. But American advertising rarely works that way. Access to network television is monopolized by a few hundred major firms. These same firms are the leading advertisers in the radio, major metropolitan newspaper, and billboard media. Most mass media advertisements contain little useful consumer information. Certainly not the beer commercials which invite you to "get all the gusto you can." Nor Exxon's homilies of the good old days; nor Pepsi's generation; Colonel Sanders' musical pageants; the man from Glad; nor the menagerie of leprechauns, Green Giants, and Tigresses who huckster breakfast cereals, frozen vegetables, and perfume. As Richard Barnet and Ronald Müller, authors of *Global Reach*, put it: "The modern ad writer sells happiness, envy, fear, and excitement, and along with them some product."

The key is association. Modern ads, with some important exceptions, serve only one economic function: they tell consumers that a brand name product exists. This is a parody of Smith's marketplace, or rather an inversion. The giant corporations exploit their privileged access to the mass media to increase general demand and specific product identification—at the expense of consumer knowledge about the characteristics and comparative advantages of products, the goods and services of smaller producers, or the less advertised virtues of thrift, conservation, self-sufficiency, nutrition, health, or safety.

Consumers, of course, pay for this lack of knowledge. Because of advertising stressing such themes as "Bayer is better," nationally advertised brands of aspirin sell for much higher prices than therapeutically equivalent unadvertised brands, and the same is true of a great many ineffective over-the-counter drugs and cosmetics. In the supermarket, brand name canned fruits and vegetables sell for 20 percent higher prices than store brands even though both frequently come from the same manufacturing plant. A study by former Pennsylvania Insurance Commissioner Herbert S. Denenberg found a 170 percent spread in the premiums charged by various companies for comparable insurance policies. Denenberg has estimated that consumers could save $3 billion each year by purchasing the "best buy" policies.

To encourage more accurate, informational advertising, the Federal Trade Commission, with much fanfare, introduced an ad substantiation program in June 1971. In the next two years, the Commission obtained substantiation of the advertising claims of a variety of products including automobiles, TV sets, cough remedies, toothpaste, and deodorants. Analysis of these claims graphically illustrated the defects in the current mode of advertising. An independent engineering firm examined 54 claims by automakers for which substantiation was submitted and found 16 adequately substantiated, 3 substantiated on a very narrow interpretation of the claim, 15 inadequately substantiated, and 20 others "completely unsubstantiated." Of the material received in response to its first four orders, the FTC found that 30 percent of the claims raised serious questions about their adequacy. Although the FTC believes its program helped curb the most blatant forms of false claims, the Commission's unwillingness to challenge "image" advertising, the extreme selectivity of the program, and the lack of real sanctions raises doubts even about that claim.

Concurrent enforcement responsibilities for the program should be given to the victims of misleading advertisements: consumers and business competitors. Before a television, radio, or major metropolitan newspaper advertisement could be communicated, each federally chartered corporation would be required to assemble substantiation of each factual claim concerning one of its products. This substantiation—in a form comprehensible to the average citizen—would be available upon request by any consumer or business competitor. Failure to prepare or forward accurate substantiation would result in money damages equal to a significant percentage, say one-third, of the cost of the advertising campaign being paid to the complaining persons in federal district court.

Given the previous failure of such programs and the reasonableness of expecting companies to possess support for their claims before they are made, these tough sanctions appear an efficient way to achieve the stated purposes of the FTC's programs: "to assist consumers in making a rational choice among competing claims . . . [to] enhance competition by encouraging competitors to challenge advertising claims which have no basis in fact . . . to encourage advertisers to have on hand adequate substantiation." But there is the danger that increasing penalties for the communication of false information to consumers may lead large companies to respond by communicating *no* information. That is, all commercials would become purely "image" ads: Kent cigarettes' husky outdoor types asserting "I smoke for taste"; or Coca-Cola's picture montages, "It's the real thing."

Legislatively, there are two possible responses. The first is to control speech. Outlaw the meaningless assertions, the pure opinions, the mood music, the appeals to happiness, envy, fear, or excitement that no single product could ever fully hope to satisfy. Quite apart from the First Amendment problems, the notion of a federal bureaucracy arguing for months, conceivably years, over whether a particular statement is fact or opinion could only please a linguist with a highly developed sense of humor or a Washington lawyer who would profit from the litigation.

It is for this reason that we rely on the second alternative: making our primary manufacturing, retail, and transportation markets more competitive. Image advertising is an attribute common to a noncompetitive industry. It is an unlikely response to the substantiated claims of a competitor who advertises a better product or one that is lower in price. For this and other economic and social reasons, Chapter VII makes the case for the deconcentration of our oligopolistic industries.

CORPORATE LOBBYING

In 1972, *Business Week* estimated that 800 of the 1,000 largest firms either have lobbying offices in Washington or use Washington law firms, public relations agencies, or consultants to exercise their right "to petition the government for a redress of grievances." Nearly every firm also belongs to several trade associations, such as the National Association of Manufacturers or the American Petroleum Institute, which perform the same lobbying functions on behalf of all industry or all corporations within a particular industry. The largest corporations maintain lobbyists not only in Washington but at state and local government levels as well. And when a particular bill or executive branch decision at any government level concerns them, the megacorporations are willing to hire additional representatives, fly in salaried executives or friendly "experts," and finance or contribute to "grassroots" organizations to create the impression that an aroused public supports their position. This generous outflow of tax deductible cash translates into massive—though usually invisible—political power.

In November 1975, for example, the Business Roundtable claimed credit for then stopping proposed antitrust legislation that would have given the attorneys general of the 50 states and private attorneys authority to recover damages on behalf of large classes of overcharged citizens. What is the Business Roundtable? A low profile lobbying organization whose 160 members include the three largest automobile manufacturers, the three largest banks, seven of the largest oil corporations, AT&T, Xerox, U.S. Steel, Alcoa, Allis Chalmers, and B.F. Goodrich. Backed by an annual budget of $1.9 million, the Roundtable specializes in bringing "limousine lobbyists" like General Electric's chairman Reginald Jones or Continental Can's Robert Hatfield to Washington. With such an ample budget, it is also adept at gathering up corporate counsel or local plant managers, as the occasion requires.

On September 11, 1975, Senator Muskie noted in the *Congressional Record* that the four major auto manufacturing corporations had launched a $750,000 advertising campaign to garner support for a five-year delay in emission standards. A single utility company, the American Electric Power Company, paid for a similar series of 36 advertisements in 260 publications to promote increased development of certain midwestern coal reserves—some of which it owned. The pricetag there was $3.6 million.

Even more significant than these one-shot political efforts are the on-going activities of established lobbies such as the oil lobby. Historically, no other lobby has done quite so well as the oil lobby: getting extraordinary State Department help for their entry into the Middle Eastern oil fields after World War I; being allowed by the State and Justice Departments to negotiate as sovereigns with foreign heads of state; winning the cooperation of the State and Treasury departments in 1951 to allow foreign oil royalties to be regarded as foreign taxes, rather than normal business expenses, for the purposes of American taxation; persuading four presidents to maintain oil import quotas that limited the import of less expensive Middle Eastern oil; and maintaining the "bonus bidding" system for offshore oil leases which effectively precludes smaller, independent oil firms from bidding on such leases, thereby leaving the majors in control of most new oil finds.

But then, no other lobby tries quite so hard as the oil lobby. Common Cause found the oil industry (including 60 oil, gas, and associated corporations) is represented by 229 individuals registered as lobbyists. In addition, there are 29 Washington, D.C. based public relations and law firms which have registered as representatives of these corporations, and 19 industry committees or associations, the best known of which is the American Petroleum Institute with over 400 employees and a $22 million annual budget. Finally, there are corporate mass mailings on the order of Standard of California's letters to its 262,000 shareholders and 40,000 employees, urging "more positive support of the efforts of Arab nations toward peace in the Middle East," as well as mass media ads such as Mobil Oil's *New York Times* sermonettes.

In 1946, Congress attempted to expose to public view such corporate lobbying in the Federal Regulation of Lobbying Act. The Act requires that any person who solicits or receives money "to be used principally or the principal purpose of which person is" to influence legislation must register with the Clerk of the House and the Secretary of the Senate and quarterly report total contributions and individual ones over $500 and total expenditures and individual expenditures over $10. Each paid representative must report his compensation. These reports are then printed in the *Congressional Record*.

Over the dissents of Justices Jackson, Douglas, and Black, the

Supreme Court upheld the constitutionality of the Act in 1954, but limited its scope to attempts to communicate directly with members of Congress. So-called grassroots lobbying—urging others to communicate with Congress—was exempted. That provision, combined with the limitation of reporting to those whose principal purpose is lobbying and the lack of an effective enforcement arm, results in far more being excluded than included. One reporter, James Deakin, author of *The Lobbyists*, estimates that $200 is spent for every dollar reported, with perhaps one quarter of the total lobbyists actually registered.

The National Association of Manufacturers (NAM), for example, has a computerized mailing list of 14,000 plants operated by 100 giant companies, divided by congressional districts. When an issue of importance to its members arises, NAM contacts executives of firms which have plants in the districts or states of key legislators and explains to them how to present the corporate position on the issue. This grassroots lobbying is not covered by the Federal Regulation of Lobbying Act. Nor are trade associations and industry groups like the American Petroleum Institute; nor the advertisements of oil and automotive companies; nor the deluge of corporate financed telegrams.

And it is not only Congress that is lobbied. As power over the past decades has gravitated toward the Executive Branch, lobbying there has commensurately increased. Occasionally an ITT or a milk price scandal will hint at the intensity of White House lobbying, but otherwise the public remains ignorant because of the limited scope of the 1946 Lobbying Act.*

The Federal Chartering Act would require each chartered corporation to disclose the names of each outside representative or employee who attempted to influence legislation or executive decisionmaking at the federal, state, or local level; the specific bills or pol-

---

* There are a few exceptions. The Federal Energy Administration, the Consumer Product Safety Commission, and certain officials in the Justice Department keep logs of their outside contacts. Between Oct. 1, 1974 and March 15, 1975, the top ten officials of the Federal Energy Administration (FEA) spent only 6 percent of their outside meeting time with environmental and consumer groups, state conservation officials, and the like. By contrast, since FEA administrator Frank Zarb took office in December 1974, 91 percent of his outside meetings have been with representatives of the oil industry.

icy decisions involved; the salaries or fees paid to such in-house or outside lobbyists; and the total annual expenses of their lobbying operations. Further, the Chartering Act would require the corporation to disclose in its annual report membership in any trade association or committee and the amount of any monies paid to such associations (whether a formal member or not). It would require corporations to disclose the name of each executive who leaves to serve in government, his or her enduring relationship to the corporation, and the name of each former government official who comes to work for the corporation. Companies would disclose in their annual reports monies spent on advertisements, shareholder or employee appeals, and organizations which attempt to influence public policy. Finally, the Act would require disclosure of all gifts, "honoraria," payments, entertainment expenses, etc., for members of Congress and their staffs and for policy-making officials in the executive branch, including employees on the White House staff.

None of these provisions will place any substantive limitations on the rights of business corporations to lobby for their own financial interests. But these proposals will require each federally chartered corporation to acknowledge how much shareholders' money they are expending and to lobby in its own name rather than through front organizations. This will give both Congress and the public a better ability to gauge the origins and weight of legislative advocacy. It will take some of Jimmy Breslin's proverbial "blue smoke and mirrors" out of politics. Or, as President James Madison understood, "knowledge will forever govern ignorance and a people who mean to be their own governors must arm themselves with the power knowledge gives."

Financial Disclosure

THE SEC'S DISCLOSURE SYSTEM

The Securities and Exchange Commission (SEC) requires disclosure of certain financial information from all publicly held corporations above a minimum size. Whenever a corporation makes a public offering of its stock or bonds, it must file a registration statement disclosing information about its properties, business, management, and financial condition. All corporations listed on one of this nation's 13 securities exchanges, or possessing assets of $1 million or more and 500 or more securities holders must also file quarterly and annual reports on their financial operations. The most detailed report, the 10-K Form, reveals the corporation's income statements, balance sheets, properties, subsidiary companies, important pending legal proceedings, increases or decreases in outstanding securities, and a good deal more.

Although this disclosure system comprises the most informative reservoir of corporate information available, its value is limited by the SEC's consistently narrow interpretation of its purpose. Under the enabling provisions of the securities laws, the Commission is empowered to prescribe such rules and regulations "as necessary or appropriate *in the public interest or for the protection of investors*" (emphasis added). The SEC has consistently interpreted this mandate to mean the protection of investors *is* the public interest. This narrowness is regrettable. Since investors are mostly concerned with making money, their interest in corporate disclosure is generally limited to financial statements that bear directly upon present and future corporate earnings. By contrast, the more inclusive public interest in an efficient economy, good health, and full employment mandates disclosure of market structure, industry-wide competition, the control exerted by dominant firms, freedom of entry for potential competitors, the true cost of products, product quality, product safety, and the social and environmental effects of production.

The consequences of indifference to the noninvestor public run throughout the SEC's interpretation of the securities laws. For example, disclosure involving control and ownership of the largest corporations is, at best, marginal. The SEC requires that reporting companies, in their proxy statements or 10-K forms, identify any person who is a record holder or is known to be a beneficial owner of more than 10 percent of the company's voting stock, and the extent of his or her holding. Disclosure of stockholdings is also required of members of the board of directors.

This list of owners, however, is very limited. One person rarely owns 10 percent or more of voting stock in an important publicly held corporation—although voluntary disclosures to Senator Lee Metcalf in 1972 found that the top 30 shareholders in

Chrysler held 41 percent of its common stock; the top 30 at Ford held 35 percent; General Electric's top 30 held 21 percent; and Mobil's, 28 percent. Moreover, the SEC has made little effort to require disclosure of the actual owners of corporate stock. Large shareholders frequently hide their identity behind pseudonyms. For example, the Bank of America uses over 100 front names—what the securities trade calls "street names," "straws," or "nominees"—to obscure the origin of its transactions; the Prudential Insurance Company trades under *noms de rue* such as AFTCO, BYECO, CADCO, CEPCO, and NINCO; even the University of Pennsylvania uses an acronym, Franklin & Co., which is one of the few street names that gives any clue to the identity of the real trader.

This game of hide-and-seek is considerably complicated by the fact that most shareholders with a penchant for anonymity do not hide behind one front name, but typically three or four separate layers of front names. The outermost is often Cede and Company, which is the stockholding name for the Deposit and Trust Company, a wholly owned subsidiary of the New York Stock Exchange. Cede is the largest single security holder in several airlines, utilities, and other corporations. Yet it is nothing more than a nominee for stock brokerage firms such as Merrill, Lynch, Pierce, Fenner and Smith; Bache & Company; and E. F. Hutton, which are members of the New York Stock Exchange. These firms constitute a second layer of secrecy; frequently they hold stock in their own names on behalf of clients. A third layer is comprised of the banks who often place the orders with the brokerage firms. According to Senator Metcalf, among Chrysler's top 30 shareholders were Kane & Co., Cudd & Co., and Egger & Co., all of which were street names for Chase Manhattan Bank; among Ford's top 30 were Berlach & Co., Stuart & Co., Thomas & Co., and King & Co., all of which were street names for First National City Bank.

Yet this is just the beginning. No self-respecting millionaire personally places his orders with the bank; rather, he gives a lawyer powers-of-attorney to do it for him. And if he is sufficiently concerned about his privacy, he transacts business with the attorney who contacts the bank through an overseas bank, a relative or friend, or a second attorney.

If regarded as a game, this may all seem terribly amusing,

what with your average major stockholder having more secret words than a Guru. But it has serious effects on tax collection, antitrust enforcement, concentration of wealth, and public policy generally. For secrecy is essential to tax evasion and incipient monopolistic practices. And knowledge of wealth distribution is necessary for state and federal legislatures to enact equitable income, trust, and inheritance tax laws.

Periodically Congress has recognized these facts and required annual disclosure of the top 30 voting stockholders in the railroads, motor carriers, water carriers, freight forwarders, oil pipeline companies, and private car lines subject to the Interstate Commerce Acts. It has also required disclosure of every stockholder with 5 percent or more of the outstanding stock in a U.S. airline under the Civil Aeronautics Act, or a waterborne shipper subject to the Federal Maritime Laws.

The SEC is presently entertaining comments on proposed regulations which would require publicly held companies to disclose the 30 largest stockholders for each class of voting securities. Yet the Commission is simultaneously hard at work to undermine the effectiveness of its proposal by limiting disclosure to "holders of record," that is, the proxy brokerage house and bank names, or, in certain instances, to the identities of individuals "with power to direct the vote"—which will probably mean a slightly more sophisticated level of front names, such as lawyers with powers-of-attorney. To reassure any anxious investors or stockholders, Ralph Hocker, Associate Director of the SEC's Division of Corporate Finance, informed the Dow Jones News Service in August 1975 that the Commission lacks authority to enforce the proposed rules in any event. And to insure that a slightly more vigorous Associate Director of Corporate Finance may not subsequently discover such authority, corporations are only required to disclose beneficial owners "if known." This is a legislative proposal of such self-defeating ingenuity that one can only wonder why the Delaware Bar Association did not propose it first.

The SEC not only fails to penetrate shareholder "nominees" to discover the real owners, but it also allows great leeway on exactly what corporations are required to report. For example, under the

10-K instructions, competitive conditions and the firm's own competitive position in the industry are to be shown only "if known or reasonably available to the registrant." It is difficult to understand how any firm could afford *not* to know its competitive position in an industry, but the SEC apparently has no desire to pry.

Information on subsidiaries is also deficient. Under SEC regulations, the "names of particular subsidiaries may be omitted if, considered in the aggregate as a single subsidiary, they would not constitute a significant subsidiary." A significant subsidiary is defined, for the largest firms, as one whose assets or operating revenues exceed 10 percent of those of the parent and its subsidiaries on a consolidated basis. As giant firms have increased in size, this exemption creates an enormous loophole in reporting. 3M Corporation, for example, states, in its 1974 10-K, that 12 of its subsidiaries were omitted. Anaconda's annual report indicates it did not consolidate its joint venture with Amax (formerly American Metal Climax). Omissions such as these allow the country's major firms to understate their actual size and obscure their direct or indirect ties with each other.

This secrecy applies as well to a company's foreign operations. Form 10-K instructions specifically exempt, except for financial data, all reporting with respect to any foreign subsidiary "to the extent that the required disclosure would be detrimental to the registrant." Names of the foreign subsidiaries are to be filed on a confidential basis with the Commission. However, the "significant subsidiary" rules can be invoked to nullify this requirement. In the case of the Economic and Development Corporation, which was the Swiss firm established by Northrop to handle payoffs on foreign sales, no report was made to the SEC.

In no aspect, however, does SEC disclosure regulation fail quite so completely as in its regulation of accounting practices. Under both the 1933 Securities Act and the 1934 Securities Exchange Act, the SEC was given absolute powers to lay down the standards under which corporations report their financial operations. After a generation of "stock watering," arbitrary depreciation, misuse of the asset term "goodwill," and more, Congress laid down the law. In the decisive prose of the 1933 Act:

Among other things, the Commission shall have authority . . . to prescribe . . . the method to be followed in the preparation of accounts, in
the appraisal or valuation of assets and liabilities, in the determination of
depreciation and depletion, in the differentiation of investment and operating income, and in the preparation . . . of consolidated balance sheets or
income accounts.

This the SEC has never done. In 1937 the SEC's Chief Accountant, troubled by the variety of techniques used in the first
three years' financial reports, reported to the Commission that immediate action was necessary to standardize accounting principles.
But at the time, the SEC was fighting the New York Stock Exchange on one front, the public utility industry on a second, and
waning congressional support on a third. Three of the five Com-
missioneers felt that it was not the right time to take on the entire
accounting profession. After acknowledging that prevalent practices seemed "improper," the Commission left the determination of
accounting standards up to the accountants.

This was a great opportunity lost. The idea that the accounting
profession was self-regulating became fixed in the Commission's
imagination. Soon the SEC turned over primary responsibility for
disciplinary questions and developing standards to the American
Institute of Accountants (now the American Institute of Certified
Public Accountants or AICPA). Later the SEC formalized this arrangement by refusing to accept financial statements which did not
follow the AICPA's recommended standards. But neither the accountants individually nor AICPA's Accounting Principles Board
collectively took their self-regulatory responsibilities seriously.
AICPA's standards were never binding on the practitioners. Instead, AICPA implored the accountants to allow each corporate
management to stipulate accounting principles for them. This is
rather like, explained one academic accountant, "having the base-
ball batter calling the balls and strikes." The whole point of disclosing financial statements is to give shareholders and others an objective measure of how well a corporation's management is doing from
year to year. Giving senior executives the power to change accounting principles when it suits them allows them the power to
artificially inflate profitability in any short run period.

The only AICPA restraint was that an accountant should not

sign financial statements unless they "present fairly the financial position of [the company] and the results of its operations . . . in conformity with generally accepted accounting principles. . . ." After three decades of AICPA interpretations, these words were about as restrictive as jello. In the Institute's official view:

1. "Generally accepted accounting principles" are those which have substantial authoritative support.

2. Opinions of the Accounting Principles Board constitute "substantial authoritative support."

3. "Substantial authoritative support" can exist for accounting principles that differ from opinions of the Accounting Principles Board.

Hence these principles logically can justify nearly any standard, and so they have been employed. Principles have been certified as "generally accepted" merely on the basis of past use in other financial statements or support in the literature. Since accounting principles are selected by management, however, the test of past use need only mean that a few accountants have agreed not to object to a management decision, while the test of support in the literature may only mean that a single accountant has published his reasons for not objecting to such a decision. "The net result," explains Law Professor Melvin Eisenberg, "is a frequent tendency toward general deterioration of both accounting principles and financial statements."

This tendency is considerably furthered by management's unlimited power to fire accountants—a power the managers of large corporations have little hesitation about employing. For example, in late 1971, Boothe Computer Corporation, a computer leasing firm, rented some $2.6 billion in IBM System 360 equipment. Since IBM had begun marketing a more desirable computer series, and since many of the leases could be canceled on short notice, Boothe's accountant, Arthur Andersen & Company, proposed to qualify its opinion by stating that the financial statements were satisfactory "subject to the effect of the outcome . . . of future events with respect to rental revenues which the computer equipment will produce." Boothe promptly fired Andersen and retained in its place Touche Ross & Co., which wrote an unqualified opinion.

By the late 1960s even Leonard Spacek, managing partner of

one of the "Big Eight" accounting firms, Arthur Andersen & Company, came to believe that "my profession appears to regard a set of financial statements as a roulette wheel to the public investor—and it is his tough luck if he doesn't understand the risks that we inject into the accounting reports." By then accounting for the large diversified firm had become a game of "massaging the numbers." You could, explained the knowledgeable 'Adam Smith,' "Change your depreciation from accelerated to straight line. If your depreciation charges are higher, then your profits are lower, so to increase profits, decrease depreciation. . . . You can change the valuation of your inventories. You can adjust the charges made for your pension fund. You can make a provision for taxes on the earnings of a subsidiary or wait until the subsidiary remits a dividend to the parent. . . ." You could also change the treatment of research and development from a one-year to a multi-year expense item or follow Litton Industries' lead and fail to distinguish normal income from extraordinary income.

By 1972, the game was no longer such fun. Big Eight firm Peat, Marwick had certified Penn Central and now the railroad was in receivership. Price Waterhouse had approved Minnie Pearl's Fried Chicken, later Performance Systems, and it was gone too. Arthur Young's name attested to the statements of Commonwealth United; Peat, Marwick had also vouched for Barchris Construction Corporation; Haskins & Sells had certified Orvis Brothers; they had all gone bankrupt. By then, Thomas O'Glove, who wrote a newsletter on accounting for a Wall Street firm, was telling his readers, "The signature [of an accountant] is worthless." David Norr, an accountant who was a member of the Accounting Principles Board, which supposedly set the standards, expressed the same sentiment: "Accounting as a mirror of activity is dead." Federal district courts began warning the legal profession to "beware of blind reliance on the adequacy of financial statements, both as a whole and in particulars." The head of a major drug company summed up, and implicitly condemned, the ethics of a generation: "One good accountant," he said, "is worth a thousand salesmen."

The SEC responded with a series of lawsuits. Ultimately, partners in Lybrand, Ross, Bros & Montgomery and Peat, Marwick were held guilty of criminal violations; Arthur Andersen &

Company was censured. By 1973, there were over 500 private and SEC claims against accountants. Private actions against Haskins & Sells, Arthur Andersen, Lybrand, Arthur Young, and Peat, Marwick had been settled for amounts ranging from $300,000 to $5 million.

The SEC also adopted new regulations requiring explanations for changes in accounting practices and disparities between the corporation's financial reports to shareholders and the Internal Revenue Service. Dismissal of an accounting firm now had to be publicly explained.

But the underlying problems remain. In 1972, with SEC support, Congress created the Financial Accounting Standards Board [FASB] to provide more rigorous standards than those being provided by the AICPA. The Commission took this unlikely occasion to publicly state that it will "continue its policy of looking to the private sector for leadership in establishing and improving accounting principles and standards . . ." It is hardly likely to receive such "leadership" from the FASB, five of whose seven original members were either accountants in private industry or in the Big Eight firms which were the principle culprits up to 1972. The FASB is perhaps the only regulatory body now operating which pays each of its members a salary of over $100,000 a year, supplied by the corporations it is supposed to regulate ($1.5 million was directly funded by the Financial Executives Institute in 1972–73). Business executives were also heavily represented on the Financial Accounting Standards Advisory Council. Not surprisingly, the FASB has broken little new ground. The magical incantation "generally accepted accounting principles" has been retained with nearly as elastic a range of meanings.

A serious aspect of this accounting legerdemain is the failure to produce meaningful line of business reporting requirements. When a corporation is small and engaged in a single field, it is fairly simple matter to design an income statement which accurately reveals its profitability and the competence of its management. As a corporation diversifies into many fields and as its consolidated income statement fails to describe the profits and losses of particular subsidiaries or divisions, its income statements become increasingly less valuable. Without knowledge of how well particular lines of business are doing, investors cannot evaluate how profitable the corporation will be in the future.

Nor are investors the only ones who need line of business reporting. Product line data are also important to assure the efficiency of the marketplace. As a Federal Trade Commission report explained in 1973, "Potential entrants will not be attracted by high rates of profit if they do not know that above-average profits exist." And government itself cannot perform its economic duties. This was graphically illustrated by former President Richard Nixon's Price Commission in 1971. Having no reliable data available on the profits of several industries, it was unable to determine whether particular price increases were justified.

The SEC recognized in 1939 that product-line data was essential: "In order either to judge the past or to forecast intelligently, an investor must have not only a record of past earnings or losses, but also the significant details as to how the particular results were obtained." It did not, however, initially enforce regulations that would provide investors these crucial facts.

By the late 1960s, the income statements of many large firms were nearly useless—except, perhaps, for their humor. Honeywell, for example, which produced a broad product line ranging from computers to cameras, reported to its shareholders that it was engaged in just one line of business—"automation." General Telephone and Electronics in 1969 reported $816 million in revenues and earnings in a single category—Sylvania—then elsewhere bragged that Sylvania "ranks among the first three domestic producers in each of the following product groups: fluorescent lamps, incandescent lamps and photoflash lamps, and radio and television tubes. . . . In addition, it is a major factor in the production of metal and plastic parts and components for use in the lighting, electronic and computer industries. . . ."

But it was the highly diversified conglomerates which reduced financial reporting to a travesty. In 1970, Ling-Temco-Vought (LTV) lumped together $3.8 billion of revenues generated by 757 separate companies under seven vaguely defined categories: steel and ferrous metal products, meat and foods, aerospace, electronics, air transportation, wire and cable, and floor covering. ITT, whose internal accounting is legendary, reported $8.3 billion sales from some 300 subsidiary firms and divisions in 1970 under just nine principal product groups: telecommunications equipment, industrial and consumer products, natural resources, defense and space programs, food processing and services, consumer services, business and financial services, Hartford Fire Insurance, and utility operations. Generously, it did relate net income as well as sales to these product groups, but it was still impossible to determine how wise had been ITT's acquisition of such major corporations as Rayomier, the leading chemical cellulose producer, Continental Baking, Sheraton, Levitt and Sons, Canteen Corporation, Avis, or Bobbs-Merrill Publishing.

Under Chairman Manuel Cohen, the SEC began nudging for improved segmental reporting requirements in 1965. After a series of modifications prompted by business opposition, Rules for Disclosure by line of business were adopted in July 1969. Corporations are asked to supply sales and income (or loss) figures for each line of business which accounts for 10 or more percent of total sales or income. But the SEC allows reporting corporations to designate any categorization they please. So the results are of no value for antitrust enforcement officers, government price and profit officers, labor negotiators, nor even many investors, since management retains the prerogative to lump a losing product line with a successful one and obscure their mistakes. Moreover, for a giant corporation, the 10 percent figure is much too large. Reporting under the SEC's new rule is little different from the reporting that Chairman Cohen criticized from 1965 to 1968:

- General Motors reports that it "considers itself to be in a single line of business, broadly defined as transportation equipment." For fuller elucidation it provides a breakdown of automotive products, and "defense and space."

- Coca-Cola, with sales of over $2.5 billion, reports that it is in "one line of business, the manufacture and sale of beverages, including soft drink, syrups and concentrates and the processing and sale of coffee, tea, frozen concentrated orange, lemon and lime juices and ades. It also cans flavored drinks."

- Minnesota Mining and Manufacturing (3M), with total sales of nearly $3 billion, lists eight lines of business with such informative captions as Graphic Systems; Tape and Allied Products; Abrasives, Adhesives, Building Service Products and Chemicals; Advertising Services and Protective Products; Photographic, Printing and Nuclear Products; and so on. Its Tape and Allied Products category includes such diverse lines as equipment for use in packaging and fastening tapes, decorative ribbons and gift wrap products, structural plastics for industrial and defense purposes, occupational health and safety products, cosmetic and allied chemicals.

In all, a staff report to the Cabinet Committee on Price Stability estimated in January 1969 that the SEC's 10 percent rule would disclose only about 14 percent of the industrial categories in which the 50 largest manufacturing companies operated. So as industry in the late 1960s grew more and more diversified, citizens and shareholders knew less and less about their giant corporations.

TO THE RESCUE, THE FTC

The Federal Trade Commission (FTC) in its long and erratic history has rarely distinguished itself for policy initiative. But, to its credit, for well over 20 years it has struggled to fill the line of business reporting gap left by the SEC, albeit achieving less than a complete success.

Starting in the mid-1950s, the Commission began seeking funds for a line of business program to determine each large company's "major products, locations of its plants, geographic areas in which it sells or buys, methods of sale or classes of customers, sales of major products and relative size in major markets." The House Appropriations Subcommittee, however, then chaired by Albert Thomas (D.–Tex.), rejected this proposal out of hand.

The idea was revived as it became evident that the FTC's Quarterly Financial Report (QFR) contained little useful information. This program classifies firms by industry on the basis of their consolidated operations. Aggregate figures are published showing total sales, profits per dollar of sales, profits on stockholders' equity, and other financial information. Governed by a commitment of confidentiality to the Office of Management and Budget, this FTC program has never released information by individual company name. During the period when industries were largely composed of specialized firms operating within a single industry, the program worked reasonably well. But when a company operated in many industries, the classification system produced less meaningful results. According to a recent statement of the commission:

It is not uncommon to have to classify large companies into one industry category on the basis of between 10 and 15 percent of their total activities. Such a classification decision contaminates the industry in which the company is classified. It also obscures the activities in the large company's nonprimary industries and leaves them unrepresentative.

The predicament is illustrated by a recently released FTC staff report on four food industries—meat, milk, bread, and beer. Because these studies were derived from QFR data, which cannot isolate out subsidiaries of many large conglomerates, many key firms in the designated industries had to be omitted—badly skewing the results. ITT's Continental Baking Company, a leading bread producer marketing Wonder Bread, was left out of the bread study since the company reports profits only on its consolidated operations. The eight leading milk producers were excluded, and only 15 percent of all milk industry sales were represented in the report. The Commission found no evidence of profiteering in the price increases in the foods studied, but had to acknowledge that there were "serious deficiencies" in the data on which the study was based.

An effort in the early 1960s to obtain more relevant and refined company data backfired. Willard F. Mueller, then Director of the Bureau of Economics, submitted to the Budget office a questionnaire relating both to product line information and corporate ownership for the country's 1,000 largest corporations. That agency's Business Advisory Council distributed copies to business groups throughout the country, triggering an avalanche of business opposition to the proposal. By mail, wire, telephone, and personal visits, businessmen protested to members of Congress. By the time the issue reached the congressional appropriations committees, the die was cast. Not only did Congress not approve the study, but a special rider was attached to the FTC appropriation specifically forbidding the inquiry.

The FTC made a similar effort in the early 1970s. Unsatisfied with the FTC's promise to maintain the confidentiality of individual company data, the OMB Business Advisory Council again marshaled all of its resources to defeat the program. It held a public hearing, attended mostly by representatives of the country's leading corporations. These representatives voiced the following complaints:

- Our "basic competitive system" would be irreparably damaged; the proposal was "outrageous"—a step "to completely regulate the economy."

- Disclosure would "greatly advantage competitors," and injure reporting firms.

- High profits do not "necessarily" connote monopoly power; the fact that two or three firms control 90 percent of a product does not determine the presence or absence of competition.

- Market shares by major firms constitute "trade secrets"; they are "proprietary information"; besides, companies lack information on market shares. Publication of such information would "create market disruptions" and damage the economy.

- Any line of business program would be burdensome and costly to industry.

- There is no need for such a program because consumers already have sufficient information "to form good judgments concerning the prices, costs and profits of suppliers."

This time the FTC and its supporters responded. Willard Mueller, by then retired as Chief Economist, testified: "Contrary to the assertions of many corporations, corporate secrecy—not corporate disclosure—is the great enemy of a market economy in a free society." Economist Robert Heilbroner discussed the elaborate information gathering large firms conduct about each other, concluding that giant corporations "know more about each other than the public knows, either as consumers or as government." FTC proponents argued that disseminating lines of business information wouldn't be expensive since any competent operating management needed to know such information to minimally perform its job. Senator Gaylord Nelson pointed out that the largest corporations had an unfair competitive advantage over small specialized firms, who already supplied detailed information on their lines of business while the larger, more diversified corporations did not.

Congress decided to help out. Shortly after the OMB's Business Advisory Council held its meeting to attack the FTC line of business proposal, Congress removed the FTC from the OMB's jurisdiction and placed the Commission under the supervision of the General Accounting Office (GAO). The FTC then developed a line of business questionnaire based upon the Standard Industrial Classification (SIC) codes used by the Bureau of Census. This proposal—to cover a projected 500 major manufacturing firms— was submitted to the GAO for clearance in March 1974. By then substantial criticism had developed. The product categories, it was argued, were too broad, encompassing too many products. Some firms complained that collection of data on a plant basis would include a substantial proportion of intracompany transactions, which would mean duplicate counting as the product moved from plant to plant. In addition, much of this movement represented transfers of goods in the manufacturing process. The figures supplied would provide no reliable picture of the sales that actually reached the marketplace. And, said business opponents, FTC rules for allocations of advertising and research costs were totally unrealistic.

The GAO's initial response was not enthusiastic. But, sensitive to prevailing congressional sentiment, the GAO eventually approved the questionnaire while "recognizing that the initial information will be unreliable at best, and may be misleading." On August 19, 1974 the FTC sent its line of business forms to 345 companies, giving them 150 days to report their 1973 operations. The first response—on August 20—was a motion by several of the companies to quash the proceedings. Upon denial, several firms filed suit in two U.S. district courts, with conflicting results. In New York, Judge Edward Weinfield refused both to grant an injunction and to issue an order enjoining the FTC from serving default notices involving fines for the companies. In Delaware, though, Judge Murray Schwartz decreed that the issues met the "ripeness" test and that, unless acted upon, the companies would be subjected to severe hardship and undue burdens. A preliminary injunction was granted. Since then, the FTC has been embroiled in continuing litigation over its line of business program.

But the Commission's practices in handling the data so far received raises serious questions about the program's potential usefulness. In an effort to persuade corporations that there will be no breach of confidentiality, the FTC permits access to the data only to the staff of the Division of Financial Statistics which publishes the QFR. With little scrutiny the information then goes directly into computers. None of the industrial economists in the Bureau of Economics may examine the information for possible reporting discrepancies. No decision has even been made as to whether even aggregate data will be published.

The FTC has also recently revived another program, the Corporate Patterns Survey. As early as 1950, the Commission secured information on ownership of affiliates and value of plant shipments by product class from the thousand largest corporations. The use of the data was largely confined to the Commission's examination of corporate mergers in the 1950s and 1960s. During these decades the FTC's staff attempted to secure publication of the shipments data obtained by each company; this was finally accomplished in the 1970s—over 20 years later. The material was then so old that companies could hardly claim that release of the information was "competitively damaging."

The resurrected Corporate Patterns Survey again proposes the collection of detailed information on corporate ownership, an area not encompassed by the Line of Business program. It parallels data required in the SEC's 10-K forms, but penetrates more deeply into interfirm relationships. Firms are to report their holdings of 5 percent or more in other domestic companies whose sales are $10 million or more. They must furnish detailed information on sales and product lines of newly acquired firms and those spun off. Joint venture arrangements must be fully disclosed, including the shares held by all parties and the nature of the business. The survey also requires submission of company data relating to value of plant shipments by broad SIC categories. Unlike the Line of Business project, which provides for annual reporting, the Corporate Patterns data will be collected every five years. The current request calls for data for 1972, conforming with the work of the Department of Commerce's Census of Manufacturers. Unlike that agency's mandatory requirement of secrecy, however, the FTC proposal includes public release of the information by company four or five years later—making it, basically, historical information for assessment of changes in corporate structure and activities.

Toward a New Financial Disclosure Program

To help assure that consumers, taxpayers, labor, antitrust enforcers, security holders, and state and federal authorities are adequately informed about the financial operations of the largest corporations, Congress should adopt the following provisions:

1. Corporate Ownership and Control—To determine accurately the structure of the United States' economy, each federally chartered corporation should reveal its investment interest in all other companies, both foreign and domestic. All joint ventures should be included, with identification of coparticipants, changes of ownership, and nature and extent of the business activity. Each firm should also disclose significant long term contracts or debt relationships with all other companies, foreign or domestic. Existing SEC rules require corporations to report information only for those holdings which constitute 10 percent or more of their aggregate assets. This standard is seriously deficient for the giant corporation, as illustrated by Standard Oil of New Jersey (now Exxon) which in 1968 had investments of about one billion dollars. It was not possible, found one scholar, "to identify from public sources even the names of all the corporations in which it had investments, and it was not possible to identify the value of the assets of *any* of these corporations."

2. Corporate Relations to Government—Over 20 percent of the federal government's 1975 budget—approximately $75 billion—was paid directly to business corporations in the form of procurement, research and development, and consulting contracts. Another $25 billion was paid to this nation's largest corporations in direct and indirect (tax) subsidies. The public has a right to know how its tax dollars are being spent. Federally chartered firms should disclose in their annual reports major sales contracts with federal agencies for the furnishing of goods or services, indicating the items involved and the dollar amounts, and any facilities that they operate for or lease from the federal government. Similar information would be supplied for significant research and development contracts, disposition of rights to government-financed research, acquisition of properties declared surplus by the government, and subsidies.

Contracts or arrangements involving federal grants or loans should also be disclosed. This should include loans from any federal agency or any international agency funded in part by the U.S. government; tax investment credits; and special tax allowances. Federally chartered corporations should report as well the identity and nature of all cases instituted, in process or settled, in which the federal government is a party. Copies of all federal tax settlements, consent decrees, or other agreements ending such controversies can easily be published in the *Corporate Register*.

Finally, each chartered corporation should publish its federal corporate tax return in the *Corporate Register*. The SEC already subscribes to this idea in principle. Under current law, "all bona fide shareholders of record owning one percent or more of the outstanding stock of any corporation" can secure a copy. By simply removing the one-percent requirement, members of the public won't have to buy several million dollars worth of stock to know whether our giant corporations are honestly paying their taxes. The State of Wisconsin, for one example, until 1953 allowed any member of the public to examine corporate state tax returns and to publish information derived from them.

3. Security Holder Disclosure—Each chartered corporation should disclose the 100 largest security holders in each class of voting stock and the name of any person or organization who holds one percent or more of any class of nonvoting stock or debt security. According to a committee representing 10 federal regulatory agencies and representatives of Senator Metcalf's Budgeting, Management and Expenditure Subcommittee in 1975, this type of information can help uncover possible conflicts of interest or illicit corporate interlocks as well as assess foreign ownership of American corporations.

Such disclosure will be meaningless, however, unless steps are taken to bar nominee or front organization ownership. Since these contrivances enable individuals and companies to evade law or public knowledge, Congress should bar nominee ownership. Each security in a federally chartered corporation should be required to be recorded in the name of its beneficial owner. If more than one person enjoys the benefits of the stock's ownership, all persons should be recorded with identification of their individual interests on the security holder list. Needless to say, compliance with this law will be the responsibility of both the securities brokerage industry and federally chartered corporations. Sanctions for failure to observe this stricture should be directed against both.

4. Management Income—Each federally chartered corporation should disclose the annual income of its 30 highest paid executives, their securities ownership, securities options, loan arrangements, and retirement benefits. As Chapter IV detailed, senior management in many large corporations has institutionalized the modern treasury raid by awarding themselves substantial income and wealth without shareholder approval, or even knowledge in some cases. The primary protection against this situation in the Chartering Act is an independent directorate to negotiate on behalf of shareholders. A secondary protection is disclosure: by giving shareholders knowledge of executive income, they may discipline directors who become unduly generous. But this requires much more comprehensive reporting techniques than those the SEC presently employs. All income or wealth benefits—including those as incidental as corporate rest and recreation facilities, chauffeured limousines, and periodic use of company apartments—should be identified, given a dollar imputation, and disclosed.

5. Financial Statements and Product Line Reporting—In 1970, Congress recognized the failure of the accounting industry to develop useful financial reporting standards by establishing the Cost Accounting Standards Board (CASB) to research and promulgate uniform cost accounting standards for contractors doing business with the Department of Defense. CASB now also covers contracts negotiated with NASA and the General Services Administration.

It is now time for Congress to extend the same protection to security holders, taxpayers, labor, consumers, antitrust enforcers, and state legislatures. The SEC should be ordered to hire sufficient staff to develop financial standards for all federally chartered firms. The importance of uniform accounting standards has been recognized by nearly every other western industrial nation. France, for example, has had a comprehensive accounting system in operation since the 1920s. The system is uniform in terminology and classification of accounts, and has standardized valuation rules. Belgium and West Germany employ similar systems. By comparison, notes Professor Robert Chatov, "the SEC's policy of disclosure without comparability is a substantially meaningless exercise."

Although this is not the place for a discussion of each item that should be disclosed in corporate financial statements, a few policy considerations deserve comment.

The SEC's primary effort here should be to standardize financial reporting among all large corporations—taking into account differing economic realities in differing industries only where absolutely necessary. "Consolidated" financial statements should represent the full operations of the firm instead of, as at present, often only partial segments, with subsidiary or affiliated corporations reporting as separate corporations. In multinational firms, statements should be broken down on a "U.S." and "all foreign" basis; in addition, there should be foreign financial reports furnished on a country-by-country basis. The flow of foreign investment, both to and from U.S. corporations, should be regularly disclosed, including identification of the nature of specific new U.S. corporate investments abroad and deposits in foreign banks as well as periodic identification of foreign loans or investment in U.S. corporations and international joint ventures.

To deal with the vital matter of line of business reporting, the SEC, in conjunction with the Bureau of Census, the Justice Department's Antitrust Division, and the FTC, should be directed to develop a reformed Standard Industrial Classification reporting system. The new system would more closely approximate the ideal of correlating all costs employed in the production of each product with all revenues and profits derived from the sale of each product. Although the technical difficulties involved in such an effort are real, they do not justify preservation of the increasingly uninformative present SIC system.

6. Corporate Management-Accountant Relations—The board of directors, not operating management, should nominate the accounting firm. The board should have no power to impose accounting principles on the outside auditor. To insure the accounting firm's independence and detachment, no firm should be rehired for more than five years. This will guarantee a rotation of accountants at the largest corporations, with the benefit that the leading practitioners will check each other's work. Lest a conspiracy of silence emerge, any accountant who discovers or ought to have discovered an earlier inaccuracy or inappropriate use of standards by a previous accountant and fails to report it to the SEC should be held co-liable in any subsequent civil or criminal suit.

7. A Multinational Study—Finally, Congress should confront the international ramifications of corporate power by ordering a study of both the social and financial impacts of U.S.-based multinational firms. Many of the problems associated with multinationals—the exporting of jobs, environmental damage, transfer pricing, tax avoidance, and exploitation of third-world countries—raise special questions of corporate disclosure which have been largely ignored by existing regulatory disclosure programs. Business secrecy in this country, though extensive, is easily surpassed by the secrecy which shields corporate foreign operations. The EEOC knows the percentage of blacks in our domestic steel industry, but not in Polaroid's South African plants. There are serious conflicts between AFL-CIO and industry data on the extent of job loss or job gain due to multinationals. And we can only guess at the extent of and cost of transfer pricing to evade taxes. Quite simply, we don't know enough about the foreign activities of multinational giants or the impact on the U.S. of these activities. The Commerce Department's Bureau of Economic Affairs has clear authority under the 1944 Bretton Woods Agreement to gather some of this data. But it has been totally stymied since its 1966 survey was completed in 1970 by the corporate-dominated National Advisory Committee on International Monetary and Financial Policy.

Defenders of the *status quo ante* argue that such added disclosure would put the United States firms at a disadvantage in their international competition with Japanese and West German firms.

Yet in some important areas other industrial countries have more stringent disclosure requirements than the United States. In Japan, for example, corporations are required to give the tax collector and the shareholders the same profit figures. When the United States adopted Subpart F of the Internal Revenue Code in 1962 to attempt to curb the use of tax havens, West Germany and Great Britain adopted similar legislation. Such parallel legislation would seem particularly likely now with the Common Market nations honing a new corporation law that emphasizes disclosure.

Congress should close this information gap by creating a joint task force—with representatives from the SEC, IRS, FTC, Census Bureau and Justice and State Departments—to prepare a study within two years examining the principal impacts of the United States based multinational corporations on the United States economy and United States international relations, and recommending what permanent disclosure and regulatory mechanisms should be enacted. Like the SEC's 1961–63 Study of Securities Markets, the multinational study should be headed and in part staffed by nongovernmental personnel—such as academics, lawyers, economists, labor and business people and consumers. This arrangement will enable the study to criticize existing government arrangements while simultaneously assuring it the benefits of as many experienced government experts as desirable.

Among other questions, the study should examine:

1. The extent of American corporations' investments abroad (i.e., subsidiary corporations, property, securities holdings, bank accounts, etc.).

2. The impact of U.S. corporations upon foreign policy formulation.

3. The effect of U.S.-based multinationals upon job opportunities within the United States and the effects of threats to relocate abroad upon U.S. labor negotiations.

4. The vulnerability of the United States economy to foreign price and production cartels—as by the Organization of Petroleum Exporting Countries (OPEC).

5. The effect of international joint ventures—such as those in the oil industry—upon U.S. national security.

6. The amount of taxes paid each country by multinationals.

7. Special governmental incentives to firms to settle where they did, including subsidies and other state-granted privileges and immunities.

8. The impact of U.S. multinationals on consumers and labor in developing countries.

9. The effect of U.S. multinationals upon the world's interdependent ecology.

VI

"Constitutionalizing" the Corporation: An Employee Bill of Rights

O, it is excellent to have a giant's strength,
But it is tyrannous to use it like a giant.

—Measure for Measure

A BASIC PURPOSE OF the United States Constitution is to distinguish the powers of government from the rights of individual citizens. Due to the widespread fear of a tyrannical national government, most of the framers agreed with Alexander Hamilton's argument in the *84th Federalist Paper* that the powers of the federal government were limited to those expressly delegated by the people in the Constitution, or those "necessary and proper" to its operation.

It is within an analogous framework that the question of corporate power should be assessed. As long as corporations were small, the Constitution's failure to mention them was a minor problem. The Supreme Court in the early nineteenth century reconciled the private corporation to the Constitution by treating incorporation as a personal property right. Later in the nineteenth century, the Supreme Court went so far as to hold that the corporation should be considered a "person" or "citizen" for the purposes of the Due Process and Equal Protection clauses of the Fourteenth Amendment.

This reconciliation broke down as the corporation's size, power and range increased. No longer was it possible to say that the corporation was a person for certain limited purposes, and otherwise ignore it. For like the state and municipal governments it overshadows, the giant business corporation *is* a government. By employing thousands of individuals, it possesses the power to rule them. It can establish employment rules restricting their conduct; grant or withhold financial rewards otherwise unavailable; or effectively destroy the career of a specialist in a monopoly or near monopoly industry. How can a Constitution, which fully restrains all levels of political government from invading the rights of citizens, then permit every business corporation to do so?

With this anomaly in mind, the Supreme Court in 1945 laid the doctrinal foundation for applying certain constitutional restrictions to the operations of the giant corporations. In the landmark case of *Marsh v. Alabama*, the question was whether a corporation could refuse to permit an individual to distribute religious literature on the "business block" of a company-owned town. Obviously, explained Justice Hugo Black for the Court, if the town of Chickasaw, Alabama, had been owned by a municipality rather than by the Gulf Shipbuilding Company, defendant Marsh's conviction for criminal trespass would have to be set aside. For no state or municipality can bar the distribution of religious or political literature consistent with the First Amendment.

Does the First Amendment cease simply because a single company has legal title to all the town? Alabama argued that the corporation's right to control the inhabitants of Chickasaw was coextensive with the right of a homeowner to regulate the conduct of his guests.

Justice Black disagreed. "The more an owner, for his advantage, opens up his property for use by the public in general, the more do his rights become circumscribed by the statutory and constitutional rights of those who use it." Black then illustrated his point. "Had the Corporation here owned the segment of the four-lane highway which runs parallel to the 'business block' and operated the same under a state franchise, doubtless no one would have seriously contended that the corporation's property interest in the highway gave it power to obstruct through traffic or to discriminate against interstate commerce." From which the Supreme Court's holding followed: It makes no "constitutional difference" that the state, instead of permitting the corporation to operate a highway, permitted Gulf to use its property as a town and to operate a business block in the town and a sidewalk on that business block. When a private corporation performs a "public function," the same constitutional standards of free speech and equal protection of the law apply as if it were the state.

Almost from the day it was decided, commentators anticipated a swift extension of the *Marsh* doctrine. What made Gulf Corporation's functions "public," Adolf Berle notably argued, was that "one corporation owned the entire town." But there is nothing special about sidewalks. "The prejudice of the owner of 90 percent of the available housing would be a public matter." So would the prejudice of the owner of any other necessary good or service. This led Berle to predict the "direct application of constitutional limitations to the corporation, merely because it holds a state charter and exercises a degree of economic power sufficient to make its practices 'public' rules."

Berle proved a poor prophet. The Supreme Court has repeatedly ruled since *Marsh* that there can be no limitation placed on a corporation's right to use its property exactly as it chooses, unless the corporation is performing a "public function" or "state action" traditionally performed by government. In one recent case the High Court said that a private utility company needn't notify a customer before cutting off service—in the same manner that a government agency must provide notice before revoking a privilege— even though the utility company had an absolute monopoly of this essential service; the Court held that the utility company was not performing the equivalent of a government function.

In an even more recent case, *Hodgeus v. National Labor Relations Board*, the Burger court flatly overruled a progeny of *Marsh* and held that striking workers do not have a constitutional right to picket peacefully in a privately owned shopping center even when the center performed many of the same functions as the company-owned streets in *Marsh*.

If the courts will not protect the rights of citizens against abuses of corporate power, then Congress should. A primary purpose of our national Constitution was to avoid the tyrannical use of collective power. It makes no meaningful difference to those who lose their "inalienable" rights to freedom of speech or due process of law that they were victimized by a giant corporation rather than by a giant government. In either case the purpose of the Constitution has been frustrated, and the Bill of Rights reduced to a bill of goods.

Potentially the giant business corporation should be subject to the fundamental restraints that the Constitution places upon state and federal government, including the right of the corporation's citizens, its employees, to participate in the governance of their workplace. But how to structure workers' participation into giant corporations is far from obvious. In the view of Mack Hanan and Isidore Silver in a pathbreaking 1967 *Harvard Business Review* article, the key is to establish an internal corporate ombudsman with the authority to intervene on behalf of employees and to dramatize and publicize *outside the corporation* complaints that do not receive proper management attention.

Other advocates of "job power" would go far further and replicate Yugoslavia's "workers councils," which possess extensive managerial powers. Or they would at least generalize the experiments of corporations such as Norway's Norsk Hydro or U.S. firms such as Corning Glass, Motorola, and Pet Foods, which have given their employees wide-ranging powers to redesign their workplaces.

Yet even short of complete "industrial democracy," Congress can act immediately in three obvious areas of constitutional rights.

FIRST AMENDMENT RIGHTS

Except within the ambit of National Labor Relations law, no present federal law assures that citizens will be as free to express themselves in the workplace as they are in the body politic. Yet the Supreme Court has reminded us that

[W]hen we balance the constitutional rights of owners of property against those of the people to enjoy freedom of press and religion . . . we remain mindful of the fact that the latter occupy a preferred position. . . . [T]he right to exercise the liberties safeguarded by the First Amendment lies at the foundation of free government by free man.

Occasional protection of union free speech is not enough.* There are numerous cases of corporations firing or otherwise penalizing employees who participated in political activity—on or off the job—or who wrote or published critical articles or expressed unpopular opinions. At several corporations, public discussion of job safety, employee privacy, or race and sex discrimination takes place in anonymous underground newspapers like *The Stranded Oiler*, the *A.T.&T. Express*, or the *Met-Lifer*.

Retaliation against outspoken employees occurs most frequently for "blowing the whistle." The conscientious employee risks losing his job for reporting practices such as the marketing of defective vehicles to unsuspecting consumers; the waste of government funds by private contractors; the industrial dumping of mercury in waterways; the connection between companies and bribery or illegal campaign contributions; or the suppression of serious occupational disease data. What Montesquieu called the basis of all political freedom—the assurance that you can do what you ought to do, and that you will not be forced to do what you ought not to do—has failed for the product testers and junior executives of our largest corporations. Men and women who should be lauded as public citizens have been intimidated and ostracized.

Men and women like George Geary. A sales executive for United States Steel, Geary objected to the sale of a new type of pipe which he believed was inadequately tested and likely to fail under high pressure. For this he was fired for insubordination, even though U.S. Steel considered Geary's charges so serious that they withdrew the product from sale pending major retesting.

Or like Henry Durham, who was demoted for protesting Lockheed's waste-ridden supply practices on the C-5A transport plane and was later forced out of Lockheed after testifying before Senator William Proxmire's Subcommittee on Economy in Government.

---

* Only five states—California, Colorado, Kansas, Louisiana, and Nevada—protect nonunion freedom of expression. Of these, the broadest law, California's, has been sharply criticized for its ineffectiveness.

Or Colt Firearms' workers Wayne Henfield and Vic Martinez, who were suspended and threatened with being "blackballed" if they publicized the defects of the M-16 rifle.

Or GM engineers Carl Thelin and George Caramanna, who were pressured not to reveal the structural defects of the Corvair.

Or Carl Houston, an engineer for Stone and Webster Engineering Company, who was fired for voicing criticism of the pipe welding of an atomic power plant even though a defect could have led to a catastrophic meltdown.

Or data analysts Kermit Vandiver and Serle Lawson, who were coerced by B. F. Goodrich executives to falsify laboratory test results on an aircraft brake for an Air Force contracted plane, and later forced to leave after they "went public" with the deception.

In each of these instances employees were punished for trying to protect the public. Yet under the present state laws of agency, they may have themselves violated their "duty of confidentiality." Section 395 of the Restatement of Agency currently enjoins an agent (or employee) from communicating information confidentially given to him by his principal (his corporation) when it will injure the principal. Comment *f* of this Section recognizes an exception where the principal is committing or is about to commit a crime—which is helpful but will not win back the employee's job. It merely bars the corporation from prevailing in any suit it may later bring against the employee. State law does not recognize an employee's right to damages for "malicious discharge" if the employee refuses to participate in immoral or tortious activity or declines to compromise professional ethics. As a General Electric official explained after three G.E. engineers quit to publicize the dangers of existing nuclear plants, corporate employees must "be willing to resign" if they exercise their First Amendment rights within a firm.

RIGHTS OF PRIVACY

Under the First, Fourth, Fifth, and Ninth Amendments, the state may not invade certain rights of individual privacy. These amendments create "zones of privacy" which government officials may penetrate only under extraordinary circumstances—such as threats to national security or "probable cause" of the commission of a crime. Otherwise they may not penetrate at all.

Under the First Amendment, the federal government normally may not question a job applicant about his religion, political opinions, or past political associations. Here, ruled the Supreme Court, "the views of the individual are made inviolate . . . the opinions of men are not the object of civil government, nor under its jurisdiction. . . ." Similarly, the census taker is enjoined from questioning about religion, political philosophy, or sexual habits or preference.

The Fourth Amendment guarantees "the right of the people to be secure in their persons, houses, papers, and effects, against unreasonable searches and seizures. . . . No warrant shall issue, but upon probable cause. . . ." As construed by the leading case of *Katz v. United States*, every citizen may "justifiably rely" upon the Fourth Amendment to protect his privacy unless the police have sought and received a search warrant. Under the Fifth Amendment, no person shall be compelled in any criminal case to be a witness against himself—either through direct interrogation or through mechanical testimony compelled by polygraph or "lie detecting" machines. And the Ninth Amendment provides that the people retain other residual rights, including, the case of *Griswold v. Connecticut* informed us, an absolute right to be secure in the marriage relationship from police inspection for illicit use of contraceptive devices.

No such niceties apply at the workplace. Eighty percent or more of our largest corporations subject the applicant to a battery of personal and psychological interviews and tests. As a condition of employment, the job applicant must answer inquiries respecting such non-job related topics as his or her reading or travel habits, nonwork interests, religious faith, relationship with parents, marital difficulties, homosexuality, sexual fidelity or abnormality, political views, "loyalty," and what Sears, Roebuck once quaintly referred to as "values."

To keep "bad apples out of the barrel," many corporations go much further. Former FBI agents or organizations such as Fidelifacts or Bishop's Service are hired to learn what they can about an applicant by talking with neighbors, former employers, and co-

workers. Not only do PEIs (pre-employment investigators) interview outsiders about the future employee's health, records at previous jobs, debts, drinking problems, drug addiction, sex deviancy,
or possible criminal violations, but many search firms and management consultants also feel it is imperative that someone—either
with the company or retained by the company—get into the man's
home for a look around. Such a home interview may establish evidence of unhappy marriage or neglect of children, whether the
applicant's spouse is domineering or otherwise a "problem."

A home interview may also determine whether the applicant is
"controversial." To quote a 1964 interview guideline offered by
Bishop's Service: "It is not necessary that the man be an active
member of a church; most aren't but they can be. But does he conform, or is he an avowed, loud rebel? . . . Whether he is Republican or Democrat is secondary, but is he what is commonly heard of
today as being an extreme liberal? Is he a Communist sympa-
thizer?" The Chicago based American Security Council kept a card
file of six million Americans including "peaceniks, draft-card
burners, pseudo-intellectuals" and others involved in "revolutionary activities." Such misplaced zeal might seem laughable except for the fact that the American Security Council was employed
by an impressive array of corporate clients including Sears, Roebuck, National Airlines, Schick Razor, Allstate Insurance, and
Quaker Oats.

Polygraph examinations take up where regular investigative
methods leave off.* Organizations such as John E. Reid and Associates, Pinkerton National Detective Agency, William J. Burns International Detective Agency, and Dale Systems, Inc. administer
tests for national corporations. For screening job-seekers, the lie detector is supposedly effective at uncovering "latent tendencies toward

---

* Since many employee surveillance techniques are morally repugnant, if not
clearly illegal, it is difficult to gather precise statistics regarding incidence. A 1974
study prepared by the Senate Subcommittee on Constitutional Rights estimated that
between 200,000 and 300,000 private business polygraph tests are administered each
year. The study indicated the figure may be as high as 500,000. A 1971 AFL-CIO
publication estimated that between 30,000 and 40,000 business enterprises use the
polygraph for personal analysis. Among them were Montgomery Ward, Armour &
Company, E. F. Hutton, and Lord & Taylor.

dishonesty"; whether or not the applicant intends to stay with the corporation "permanently"; "dangerous habits" such as alcohol, gambling, girl friends on the side, or homosexual "tendencies."

On the job, surveillance may become even more intensive. Vance Packard interviewed executives at the William J. Burns Detective Agency and Norman Jaspan Associates ("with a hundred clients who are listed on the New York Stock Exchange") to document the extent "of hidden cameras, hidden microphones, one-way mirrors, and peepholes to watch the already well-screened employees." He concluded that the practice of surveillance is so widespread that in a single year "13,500,000 Americans—or approximately one-fifth of all jobholders—were being scrutinized under some sort of security or loyalty program." A 1966 American Broadcasting Company report similarly estimated that one out of every five businesses in the country eavesdrops on its workers.

The rights of union leaders, rival businessmen, and corporate critics are particularly susceptible to abuse. Former Senator Edward Long was impressed by a 1962 survey of industrial espionage conducted by the trade magazine *Industrial Research:*

An interesting paradox was reported: nearly everyone questioned thought that wiretapping was dangerous, and "dirty pool," yet one-third of the firms with formal intelligence operations reported they tapped phones or hired someone to do it for them. Another third of these firms carefully refused to say whether they did or did not tap. . . .

Not all industrial espionage is carried out by electronic means. One company installed a false ceiling with peepholes in a room used for union meetings. Arrangements have been made with janitors and cleaning people to purchase the contents of a competitor's waste basket. Secretaries of key executives have been wooed. Blackmail, bribery, and burglary have all been used. And one widely used tactic of proven effectiveness is the planting of a spy in a competitor's business.

Since 1962 the methods deployed by corporations have become more sophisticated. In 1967 *The New Republic* described an internal General Motors document purportedly sent from a systems development company to the management of General Motors, urging GM to set up a corporate CIA with the purpose of gathering and analyzing information about GM's rivals. *The New Republic* found no reason to doubt General Motors' assertion that it had rejected this plan. "Nonetheless," the magazine continued,

the plan is interesting because it suggests what the future of the spy business could be. The 19-page memorandum predicts that "within five years the gathering of intelligence as currently practiced by governments in both military and diplomatic affairs will become a formal, recognized activity in corporate management." "A technological revolution in information handling has taken place," the memo says, "and there is no choice but to respond to it." First, modern computers are able to store and retrieve information at costs low enough so that "information handling cost, however calculated, is no longer dominant even when the vast bulk of what is recorded is never used." Second, sensory devices for getting information are "startlingly successful."

The memorandum lists a variety of activities that a corporate CIA might undertake: recording all telephone conversations without the callers' knowledge; "bugging" the hotel room of a competitor; observing a competitor's equipment during a technical meeting "field trip"; confusing a competitor's test marketing equipment; hiring a competitor's employee; planting an agent in the employ of a competitor; investigating the "personal history" of a competitor's executive group.

It is technically possible to simulate the decision-making processes of rival firms, based on a systematic accumulation and analysis of large amounts of data, and thereby predict their probable behavior. . . . The business espionage of the future will begin "formulating more sophisticated models of competitors' activities than (is) conventionally done and using these models to find the binding constraints on competitors' activities." The basic goal will be a "higher level of understanding of how one corporation can cripple another."

Within five years, much of what the memorandum had prophesied had become fact. In the largest corporations, computer data banks frequently include "personal dossiers" containing information on an employee's education, military record, medical history, employment background, aptitude and psychological testing performance, as well as subjective appraisals of his character and skills. A corporation may integrate pre-employment "loyalty" or polygraph checks, conviction and credit records, as well as anonymous or unattributed complaints. Since no safeguards assure "contextual accuracy" and computer dossiers are freely disseminated, the individual's ability to maintain control over personal information has disappeared.

Paralleling the cybernetics revolution has been a "bug boom." Wiretapping, hidden television cameras, spike and parabolic microphones, remote sensing devices, and infrared photography have become less expensive and more effective. *Newsweek* recently reported that:

> [I]n these post-Watergate days, it is as easy to buy a bug in this country as it was to get bootleg booze during Prohibition. Electronic-parts distributors across the country sell listening and recording devices that as often as not end up in the hands of would-be political snoopers, industrial spies and just plain nosy neighbors both over the counter and through the mail as openly as they peddle tape cassettes.

What's more, the bugging equipment comes cheap. We interviewed representatives from the American Society of Industrial Security, the National Wiretapping Commission, and private firms such as the Spy Shop, a basement "consulting" firm until recently located just two blocks from the White House. Microphones can be installed in P.A. speakers already operative in washrooms, loading docks, lounges, or offices for as little as five to ten dollars. Phone taps or phone listening devices which audit all conversations within a room cost little more. Even quite sophisticated equipment such as long distance "snooper" antennae or bugs that "broadcast" detected conversations to distant receivers are well within reach of the security-conscious corporation.

Simultaneously, corporate employment of "outside specialists" to deploy the new sophisticated electronic devices has surged. The giant detective agencies, Pinkerton's, William J. Burns, Wackenhut, and Norman Jaspan Associates, are increasingly hired for "undercover" assignments. Not only rival businesses and unions, but also fellow executives are surreptitiously observed or followed to assure they are not leaking corporate secrets or otherwise being disloyal. One indication of how commonplace these activities have become is a full-page advertisement in the October 1975 issue of *Fortune* magazine. For $15,000, Dr. Robert S. Aries offers to sell to the "managements of the world's largest corporations" an *Industrial Espionage Encyclopedia* treating such topics as "How to fabricate fake memos for competitors' consumption" and "How to make your competitors' R&D [that is, Research & Development] work in the wrong direction."

Aries knows a market when he sees one. A survey in the November–December 1974 issue of the *Harvard Business Review* reported that 72 percent of the respondents felt their "company should have a more systematic method of gathering, processing, analyzing, and reporting information about competitors." In addition, 39 percent of 1,211 responding executives *admitted* their corporations either "occasionally" or "often" engaged "undercover operatives for in-house checking on embezzlement, stealing, and so on." Similarly, 38 percent admitted their corporations engaged in "electronic surveillance of high-risk areas"; 24 percent acknowledged their companies surreptitiously conducted locker checks.

This is very far astray from the free society the Bill of Rights sought to promote. As General Robert E. Wood, former chairman of the board of Sears, Roebuck & Company, explained, "We complain about government and business, we stress the advantages of the free enterprise system, we complain about the totalitarian state, but in our individual organizations . . . we have created more or less of a totalitarian system in industry, particularly in large industry." Yet presently statutory law provides virtually no protection to corporate employees. Most employee surveillance techniques—non-work related pre-employment testing, polygraphs,* the ubiquitous television cameras, peepholes, and company spies—are probably lawful. Even when the surreptitious or unexpected nature of corporate surveillance might otherwise sustain a civil claim, the courts are reluctant to protect employee rights. Professor Arthur R. Miller has concluded:

Perhaps the most significant weakness in today's common law privacy action is the frequency with which it is barred by a successful assertion that the injured person waived his right to sue by engaging in activity inconsistent with a desire to maintain his privacy or that he consented to the dissemination of personal information. The utilization of these concepts by the courts has been somewhat Draconian and has resulted in an understandable dampening of enthusiasm for pursuing the privacy theory.

---

* As of 1974, 13 states limited or outlawed corporate use of polygraph tests.

An exception is wiretapping. Under the 1968 Omnibus Crime Act, wiretapping and electronic surveillance have been made a federal crime. Yet for the corporate employee this is more prayer than law. An elaborate procedural framework regulates federal and state law enforcement wiretaps. Government wiretaps are initiated and reviewed under court supervision. They are preserved and indexed, and sanctions are imposed for government failure to produce such records upon a legitimate demand. Although there have been government violations of this law, it still contrasts favorably with the business-initiated wiretap; for it is nearly impossible for a corporate victim to confirm he was tapped. No corporation is compelled to answer a victim's inquiry, nor need it preserve any records. Congressional prohibitions on the manufacture or possession of eavesdropping equipment or bans on broad categories of corporate espionage have not been adopted. As former Senator Edward Long put it, "While technology races, legislation has crawled."

EQUAL RIGHTS

An essential right guaranteed by the Constitution is that of legal equality. Again and again equal protection is required by the Constitution: in the First Article's two prohibitions of titles of nobility; in the Sixth Article's preclusion of religious tests; in the Thirteenth, Fourteenth and Fifteenth Amendments; the Nineteenth; and the Twenty-fourth.

This constitutional principle, unlike those previously discussed, has already been applied to corporations to a limited extent. Title VII of the Civil Rights Act of 1964 forbids employers and unions to discriminate on the basis of race, color, sex, religion, or national origin. Executive Order 11246 not only forbids discrimination by government contractors, it also requires the implementation of "affirmative action programs" to assure the attainment of equal employment objectives. Under the Civil Rights Act of 1964, corporations which own public accommodations such as hotels or motels, restaurants, cafeterias, motion picture theaters, sports arenas, or other places of exhibition and entertainment are prohibited from discriminating on account of race, color, religion, or national origin. The 1968 Civil Rights Act similarly enjoins discrimination in the sale or rental of housing. Congress has also occasionally legislated control over what the late Professor Berle called "the great and ill-defined field of access to business opportunity." The Federal Automobile Dealer Franchise Act of 1956, for example, prohibits automobile manufacturers from terminating dealerships without just cause.

But Congress has never fully applied the concepts of equal protection and equal opportunity to the largest corporations. Ad hoc application has left the law both curious and anomalous. Why protect automobile dealerships and not dealers of other products or services? Why assure equal protection in housing or restaurants or places of entertainment and not to the consumers of wholesale or retail goods? These contradictions become even less explicable when thought of in terms of economic impact. If you deny a user of a public accommodation equal rights, you may inconvenience him or her for a meal or a movie or, at most, a night. If you deny a distributor of a giant corporation equal rights, you may bankrupt an entire business. A dramatic example of this occurred during the 1970–74 gasoline shortages. Thousands of independent gasoline service station operators were driven out of business because the major oil corporations gave their wholly owned stations preference in drawing upon supply. Denying independents equal protection ultimately drove them to work directly for giant corporations—or not to work at all.

True, it has long been a cherished value in this country that an owner may employ his property as he wishes. But the man's-home-is-his-castle concept makes little sense when applied to super-corporations. The executives who control corporate property do not own it. They do not receive instructions from shareholders who do. A giant corporation is more like a public utility than a person's home. If it should achieve a position of monopoly or shared-monopoly, consumers, suppliers, and distributors come to depend upon that corporation for particular goods or services. To permit such a corporation to discriminate against women or against blacks or against independent dealers effectively means that such groups may never use a particular good or service or supply or distribute that good or service.

There is neither moral nor economic justification for such corporate prejudice. A giant corporation, unlike a human being, has no inherent rights. It achieves its powerful social and market position only because the government allows it to. This consent is premised on a general belief that free interchange between private economic firms and consumers is the most efficient method of distributing goods and services. When a corporation betrays this premise by an act of discrimination, it deserves neither the respect we accord the individual property holder nor the support of the legislature.

The Constitution becomes merely a paper right to the extent that we permit crucial aspects of American life to be conducted outside its scope. When we say the corporation should be "constitutionalized"—that is, the corporation should be made subject to applicable principles of the Constitution—we are not only asserting that the individual rights of those affected by a corporation are more valuable than certain property rights of the corporation, but also that the legitimacy of our Constitution itself is at stake. The Constitution is our First Law because it reflects a general political understanding about our social values. It is seriously devalued, if not undermined, when important activities of American citizens are not protected by its guarantees.

AN EMPLOYEE BILL OF RIGHTS

The burden should be placed squarely on the giant corporation to justify any act which contravenes basic constitutional rights. Corporations under the Federal Chartering Act, to the same extent that the Constitution requires of the United States Government, should in every transaction, practice, or occurrence:

- observe the First Amendment requirements of freedom of religion, freedom of speech, freedom of the press, and peaceable assembly;

- respect the rights of privacy of its employees and all other United States citizens; and

- not discriminate on account of race, religion, creed, or sex.

To elaborate, the First Amendment rights of "whistle blowers" will be defined to prohibit retaliation against any employee who in good faith communicates to the board of directors, the United States Congress, state legislatures, local governments, or any appropriate law enforcement agency information concerning corporate violations of state or federal law; information which would tend to impeach the testimony of corporate representatives before state or federal courts, agencies, or legislatures; information concerning inaccurate public statements of the corporation; or information concerning unethical conduct by the corporation or any of its employees. Thus, a company could not retaliate against an employee who exercises his or her constitutional right to dissent or petition public authorities, without due process of law—such as an impartial grievance procedure.

Second, the rights of privacy of employees should prohibit specific types of pre-employment testing and on the job surveillance, such as the use of mandatory polygraph tests and the gathering of confidential credit information. Other pre-employment tests would be permitted only to the extent that the corporate employer can demonstrate a functional relation to the job under consideration. The use of hidden microphones or television cameras, which violate the privacy of numerous innocent employees, would be proscribed. Further, the Federal Chartering Act would allow employees the right to examine their corporate personal files. This proposal is similar to recent federal laws which enable students and citizens to inspect their personal files at universities and federal agencies (including the F.B.I. and C.I.A.) to determine whether the collected information is accurate. Some corporations, including IBM, have already recognized the propriety of this right.

Third, the reach of the corporate equal rights provisions is described by the legal term "every transaction, practice, or occurrence." Although it is impossible to anticipate every instance in which a corporate employee, consumer, distributor, or pensioner might be discriminated against on account of race, religion, creed, or sex, the comprehensive language of this definition indicates that in no instance will such discrimination be permitted.

A fourth section would give teeth to these substantive rights by creating a new federal cause of action. Under present state law, a corporation may dismiss an employee or sever an economic relationship at will. The tenor of state law was succinctly described by a Tennessee court in 1884: All employers "may dismiss their employees for good cause, for no cause, or even for cause morally wrong, without being guilty of legal wrong." The Employee Bill of Rights would reverse this rule only when the corporation fires, penalizes, or intimidates an individual in violation of his constitutional rights to freedom of expression, equal rights, or privacy. In such cases, the injured person could seek money damages from either the corporation or the corporate executives or employees involved; and if the injured person were an employee or dealer of the corporation, he or she may also seek job protection. To effectuate such suits, the federal courts would be given power to enjoin the corporation from dismissing or penalizing an employee or dealer during the litigation process. The courts would also have the powers to award the injured person attorneys' fees and costs and to transfer or dismiss corporate executives or employees who willfully violate these constitutional rights.

Such a remedy would expand an already existent federal policy of protecting employees from "unjust dismissals." For example, the 1964 Civil Rights Act forbids employers from discriminating against employees on account of race, color, sex, religion, or national origin; the National Labor Relations Act authorizes union members to seek damages (in the form of back pay) and reinstatement if they are discharged because of their involvement in certain labor union activities. The National Labor Relations Act also enables unions to insert "just cause" provisions in their collective agreements to protect their members from discharges for ulterior purposes, for unstated reasons, or for reasons erroneously believed by the employer to be true. Similar protection is provided by the Federal Fair Labor Standards Act, which prohibits the discharge of employees who complain or testify about violations of federal wage and hour laws; the 1972 Muskie Amendments to the Federal Water Pollution Prevention and Control Act, which prohibits discharge, harassment, or discrimination against an employee for reporting suspected violations of federal water quality to federal authorities; and the Federal Automobile Dealers Franchise Act of 1956, which authorizes automobile dealers to bring a damages action against any automobile manufacturer who attempts to intimidate, coerce, or threaten them.

By generalizing the selective protection of these acts, the Employee Bill of Rights would fairly balance the corporation's general power to make or sever economic relations against the constitutional rights of those affected by the operations of our largest corporations. This rule would effectively announce that accountability in the workplace is an essential corollary of democracy in society and that corporate tyranny will not be the price of efficient production.

VII

Corporate Monopoly:
Failure in the Marketplace

The trouble is that so many witnesses come and say, "Monopoly is wrong, of course. We condemn it. These dishonest devices which are used are utterly wrong. They should not be tolerated." But the minute anyone suggests a method by which they may be prevented, then the cry is, "No, don't do anything."

—Senator Joseph O'Mahoney, 1938

A SKETCH OF LAW AND LAW ENFORCEMENT

AMERICANS have long been hostile to concentrated economic power. The Revolutionary War was in part a reaction against an absentee government protecting British traders from colonial competition. Thomas Jefferson, writing from Paris in late 1787 to James Madison, regretted that the Constitution lacked a specific provision restricting monopoly—though at least English consumer law, adopted by United States courts, did usually consider restraints of trade illegal. The successful Jacksonian drive to break up the Second Bank of the United States further indicated that a young nation of small merchants, farmers, and frontiersmen would not genuflect to monopoly power.

By the late 1800s, however, industrial technology and corporate illegality threatened to overwhelm this native antipathy to big business. Communications and transportation improvements, along with the growth of large financial institutions, combined to encourage companies of nationwide size. The invention of the trust device and New Jersey's legalization of the holding company (discussed in Chapter II) provided the catalysts for the rise of monopoly in America. After the establishment of the Standard Oil Trust other trusts and monopolies emerged to dominate the industrial landscape: cottonseed oil in 1884; linseed oil in 1885; the whiskey, lead, and sugar trusts in 1887; the match trust in 1889; the tobacco trust in 1890; the rubber trust in 1892.

These activities triggered widespread public opposition. Farmers especially felt the pinch. By 1888 one observer could report that "the public mind has begun to assume a state of apprehension, almost amounting to alarm, regarding the evil economic and social tendencies of these organizations." That same year both the Republican and Democratic parties had antimonopoly planks in their platforms. The Populist Party put it most bluntly: "The fruits of the toil of millions are boldly stolen to build up colossal fortunes for a few. . . . From the same prolific womb of governmental injustice we breed the two great classes—tramps and millionaires." The result of this consensus was the 1890 Sherman Act.

The Act prohibited "every contract, combination . . . or conspiracy in restraint of trade" and made it criminal to "monopolize or attempt to monopolize" any line of commerce in the United States. Despite its popularity and the apparent clarity of its message, the Sherman Act was nearly stillborn. Of the first seven cases brought under it, the government lost six—including the 1895 *Sugar Trust* case, where the Supreme Court actually upheld a combination controlling 98 percent of all sugar production because "manufacturing" was not "interstate commerce" within the meaning of the Act! Attorney General Richard Olney (1893–95) seemed not at all displeased with the result; announcing that the Sherman Act was merely "an experimental piece of legislation," he failed to file a single case under it during his term in office. It was not until 1903 that the federal government appropriated funds for antitrust activities at the Justice Department. In March of that year one William A. Day, along with five lawyers and four stenographers, began an Antitrust Division of the Department of Justice.

Federal antimonopoly policy showed signs of resuscitation in the 1903–14 period. The Supreme Court, in the 1903 *Northern Securities* case, enjoined a holding company from exercising any control over competing railroads. President Theodore Roosevelt's preachings against "the malefactors of great wealth" earned him the mantle of The Great Trustbuster and a reputation that has survived for seven decades. His administration's antitrust cases against the Standard Oil and American Tobacco trusts culminated in two seminal 1911 Supreme Court decisions which, for the first time, actually broke up illegal industrial combinations. And by 1914, Congress tightened antimonopoly law enforcement when it passed the Clayton Act and created the Federal Trade Commission. That statute, among other provisions, prohibited interlocking directorates between competitors and stock acquisitions where their effect "may be substantially to lessen competition."

But there was less here than met the eye. Roosevelt managed to equivocate between attacks on "the plundering rich" and attacks on "muckrakers," between denunciations of the trusts and assertions that "the man who advocates destroying the trusts by measures which would paralyze the industries of this country is at least a quack and at worst an enemy to the Republic." His contemporary, Senator Robert LaFollette, ridiculed the way his "cannonading, first in one direction and then in another, filled the air with great noise and smoke, which confused and obscured the line of action, but, when the battle cloud drifted by and quiet was restored, it was always a matter of surprise that so little had been accomplished." Further, the 1914 Clayton Act, however well intended, was seriously flawed. It prohibited *stock* acquisitions which could become Sherman Act violations, but not comparable *asset* acquisitions—which, predictably, soon proliferated.

The most enervating development of this formative era, however, was the very first break-ups themselves. After the Supreme Court approved of the divestitures in those cases, it went on to adopt a standard the Court had twice before rejected: the "rule of reason" test. Not every restraint of trade, but only "unreasonable" restraints of trade, would be illegal; not every trust, but only "bad" trusts formed by individuals "intending to monopolize" and engaging in predatory practices would be illegal. Antitrust proponents thought this standard would possess all the strength and viability of the Articles of Confederation. The Congress in 1909 had specifically refused to consider a "rule of reason" test, explaining why in a Senate Judiciary Report:

The injection of the rule of reasonableness or unreasonableness would lead to the greatest variableness and uncertainty in the enforcement of the law. The defense of reasonable restraint would be made in every case and there would be as many different rules of reasonableness as cases, courts and juries. . . . To amend the Antitrust Act, as suggested by this bill, would be to entirely emasculate it, and for all practical purposes render it nugatory as a remedial statute.

But the Judiciary did what Congress wouldn't. The Supreme Court later showed precisely how its new rule would work. It refused to approve the divestitures of U.S. Steel and International Harvester, in 1920 and 1927 respectively, because those giants had not exhibited the predatory intent or practices of a Standard Oil. "The law . . . does not make the mere size of a corporation, however impressive, or the existence of an unexerted power on its part, an offense, when unaccompanied by unlawful conduct in the exercise of its power." Thereafter, antitrust enforcement would be saddled with the often metaphysical search for an industrialist's "intent" at a given time. The mere fact of monopoly power would not be enough to make out a violation; instead of proving a bad market *structure*, the government had to prove the existence of bad *practices* and *motives*.

Since this early period, there have been few surprises in federal antimonopoly law enforcement. Still, in the past six decades, there have occurred three major developments which have either reshaped, or had the potential to reshape, the government's approach to concentrated economic power.

First, in 1938 Yale law professor Thurman Arnold took a sleepy Antitrust Division of a few dozen and, by the end of his tenure as Division Chief in 1943, turned it into an agency of almost 200 highly motivated lawyers. Though he brought few cases involving the monopolistic structure of industry, Arnold did file a large number of cases against anticompetitive practices, and he possessed the Rooseveltian gift of attracting headlines and followers. Such publicity unnerved Attorney General Francis Biddle—who, tiring of reading about Arnold's forays in the morning papers, finally told him: "There is only one Attorney General in this Department and that's me!"—but it also generated crucial and widespread public support for antitrust efforts.

Second, in 1945 U.S. Appeals Court Judge Learned Hand handed down the landmark *Alcoa* decision. Hand ruled that Alcoa's 90 percent control of the virgin-aluminum ingot market was an illegal monopoly—which by itself was not unusual. But his reasoning broke with the 1911 line of cases. Unless a monopoly had been "thrust" upon a company due purely to skill, foresight and industry, it would be illegal. "No monopolist monopolizes unconscious of what he is doing." He went on to add that market control of only 33 percent would certainly not be a violation, though market control over 64 percent might be. His monopoly *per se* analysis, however, has remained of interest largely to antitrust historians rather than law enforcers. Since subsequent prosecutors have neglected his reasoning, the *Alcoa* decision remains more an aberration than a precedent.

Third, the Celler-Kefauver Act of 1950 closed the loophole in the 1914 Clayton Act by prohibiting *asset* acquisitions which tended substantially to lessen competition. The Justice Department no longer had to show that a merger revealed a restraint of trade; it would be sufficient merely to show that it tended "substantially to lessen competition." It was not until 1962 that the Supreme Court found that the Act's purpose was to stem "a rising tide of economic concentration in American industry." But it is now clear that the Celler-Kefauver Act has significantly reduced the number of anticompetitive mergers which were either "horizontal" (between competitors) or "vertical" (among suppliers, producers, and dealers).

In sum, the history of federal antimonopoly enforcement has been one of bipartisan support and deficient performance: perhaps the only thing more predictable than the endorsement of competition by Democratic and Republican Administrations was their unwillingness to back up their words with deeds. The gap between antitrust promise and performance remains large, for several reasons:

● *Resources*—"Even if the Antitrust Division and the Federal Trade Commission enjoyed appropriations five times as large as they now have," Professor Edward S. Mason wrote in 1949, "they could not conceivably bring a tenth of the cases it would be possible to bring." It's still true. In 1950, the Antitrust Division had 314 lawyers and staff economists. In 1976, with a real GNP more than double that of 1950, the Division has 427 professional staff. The Federal Trade Commission's antitrust effort has had a comparable incremental growth. But together their approximately $40 million budget still totals one-seventh the budget of the Fish and Wildlife Service and less than one-half the cost of a single B-1 bomber. These few hundred antitrust policemen are simply inadequate to patrol an economy with 203 industrial firms worth over $1 billion; 85,000 with over a million dollars in assets; and 1.8 million firms in all.

An inadequate staff becomes especially glaring when pitted against the army of attorneys corporate defendants can throw into antitrust battle. It has been reported that IBM's legal expenses in its defense against the current Justice Department suit are larger than the entire annual budget of the Antitrust Division. The numbers of corporate lawyers, their techniques for intentional delay, and the government's burden of showing "intent" in monopolization cases lead to the decade-long cases that throttle the antitrust process. Too few staff also encourages the trivialization of antitrust: to keep up a respectable numerical record, many small cases in, for example, the chrysanthemum or swimming suit industries are preferred to big cases in, say, the auto or steel industries.

• *Politics*—With so much potentially at stake for the defendant firm in an antitrust case and with elected officials so dependent on business support, it should hardly be surprising that politics has often compromised antitrust efforts. The problem long predates ITT's clumsy though successful politicking to settle its merger cases in 1971. Members of Congress as powerful as James Eastland, Emanuel Celler, or Everett Dirksen—on behalf of, respectively, Mississippi banks, Schenley Industries, and United Fruit—pressured the Justice Department into favorable settlements. And Attorneys General like Eisenhower's Herbert Brownell or Johnson's Nicholas Katzenbach proved attentive to such importunings. With the appearance of the Eisenhower Administration in 1953 came the collapse of the first ATT-Western Electric case and of the so-called Oil Cartel case. And when Senator Allen Ellender (D.-La.)—then chairman of the Senate Agriculture Committee—asked Katzenbach to go easy against two Louisiana rice milling firms, the Attorney

General obliged, later explaining in an interview, "Why not get a political benefit from what you are going to do anyway?"

• *Penalties*—Penalties for antitrust violations are both inadequate and underapplied. Between 1955 and 1974, the maximum penalties were a $50,000 fine and one year in prison. But corporate fines averaged only $13,420 and average individual fines $3,365—penalties, said one Antitrust Division chief, which were "no more severe than a $3 ticket for overtime parking for a man with a $15,000 income." And in the Sherman Act's first 82 years, there were only four instances when businessmen actually spent time in jail; sentences were invariably suspended by sympathetic judges. Indeed, one analyst in the Law Department of New York City made a cost-benefit analysis of antitrust crime in six case studies and concluded that crime pays. "Indictment by a federal grand jury, punishment inflicted through criminal action, the payment of trebled damages resulting from civil trials, all legal costs incurred in the process—none of these nor any combination of them succeeds today in denying the price-fixer a profit realization at least double a normal level." Plaintiffs' treble damage cases have greatly increased in the past decade, but they are invariably settled far short of actual triple damages and they almost never succeed against a monopolistic structure.

In 1974 the antitrust law was amended to increase penalties to a maximum of $1 million for corporations and three years in prison for individuals. Given the net income of *Fortune's* 1000 and the historic proclivity of judges, however, the fines actually imposed will undoubtedly still be a mere cost of doing business to the antitrust violator; and potentially longer jail terms are hardly of consequence when business lawbreakers don't go to jail anway. As Thomas Kauper, Assistant Attorney General in charge of Antitrust, complained in an April, 1976, address:

Some of the recent sentences in antitrust cases have been inappropriately mild by any conventional sentencing standards. Reporters who have followed antitrust sentencing tell me that some convicted defendants, who have been ordered to give speeches on business ethics as part of their sentences, candidly tell their audiences that their violations were simply 'technical.' No matter how strongly the Congress or the Department feels about price-fixing violations, businessmen and women are unlikely to take the Sherman Act seriously until District Court Judges do.

These persistent defects have produced a desultory federal antitrust record. To be sure, if there were no federal antitrust law, economic concentration and anticompetitive behavior would be far worse. "The success of antitrust," said economist Almarin Phillips, with only slight exaggeration, "can only be measured by the hundreds of mergers and price-fixing situations that never happened." But what about all that monopolization that *has* happened?

THE ROAD TO MONOPOLY

The road to monopoly has been paved by mergers. Due to the early neglect of the Sherman Act, the first great merger movement occurred in 1898–1902. There were 2,653 important industrial consolidations in this four-year period—or an average of 531 a year as against just 46 for each of the previous three years. Many firms consolidated in this period are still the leading firms in their industries, such as DuPont in chemicals, General Electric in electrical machinery, Swift in meat packing, United Shoe in shoe machinery, International Paper in paper, American Can in metal cans. By 1904, 319 industrial trusts, capitalized at $7 billion, had taken over 5,300 companies; and 127 utilities, capitalized at $13 billion, had absorbed 2,400 firms. In all, the trusts then controlled 40 percent of the manufacturing capital of the country.

A second merger wave swept American industry in 1925–29. Although the average size of these consolidations was smaller than their turn-of-the-century predecessor, the number involved was nearly double. In these five years there were 4,583 mergers, with a peak of 1,245 in 1929. A buoyant stock market inspired many of the mergers, and a crashing stock market ended them.

Beginning in the mid 1950s, a third merger wave began slowly building, cresting only in 1969. From 1955 to 1959, there was an annual average of 1,162 mergers; in 1960–66 there were 1,664 mergers a year; by 1967–69 there was an annual average of 3,605 mergers, or more per year than had occurred in the entire first merger wave. These were largely "conglomerate" consolidations, with large acquiring firms purchasing smaller firms in unrelated industries. Companies like ITT, Ling-Temco-Vought, and Gulf & Western became familiar names during this period. By 1970, a sagging stock market, a series of antitrust lawsuits against conglomerate mergers, and cutbacks in defense spending—on which many conglomerate firms depended—finally blunted this merger drive.

In all, the largest 200 industrial firms acquired more than $50 billion in assets between 1948 and 1968. Over 1,200 manufacturing companies worth $10 million or more were acquired in this period. During the 1960s eight giant companies alone acquired more than $13 billion in assets. And between 1962 and 1968, fully 110 of *Fortune*'s 500 largest industrials disappeared as the result of mergers.

Why this urge to merge? At best, acquisitive managers may believe that they can revive a languishing company and make it more productive and competitive. They may believe that the merged firm will possess economies of scale or other synergistic benefits that each company separately lacks. Or they argue, as industrialists have long argued, that the joining together of companies is historically inevitable and quite natural.

To which Louis Brandeis once responded, "Combination is not natural any more than any of the other things in life are natural which it is easier to do if you have no occasion to count the cost." President Lyndon Johnson's Cabinet Committee on Price Stability concluded that the merger waves were "not rooted in technological imperatives."

"The history of corporations," Eugene Rostow wrote three decades ago, "is the best evidence of the motivation for their growth. In instance after instance [it] appears to have been the quest for monopoly power, not the technological advantages of scale." More recently, the FTC's *Economic Report on Conglomerate Mergers* in 1971 reported that merger booms "cannot be explained in terms of a quest for efficiency, particularly when large firms merge with one another."

More likely motives for mergers—beyond the desire to monopolize—include the temptation to aggrandize personal power and exploit financial gimmicks.

For most managers it is more exciting to govern a large empire than a small one—and more enriching as well. Samuel Richardson

Reed, who has conducted the most comprehensive merger studies, concluded in a 1968 book that "Managers' personal and group goals of security, power, prestige, increased personal income and advancement within the firm may well be identified more with firm growth . . . than with classical profit maximization." Harold Geneen made the cover of *Time* magazine because he heads ITT —now worth $11 billion in sales annually and with 409,000 employees in 90 countries—not Flavorland Industries of Omaha, Nebraska. Corporate perquisites such as large advertising accounts, company jets, and ample expense accounts and salaries are more characteristic of giant rather than medium-size firms. At the height of the 1968 merger frenzy, the *Wall Street Journal* headlined a front page article, "Some Officials Scored for Personal Bargaining When Companies Join."

Tax rules also provide a financial incentive to merge. Although in most mergers significant premiums are paid over the market value and certainly over the basis of stock, there is generally no taxation on the transfer of stock. Under the provisions of the Internal Revenue Code, for example, 14 of the largest 18 mergers in 1967–68 were tax free. The FTC estimates that in 1968 alone "taxes uncollected on the capital gains from these mergers amounted to at least several hundred million dollars." Although the 1969 Tax Reform Act limited the deductibility of interest on debt instruments used in acquisitions, the tax structure still invites mergers.

If mergers are the bricks of existing monopolies, "high entry barriers" are its mortar, keeping market power intact over time. In the language of economists, an entry barrier discourages a potential competitor from entering an industry. The threat of a new entrant can keep existing firms from raising prices so high as to induce new competitors to enter the market. But various "barriers" can make entry into an industry difficult: the large capital outlay initially required, given an imperfect capital market, discriminates against the new firms; due to superior production techniques, managerial talent, control over special resources or special patents, established firms may be able to maintain an absolute cost advantage; existing firms may have all distribution outlets tied up by "exclusive dealing" contracts, requiring a new firm to enter on both a production and a distribution level.

One major entry barrier can be massive advertising whose aim is to generate consumer brand loyalty by emphasizing "product differentiation"—i.e., when one product is made to seem far different and far better than comparable, competing products. In concentrated markets, "competition" in gadgetry, trading stamps, style, and clever advertisements then replaces price competition. The result is higher product prices, for two reasons: the costs of lavish ad campaigns are passed onto consumers and companies charge buyers more for the privilege of purchasing a brand name product. Thus, Exxon costs three cents a gallon more than "Clark" gasoline in St. Louis and Bayer aspirin costs more than three times as much as Safeway aspirin in Washington—even though all gasoline and all aspirin are basically the same chemical compounds.

A new competitor must now not merely have a viable product but an expensive advertising campaign before it can challenge an industry's dominant firms. That is, *if* it can get on television. A study of 1,697 advertisements in March 1966 found that 20 percent of all commercials were placed by just five companies. Big firms which are big advertisers—Bristol Myers, Procter & Gamble, General Foods—have easy access to television time while more modestly sized firms do not, and they have in the past obtained discounts beyond cost savings that discriminate against smaller buyers.

As a result, massive advertising in concentrated industries entrenches market power and monopoly profits. Economist John Blair compared the concentration figures for 33 consumer goods industries, which advertised heavily on television, for the years 1947 and 1963—before and after the television explosion. He found that 25 industries—such as chewing gum, cereals, refrigerators, malt liquor, and margarine—recorded significant increases in concentration. According to Donald Turner, law professor, economist, and former assistant attorney general in charge of the Antitrust Division, "Industries with high advertising outlay tended to earn profit rates which were about 50 percent higher than those which did not undertake a significant effort. . . . It is likely that these additional returns represent monopoly rewards."

The consequence of inadequate antitrust efforts, periodic merger waves, and high entry barriers is a level of economic concentration which sharply conflicts with the cherished notions of economic traditionalists.

Any sanguine assumptions about the competitiveness of American industry that had survived the trust movement were shattered by a series of pioneering analyses in the 1930s. In that decade, Gardiner Means' now famous memorandum to the Secretary of Agriculture, Joan Robinson's *The Economics of Imperfect Competition*, and Edward Chamberlain's *The Theory of Monopolistic Competition* all explained how concentration, not competition, was the rule in American industry. In the eyes of the economist, this occurs when an industry is an *oligopoly*—which is Greek for "few sellers." A popular measure of the existence of industrial oligopoly is the concentration ratio, the percentage of shipments accounted for by the leading firms in an industry. Most industrial economists agree that when an industry had a four-firm concentration ratio of 50 percent or more—i.e., when four or fewer firms control 50 percent or more of a market—it tends to act like a cartel or monopoly.

Based on the use of concentration ratios, the Temporary National Economic Committee in the late 1930s found that more than half of U.S. manufacturing and mining were concentrated, and that these sectors were larger in size and more important than unconcentrated markets. In 1959, professors Carl Kaysen and Donald Turner concluded in their now classic *Antitrust Policy* that "There are more concentrated than unconcentrated industries in manufacturing and mining, they are larger in aggregate size, and they tend to occupy a more important position in the economy." Over a decade later two other students of Corporate America corroborated this estimate. Professors William Shepherd and Richard Barber both calculate that oligopolies control nearly two-thirds of our manufacturing sector. For example, the four largest American firms in a particular industry controlled domestic production of 98 percent of locomotives, 96 percent of aircraft propellers and parts, 96 percent of automobiles, 93 percent of electric lamps, 88 percent of chewing gum, 81 percent of cigarettes, 72 percent of soaps and detergents, and 71 percent of tires and inner tubes.

Defenders of industrial structure point out that concentration data are flawed* and that market concentration hasn't seriously increased since the late 1940s. The latter point is widely held, though not entirely accurate. The average four-firm concentration ratio, according to the Cabinet Committee on Price Stability, went from 35.3 percent in 1947 to 39.0 percent in 1966. Based on the most recent 1967 concentration ratios, Blair has found that for the 209 industries tabulated in 1947–67 concentration data, 95 showed increases, 75 decreases, and 39 were relatively stable. Notwithstanding this evidence, it misses the point to contend that concentration has not significantly increased in the past thirty years. The more relevant issue is whether it was and still is too high. That economic concentration has remained excessive for three decades is hardly an argument in its favor.

The seriousness of this level of *horizontal concentration* is exacerbated by the existence of *vertical integration*—when a single firm owns subsidiaries in various stages of the production process, such as manufacturing, transportation, and distribution. Control of supply and access to markets can enable one "integrated" competitor to squeeze its "independent" competitor (one lacking its own supplies or outlets). "When at the turn of the century U.S. Steel acquired the iron-ore deposits of the Mesabi Range," argues Blair, "no elaborate analysis was needed to understand how ownership by one company of vast iron-ore resources could injure competition."

* It is true that mere reliance on concentration data can overstate market power in specific instances. They do not include import shipments, they fail to account for substitute products (plastics for steel), and they include multi-products within one product category—e.g., GM is catalogued under automobile production though it also produces refrigerators, electrical appliances, and locomotives.

Overall, however, concentration ratios probably understate the extent of corporate power in America. They deal with national averages when competition usually occurs at the regional or local level. The four-firm concentration ratios for bread and cement nationally in 1963 were 23 percent and 27 percent, respectively; yet the average local market concentration ratios were 57 percent and 73 percent respectively. Consider, also, the drug industry. Walter Measday, an economist with the Senate Antitrust and Monopoly Subcommittee, observes that "the overall drug industry is fragmented into a number of separate, noncompeting therapeutic markets: antibiotics are not substitutes for antidiabetic drugs, and tranquilizers are not substitutes for vitamins. Manufacturers do not compete on an industry-wide basis, and hence competition must be evaluated within the various therapeutic groups of drugs in which competition does occur."

It was similar reasoning about the evils of vertical combinations that compelled the Supreme Court, in its landmark *GM-DuPont* decision in 1957, to require DuPont, which provided GM with much of its auto paints, finishes, and fabrics, to divest itself of its 23 percent holding of GM stock. The Court was understandably influenced by a DuPont executive's memorandum—at the time of the GM purchase in 1917—which stated: "Our interest in the General Motors Company will undoubtedly secure for us the entire Fabrikoid, Pyralin, paint and varnish business of these companies [GM's divisions], which is a substantial factor."

This discussion has thus far focused on *market concentration*—when a few firms control a particular industry, such as GM, Ford, and Chrysler in autos; or GE, Westinghouse, and Sylvania in electrical machinery. Another criterion of business power is *aggregate concentration*—when our largest conglomerates control the assets of various industries, such as Textron in aircraft, golf carts, and poultry farming. Market concentration is concerned with a firm's percentage of a particular industry; aggregate concentration is concerned with a firm's asset size, which often cuts across several industries. Due in large measure to the conglomerate merger wave of the late 1960s, aggregate concentration has significantly increased in the past few decades. In 1947, the largest 200 manufacturing corporations accounted for 47.2 percent of total manufacturing assets. By 1968, according to the FTC, it had jumped to 60.4 percent—or almost a one-third increase in 20 years. The next year Dr. Willard Mueller, then the chief economist at the FTC, testified before the Senate Antitrust and Monopoly Subcommittee:

You may recall that I testified before this Committee in 1965 that, should postwar trends in aggregate concentration continue, by 1975 the 200 largest manufacturing corporations would control two-thirds of all manufacturing assets. Unhappily, we have reached this level ahead of schedule. Today the top 200 manufacturing corporations already control about two-thirds of all assets held by corporations engaged primarily in manufacturing.

The 100 largest corporations today have a greater share of all manufacturing assets than the 200 largest did in 1950. And the top 200 today control the same share of assets the 1,000 largest held in

1941, the year the Temporary National Economic Committee submitted its final report to Congress recommending an "Investigation of Concentration of Economic Power."

Even these descriptions of the extent of both market concentration and aggregate concentration probably understate how much industrial power is concentrated in a few hands. First, interlocking managers and directors in an industry are prevalent, as described in Chapter IV. Second, joint ventures, especially in the oil industry, are common forms of business. And "businesses that are partners in one market," says the Cabinet Committee on Price Stability, "may be disinclined to behave independently when they meet as rivals in others." And third, by 1967 just 49 banks were trustees of $135 billion in assets. These banks held 5 percent or more of the outstanding shares of one or more classes of stock—which can constitute a controlling interest—in 5,270 companies (many being direct competitors). In a study of the largest manufacturing corporations, Jean-Marie Chevalier observes that commercial banks have not historically exploited the influence of their ownership shares in corporations. But he goes on to ask, "Will they be in a position to *not* make use of the formidable power lawfully conferred on them when, in 1980, they are responsible for close to $225 billion in [corporate] assets? It is a legitimate question."

THE COST OF CONCENTRATION

So what, reply big businessmen. To them bigness is goodness, oligopoly is inevitable, and competition is anachronistic. "Big corporations are the only ones that can compete with big corporations in world markets," contends Douglas Grymes, the president of Koppers Co., who adds that our 26 steel companies should merge into five or six so they can "get together, produce together, sell together." Dow Chemical chairman Carl Gerstacker agrees. "It has been abundantly proved that size is often a gigantic advantage, and often, for certain tasks, a necessity. The problems of our times will require greater, bigger organizations than we now have. . . . We must discard our outmoded notions of size and our fear of bigness."

Perhaps Dow's annual reports have "abundantly proven" this contention, but the overwhelming weight of economic evidence leads to a very different conclusion. The costs of corporate oligopoly and giantism—to the consumer, to the small businessmen, to the worker, to the economy—are substantial:

Higher Prices and Profits—It seems like ancient history, but prior to the 20th century prices would rise *and* fall, depending on such classic variables as supply and demand. No longer. Price in concentrated industries is, as economists say, "sticky downward." Which means, as consumers know, that it tends only to go up and up.

The phenomenon of "administered prices"—a term developed by Gardiner Means—is simple in its operation. A monopoly or well-coordinated cartel could obviously charge a higher-than-competitive price and make it stick since the consumer would lack a cheaper alternative. Yet when a few firms dominate an oligopolistic industry, a system of mutually beneficial "parallel pricing" or "price leadership" can achieve the same result. For example, an industry leader, such as U.S. Steel, announces a price increase of 6 percent on certain major items; within days all other firms in the industry increase their prices by a comparable or identical amount. Since different firms have different costs, only a system of noncompetitive price leadership can enable them to charge similar prices. Each firm gladly increases its profit margin by getting the same share of a larger pie. There is no incentive to keep price down, for then all the other firms will have to come down to that price—which means the same share of a smaller pie.

So price only rises, regardless of such nagging problems as falling demand. In 1951–55, with steel capacity down from 94 percent to 71 percent utilization and the wholesale price index falling 0.9 percent, the price index for steel *rose* 4.8 percent a year. In 1974–75, with new car sales down 25 percent due to a recession and the explosion of gasoline prices, some new car prices were $1,000 higher. This tenacity for sticking with its administered price, however, is not costless to an oligopoly. If it won't give the consumer a choice, foreign firms will try to. Consequently, auto imports have increased from a negligible amount in the mid-1950s to 22 percent of all new car sales in the mid-1970s. "It is difficult to resist the conclusion that the American steel industry during the last 20 years has tended to price itself out of the market," Walter

Adams concludes in his study of this industry, adding that "as a consequence, it has suffered from incursions into its domestic market for imports. . . ."

Quite predictably, prices and profits are comparably higher in concentrated than in competitive sectors. Economist Leonard Weiss of Wisconsin has collected and analyzed virtually all econometric studies of concentration and profits: of 45 studies, 38 showed a significant positive correlation and seven showed an insignificant or zero correlation. Weiss concludes: "The bulk of the studies show a significant positive effect of concentration on profits or margins. . . . [A]ll the studies together reflect a wide range of experience—from 1936 to 1970, and covering Britain, Canada, and Japan as well as the United States."

Inflation and Unemployment—Oligopolistic pricing patterns also affect both the rate of inflation and unemployment in the United States.

The "Phillips Curve" has long been an article of faith among economists. It predicted a trade-off between inflation and unemployment: as unemployment rose, demand would fall and so would prices; as employment rose, so would demand and inflation. But administered prices have effectively repealed the Phillips Curve. Steel prices throughout the 1950 recessions proved that the predicted trade-off was inoperative in that industry. By late 1975, even *Business Week* realized something was structurally wrong in much of big business:

Something strange is happening in the heartland of corporate America. . . . Despite slack demand and low capacity utilization rates, a number of major industries from aluminum and autos to chemicals, lead, steel, and zinc have unexpectedly started to raise prices—just as the U.S. economy is beginning to extricate itself from the worst recession since the 1930s.

The persistence of perennially high prices can aggravate inflation in two ways. First, countercyclical monetary and fiscal policy assume that an increase in interest rates or reduction in government spending will reduce aggregate demand, cool off the economy, and control inflation. But oligopolies can frustrate such governmental efforts, maintaining high prices or even increasing them since consumers may have nowhere else to go. Hence, when the Nixon and

Ford administrations prescribed the classical Keynesian cure of tight money, this oligopoly power contributed to a new disease dubbed "stagflation," which combines inflation and recession.

Second, studies by Blair and Means indicate that prices rise faster in concentrated than unconcentrated industries. From December 1969 to December 1970, with aggregate demand contracting, Blair found that average prices rose 5.9 percent in industries with four-firm concentration ratios of over 50 percent and fell 6.1 percent in industries with four-firm concentration ratios of under 25 percent. Means looked at the 12-month period beginning in September 1973 and documented that wholesale prices increased 27 percent for oligopolistic firms while prices rose less than 5 percent in competitive industries. These critics of course recognize the multiple causes of inflation—e.g., shortages, the cost of the Vietnam War—but conclude that the 1970s inflation is largely an administered inflation.

Their analyses are hotly disputed by other economists who have conducted other studies. These show that in 1967–69, and in December 1970 to December 1971, concentrated industry prices rose *less* than relatively unconcentrated prices. Leonard Weiss thinks that the pricing behavior of concentrated and unconcentrated industries differs during periods of cost-push inflation (which the former can pass on to consumers while the latter cannot) and demand-pull inflation (which affects competitive firms but not oligopolistic ones).

What appears beyond doubt, however, is that administered pricing does create an inflationary bias in the economy. At the least, concentrated industry prices increase even in recessions, increase rapidly in cost-push inflation, and set a standard for less concentrated industries to reach for in a demand-pull inflation.

Oligopoly-induced unemployment is the mirror image of oligopoly-inspired inflation. Again, corporate power frustrates a Keynesian prescription. Here expansionary monetary and fiscal policy increases demand but fails to increase industrial output—because oligopolies prefer to increase price rather than production. Frederic Scherer has estimated this lost production, due to restricted output and monopoly inefficiencies, at 6.2 percent of GNP, or some $87 billion in 1974. In other words, some significant percentage of our approximately one-third idle industrial capacity lies unused because that's the way oligopolies want it. And idle capacity means idle workers.

Distribution of Income and Wealth—Economic concentration not only misallocates resources through perversion of the price mechanism but it misdistributes income and wealth among citizens as well. Clearly, consumers pay more in these industries than in unconcentrated industries, though exactly how much they are overcharged is difficult to determine. One FTC study, computing the "adjusted monopoly margin (as percent of sales)" of 100 industries, concluded that consumers had overpaid more than $15 billion a year. Economists William Shepherd and Frederic Scherer estimated the overall income transfer at 3 percent of GNP, or some $42 billion annually.

That monopoly has unequal distribution effects was demonstrated in an important, and overlooked, 1973 study by economists William Comanor and Robert Smiley of Stanford University. Assuming that monopoly power can overcharge consumers 2 to 3 percent of GNP annually and that the degree of monopoly has been fairly constant between 1890 and 1962, they concluded that the presence of past and current monopoly has had a major impact on the degree of inequality in the current distribution of household wealth. For example, they specifically found that in the absence of monopoly power, (a) 2.4 percent of American families would control not 40 percent of total wealth but only 16.6 percent to 27.5 percent, and (b) 93.3 percent of American families would be better off and only the wealthier 6.7 percent worse off. Without historic monopoly, they estimate that our current maldistribution of wealth would be as much as *50 percent less.*

Economies of Scale and Efficiency—The *raison d'être* of big business is its efficient size and inventiveness, which, say business managers, is impossible in a nation of cottage industries. Hence they emphasize a substantial minimum efficient scale and deride the "Small is Beautiful" ethos of the Schumachers and antitrusters as antihistorical, if not downright silly.

As Joe Bain showed in his classic *Barriers to New Competition*, efficiency does increase and unit cost does decline as plants become larger—but only up to a point. The efficient unit of production is essentially the local plant, not the national firm. Beyond a certain point in plant and firm size, therefore, there are either no further efficiencies to be gained or, in fact, actual inefficiencies incurred.

The best research indicates that most large companies are far larger than required by minimum efficient scale. "Referring to the first four firms in each of our industries," Bain concluded in an intensive study of 20 industries, "it appears that concentration by the large firms is in every case but one greater than required by single plant economics, and in more than half of the cases very substantially greater." Several economists studied 26 British industries in 1969 and concluded that in only seven did the minimum efficient scale require plants producing 10 percent or more of a market. Another study of 12 American industries found only one, refrigerators and freezers, requiring a minimum efficient plant of over 10 percent of U.S. consumption—although the concentration ratios for all the industries far exceeded minimal economies. Combining these three studies (and converting the British examples to the American experience), Scherer concluded that "only in ten of the forty-four is MOS [minimum optimal scale] plant volume sufficient to justify four-firm national concentration ratios of forty or more. . . . Thus, the three studies all point toward the same conclusion: that nationwide oligopoly and higher seller concentration cannot be viewed primarily as the inevitable consequence of production scale economies at the plant level." These studies indicate that very few firms need be larger than 7 percent of their industries in order to be as efficient as size allows.

Consider, for example, the automobile industry. Reasons of efficiency do not compel General Motors to control over 50 percent of the domestic auto market—or some 4–5 million cars a year. George Romney, then president of American Motors, told a Senate Committee in 1958 that a small auto company could efficiently produce 180,000 to 220,000 cars a year. Bain put it at 300,000 to 600,000 cars and Lawrence White, fifteen years later in his *The Automobile Industry Since 1945*, at 400,000 to 800,000. It is understandably why economist Robert Lanzillotti, a former member of President Nixon's Cost of Living Council, thought there was ample room for at least 10 domestic car manufacturers, not just four as today.

Beyond any production efficiencies at the plant level, there may appear to be several advantages to a large multiplant firm: a multiplant firm can keep transportations costs down by reliable intrafirm shipments; it may be able to raise capital more easily, since large firms have larger deposits and more interlocks with major banks; it may be able to get discounts from suppliers or distributors, due to savings or the ability to wrest concessions; and perhaps it can obtain preferential access to outlets or advertising markets. But all of these benefits trace either to the breakdown of competition or to one firm benefiting at the expense of another. For example, competitive and inexpensive trucking firms should be able to transport products more efficiently than a Gulf & Western trying to run its own trucking concern. Or if large and powerful Bethlehem can wrest a better deal buying its raw materials or getting on television because of its size than Inland Steel, Bethlehem may benefit but society does not. Instead of favoring huge multiplant firms, these "advantages" argue for more competition and less distributive injustice.

And giant multiplant conglomerates may be so large as to be managerially inefficient. All chairmen and vice-presidents have the same 24-hour day as the rest of us, and if they try to manage 100 subsidiaries rather than two, there will be too little time to make quality judgments about the numerous issues that fly by one's desk. And the bigger a firm, the bigger the costs of bureaucracy: excessive paperwork; committees reviewing committees; undetected sloth; institutional caution and delay; and Parkinson's law that superiors like to proliferate subordinates. "[T]here is no obvious association between firm size and such dimensions of managerial quality as dynamism, intelligence, awareness, and skill in interpersonal relations," said Scherer after 86 interviews with business managers. "I am inclined toward the view that the unit costs of management, including the hidden losses due to delayed or faulty decisions and weakened or distorted incentives . . . do tend to rise with the organizational size." Acknowledging that economists have not systematically studied the subject, he has also noted that "How typical it is for firms insulated from competition to operate with copious layers of fat can only be guessed. My own belief is that padding as high as 10 percent of costs is not at all uncommon."

Such "managerial diseconomies" make it not implausible that our largest firms may grow so large as to risk falling of their own weight. In an era of Penn-Central, Lockheed, and Litton, cheerleaders of the bigness-is-goodness school cannot be quite so enthusiastic. Yet they can be confident. For in the ultimate perversion of the marketplace, our dinosaur firms may grow so large that, whatever their inefficiencies, the government cannot afford to let them fail. But if the marketplace is no longer allowed to "penalize" poor managerial decisions, then business has less discipline or incentive to make good decisions and revise bad ones. No wonder, then, that entrepreneurs prefer big to small: it is the ultimate insurance policy. John Cobbs in *Business Week* understood the dilemma:

In the years before World War I, Germany invested so heavily in battleships that, when the war came, it did not dare let them fight. As the U.S. economy slides deeper into recession, the federal government finds itself in a similar position. The huge U.S. corporations have become such important centers of jobs and incomes that it dare not let one of them shut down or go out of business. It is compelled, therefore, to shape national policy in terms of protecting the great corporations instead of letting the economy make deflationary adjustments.

Innovation—Economists as renowned as Joseph Schumpeter and John Kenneth Galbraith argue that big firms can innovate better because they can afford to risk large investments in research and development (R&D). "[A] benign Providence," Galbraith has written, "has made the modern industry of a few large firms an excellent instrument for inducing technical change." Again, however, this is more assertion than fact, for economic and industrial studies indicate that the present huge size of many corporations is unnecessary or even counterproductive.

In a 1955 study of 352 large manufacturing firms, the four biggest accounted for 19.9 percent of the 352 firms' sales but only 9.7 percent of their R&D employment. Large firms are also more likely to sit on those patents they do develop. (For one notorious example, Standard Oil of New Jersey and foreign "competitors" like A. G. Farben retarded the growth of the synthetic rubber industry in the United States by not developing their relevant patents—which later had the effect of impairing the U.S. war effort.) Having examined many R&D expenditure analyses, Leonard Weiss concluded, "Most studies show that within their range of observation, size adds little to research intensity and may actually detract from it in some industries." Scherer, based on his own compilation of studies correlating firm size and innovation, observed that there were economies of scale for innovation for firms up to 5,000 employees (*Fortune*'s 500th firm in 1974 had 6,450 employees), but no advantage beyond that.

The famous Jewkes study of invention showed that of 61 basic inventions examined, only 16 resulted from organizational research by large companies. For example, the ballpoint pen was invented by a sculptor, the dial telephone by an undertaker. The firms which introduced stainless-steel razor blades (Wilkinson), transistor radios (Sony), photocopying machines (Xerox), and the "instant" photograph (Polaroid) were all small and little known when they made their momentous breakthroughs.

The records of innovation by the steel, auto, and electrical appliance industries—all dominated by very large firms—corroborates that big is not synonymous with innovative.

● Of the three major breakthroughs in steelmaking—the Bessemer, open hearth, and basic oxygen processes—the U.S. Steel industry developed none. Our domestic companies in the 1960s wrongly invested in the open hearth furnace instead of the newer oxygen furnace, which had operating savings of $5 a ton. It took a small Austrian company, one third the size of a single U.S. Steel plant, to perfect and introduce the oxygen steelmaking process. The first American company to adopt it was McLouth Steel, which had less than one percent of industry capacity. According to the National Science Foundation, in 1964 the steel industry spent only .6 percent of sales revenue on R&D as compared to 1.9 percent for all manufacturing.

● It took an electrical engineer employed by a shipbuilding firm in the 1930s to develop the automatic transmission—a development which was, according to Ford Vice President Donald Frey in 1964, "the last major innovation of the industry."American inventors of a nonpolluting Freon-powered engine and a hydraulic bumper attachment absorbing collisions up to 30 mph failed to interest any of the four American auto manufacturers; the inventors then went abroad, where their discoveries were quickly picked up by Japanese and German manufacturers. As Detroit complains it cannot meet federally mandated clean air act provisions by 1978, Japan's Honda has announced that it can already meet them. There is substantial evidence documenting that our domestic auto firms suppressed the development of an antipollution exhaust device between 1953 and 1969, the year the Justice Department sued them for jointly hindering this development.

• What of General Electric, where "progress is our most important product"? In the household appliance field alone, the late T. K. Quinn, a former vice president of GE, credits small companies with the discovery and initial production of: electric toasters, electric ranges, electric refrigerators, electric dishwashers, vacuum cleaners, clothes-washing machines, deep freezers, electric hot irons, and electric steam irons. Quinn summarized his own experiences at GE: "I know of no original product invention, not even electric shavers or hearing aids, made by any of the giant laboratories or corporations, with the possible exception of the household garbage grinder, developed not by the research laboratory but by the engineering department of General Electric. . . . [T]he record of the giants is one of moving in, buying out, and absorbing the smaller concerns."

It appears that the best innovation usually emerges from solo inventors or small and medium-sized firms—not our giant corporations. Why this is so baffles many people, who understandably assume that these companies can best afford the investment and risk of pursuing a technological breakthrough. They may be able to *afford* it, but do they *desire* it? If you already dominate an industry, where is the incentive to take a chance on a new and costly approach? We don't associate inventiveness with the centralized planning of socialist economies, though the planners have substantial R&D resources under their control. The reason is that they, like big businessmen, are not eager to give the green light to new ways which threaten their investment in old ways.

Consider the bizarre problem of Jacob Rabinow when he first

designed the "automatic regulator," now a standard part of clocks and many watches. Manufacturers he approached conceded it made watches more accurate, but they refused to buy his innovation. One manufacturer explained, "You know, we advertise a *perfect* watch." When Rabionow said that of course no watch was perfect, the manufacturer replied, "It's not important what the watch is. What counts is what the customer thinks it is. They think it's perfect. Who needs an automatic regulator to make a perfect watch more perfect?"

Social and Political Consequences—The Sherman Act was written not by economists but politicians, as Hans Thorelli, chronicler of antitrust history, realized. "In safeguarding rights of the 'common man' in business 'equal' to those of the evolving and more 'ruthless' and impersonal forms of enterprise, the Sherman Act embodies what is to be characterized as an eminently 'social purpose.' " Judge Hand, too, recognized that beyond the economic costs of monopoly power "there are others, based upon the belief that great industrial consolidations are inherently undesirable regardless of their economic results."

For example, one 1969 study indicated that firms in concentrated industries have the market power to afford to racially discriminate against black employees in white collar positions—and they do. Those competitive firms who had to hire the best employees—white or black—were found to discriminate less.

Another social cost is the profound effect an absentee corporation can have on a local community. A study by Jon Udell of the University of Wisconsin indicated that firms acquiring Wisconsin companies tended to use fewer professional services in local communities after a merger. "Most of the acquired firms covered in the survey now use the financial institutions, legal services, and accounting services of parent companies." So after the Chase Manhattan Bank extended a line of credit to Gulf & Western to make acquisitions, G & W reciprocated by moving the acquirees' financial services from local banks to Chase. Following a West German firm's takeover of a Detroit chemical company, Senator Philip Hart (D.-Mich.) asked, "to what extent will a firm whose headquarters are in another state or another country be disposed to play a significant role on something like the New Detroit Committee?" This erosion of community by absentee business control especially worried former Supreme Court Justice William Douglas. In 1949 he wrote:

Local leadership is diluted. He who was a leader in the village becomes dependent on outsiders for his action and policy. Clerks responsible to a superior in a distant place take the place of resident proprietors beholden to no one. These are the prices which the nation pays for the almost ceaseless growth in bigness on the part of industry.

There is not only the price to the community but to the individual. In feudal Europe land was the principle source of economic productivity and wealth. Land tenure was also the cornerstone of the political system; landlords ruled, serfs did not. For most people today, their work is their wealth. But with company towns and "company states" come a restriction of job mobility and an increase in employee dependence. Individualism gives way to conformity. As more people work for fewer and larger companies, as their tasks are increasingly compartmentalized, and as they even come to depend on "their" firm for their social life, we encounter a kind of corporate feudalism more characteristic of the Japanese Zaibatsu or Soviet bureaucracy than the "rugged individualism" we customarily associate with American enterprise.

Politically, large oligopolies and conglomerates can impair the ability of federal or state government to operate effectively and democratically. "When a major corporation from a state wants to discuss something with its political representatives," Senator Philip Hart has said, "you can be sure it will be heard. When that same company operates in 30 states, it will be heard by 30 times as many representatives." This technique was employed by ITT in its effort to merge with the ABC network in 1968. It enlisted 300 Congressmen and Senators to complain to the Antitrust Division about its intervention at the FCC in opposition to the merger.

Ling-Temco-Vought, another huge conglomerate, understood the tactic. An internal Ling-Temco management document in 1962 gave the following justification for its then-pending merger with Chance-Vought, another large Texas defense contractor.

It is tacitly recognized in the industry that a depressed labor area with a large, capable, highly qualified defense contractor backed by purposeful and dedicated congressmen represents a significant additional factor considered by the government in awarding new contracts.

Undue corporate power is incompatible with democracy for two reasons. First, democracy assumes the clash of many voices in the political marketplace, a clash big business can dominate by its size and resources.* And second, though corporate executives decry the rise in government bureaucracy, their own actions may make it inevitable. Unless business comes to completely control government—a flash point we have not yet reached—a democratic government must eventually attempt to impose some form of public authority over private power.

Conglomerates—The large multiplant conglomerate firm—i.e., one possessing holdings in several industries though not necessarily dominating any one industry—can also suffer from the diseconomies of elephantiasis and can inflict substantial social and political costs on the polity. Still, when economists talk about monopoly power and economic concentration, they are usually referring to market concentration and oligopolies rather than aggregate concentration and conglomerates. The economic problems of conglomerates warrant separate mention.

It seems clear that the 1950 Celler-Kefauver Act helped stunt the growth of horizontal and vertical mergers, but not conglomerate ones. In 1950 the number of firms among the top 1,000 which produced 16–50 products was 128; by 1962 it was 236. According to 1963 data, in 44 percent of industries surveyed, at least one-third of the output came from companies which were among the eight leaders primarily engaged in some *other* industry. Between 1948 and 1971, conglomerates accounted for 72.8 percent of all large industrial mergers.

Conglomerate mergers, which by definition are not mergers between direct competitors or between suppliers, producers, or

---

* Of course small businesses—such as milk co-ops or retail pharmacists—can organize together and have substantial political impact. But that impact requires a broad consensus among many entities on a relatively narrow range of issues. A few big business firms, on the other hand, can more easily agree on a broad range of political issues. Which is why firms like ITT and groups like the Business Roundtable are so politically influential on so many business-related issues.

dealers,* are comparatively less anticompetitive and costly. Indeed, conglomerateurs plausibly argue that their mergers can be procompetitive: a "toehold" acquisition of a lethargic firm in a lethargic industry can be a stimulant; there can be managerial or administrative economies by bringing two particular firms together; the new entity can have easier access to the capital market. These benefits are possible but, as studies indicate, unlikely. An FTC report says there is little evidence that conglomerates make small "toehold" acquisitions rather than more substantial ones. And since more than 70 percent of acquiring conglomerates in recent years have been larger than $400 million, increasing their size still more would not enable them to borrow better. Indeed, five separate and recent economic studies have all concluded that there was no relationship between conglomeration and efficiency, as reflected by profitability.

A conglomerate merger may be less anticompetitive than horizontal or vertical mergers, but that should hardly commend it. For when a giant corporation merges into a moderate size industry—say a corporation with the deep financial pocket and political muscle of an ITT—the competitive nature of that industry will be altered. Economist Walter Adams, with typical flair, has said: "Pretending that a firm with ITT's absolute size and aggregate power is a run-of-the-mill newcomer to the grass seed business is not unlike the suggestion that injecting Kareem Abdul Jabbar into a grade school basketball game would have no impact on pre-existing power relationships or the probable outcome of the contest." More specifically, large conglomerate mergers can lead to:

• *A loss of potential competition*—Since LTV might have entered the steel industry via internal expansion or the acquisition of a small steel firm, there was a diminution of potential competition when it took over Jones & Laughlin, the sixth largest steel company. The threat of potential entry by a major firm hovering outside an industry can discourage the use of monopoly power to raise price by dominant firms in that industry.

---

* Specifically, there are three kinds of conglomerate mergers: "product line extension mergers" add related products to a company's existing line of products; "market extension mergers" involve two firms each selling the same product but in different geographic markets; and "pure" conglomerate mergers, which lack all such links between the merging firms.

• *Reciprocity*—A large multiplant firm may buy and sell among its many subsidiaries. Such interrelationships foreclose the market to more efficient competitors, who lose out not to a superior product but to an intrafirm *quid pro quo*. As *Fortune* once complained, "The U.S. economy might end up completely dominated by conglomerates happily trading with each other in a new kind of cartel system."

• *Entrenchment of leading firms*—Clorox was the leading firm in the bleach industry, but when Procter & Gamble acquired it in 1957, the firm became the unassailably dominant leader in the industry. As the Supreme Court said in 1967, smaller competitors and potential competitors, appreciating P&G's financial ability to underwrite huge advertising campaigns or cross-subsidize its subsidiary if necessary, "would become more cautious in competing due to their fear of retaliation by Procter."

• *"Mutual forebearance"*—An anticompetitive community of interest can arise among huge conglomerate enterprises, as each understands it should not invade the industries of another lest it invite retaliation. As Corwin Edwards put it, "Like national states, the great conglomerates may come to have recognized spheres of influence and may hesitate to fight local wars vigorously because the prospect of local gain is not worth the risk of general warfare."

• *Corporate secrecy and aggregate concentration*—It is worth recalling what has been elaborated previously: Conglomeratization facilitates corporate secrecy, since a conglomerate's consolidated financial statement gives overall data, not data by subsidiaries; this shielding of subsidiary performance frustrates the ability of shareholders to assess which divisions are efficient or laggard and it frustrates the ability of potential competitors to know when to enter a lucrative market.

It was such a catalogue of costs that inspired Richard McLaren's crusade against the conglomerates in 1969. As head of the Antitrust Division, he brought suit against several of the conglomerate acquisitions of ITT, LTV, and Northwest Industries. Yet after repeatedly announcing that he would take such precedent-setting cases to the Supreme Court, he about-faced and settled the ITT merger cases in mid-1971, weakly explaining that "it is a lawyer's job to get a satisfactory conclusion to a case as rapidly as possible." Thus, there was no High Court determination of many of the unresolved issues concerning the applicability of the Celler-Kefauver Act to conglomerates.

True, the conglomerate surge slowed after 1969, the victim of a sluggish economy. But what happens when the economy picks up? The lure of industrial empire and funny-money profits may well attract budding Jim Lings and Harold Geneens—and there would be little settled law to stop them.

THE DECONCENTRATION ALTERNATIVE

If many of our largest corporations dominate their industries—leading to overcharging, underproducing, waste, and retarded innovation—the obvious remedy should be deconcentration to provide for more competition. In recent years the deconcentration alternative has had varied proponents. Carl Kaysen and Donald Turner proposed it in their 1959 book, *Antitrust Policy*. President Johnson's Antitrust Task Force, headed by Chicago law dean Philip Neal, endorsed it in 1968, saying "The judgment of most of the members of the Task Force is that enough is known about the probable consequences of high concentration to warrant affirmative government action in the extreme instances of concentration." In 1972 Senator Philip Hart, chairman of the Senate Antitrust and Monopoly Subcommittee, unveiled his major proposal for the deconcentration of dominant firms. And in October 1975, 45 Senators voted to vertically divest the petroleum industry into its constituent functions—exploration, refining, transportation, and marketing.

Not just liberal Democrats support this structural antidote to market power. For *bona fide* conservatives are concerned about bureaucratic red tape, waste, and inefficiency, not only in big government but in big business as well. Henry Simons, the founding father of what has come to be called the Chicago school of economics, wrote in 1948:

Few of our gigantic corporations can be defended on the ground that their present size is necessary. . . . Their existence is to be explained in terms of opportunities for promoter profits, personal ambitions of industrial and financial "Napoleons," and advantages of monopoly power. We should look toward a situation in which the size of ownership units in every industry is limited by the minimum size of operating plant requisite to efficient, but highly specialized, production—and even more limited, if ever necessary to the maintenance of freedom of enterprise.

In 1973, Pierre Rinfret, the well known economic consultant and former advisor to President Richard Nixon, strongly endorsed Senator Hart's bill. That same year, Federal Reserve Chairman Arthur Burns complained to the Joint Economic Committee and Senator Hart's subcommittee about the economic power of large corporations, saying that "We urgently need to revitalize competition in our economy through structural reform."

The deconcentration remedy still frightens many observers who worry that "atomizing" large companies might destroy them and that deconcentration is hopelessly complex, if not impossible. Of course, breaking up bloated corporations does not mean that firms are put out of business or that workers are laid off. Rather, several firms exist where one did before, jobs remain, and economists predict *more* jobs will be created as artificial constraints on production ease. While some exaggerate the costs of deconcentration, there is also the cost of *not* deconcentrating—higher prices, reduced output, wealth maldistribution, and employee alienation.

As for the complexity or impossibility of widespread divestiture, judicially and legislatively decreed divestiture has a long lineage. "The first antitrust statute was surely an urgent mandate," said Columbia law professor Harlan Blake, "to 'deconcentrate' the American economic system by, among other things, dissolving the trusts." George Hale, discussing the divestitures of Standard Oil, American Tobacco, and the powder and photographic equipment trusts, concluded that "commercial triumphs among the successor units are almost universal." He added that "whatever doubts may be entertained as to the efficacy of dissolutions of the past, it seems clear that the mechanics of separating monopolistic combinations . . . have not presented insuperable problems." The 1906 Hepburn Act required railroads to stop producing coal and other commodities; the 1932 Glass-Steagall Act compelled financial institutions to surrender either their commercial or investment banking activities; the 1934 Air Mail Act made several firms divest either their air carrier or aircraft manufacturing facilities—as a result of which GM sold off its interests in Eastern, Western, United, and TWA airlines.

Finally, of course, there was the momentous Public Utility Holding Company Act of 1935. By the late 1920s, 16 holding companies controlled 92 percent of all power produced by private sources. The Act, among other provisions, required the SEC to limit each public utility holding company to one integrated public utility system. Opponents of the Act predicted that massive divestitures would destroy our power system; they didn't.

Actually, the decentralized internal structure of most multidivision firms would make a divestiture program today very feasible. Citing this divisional structure in Senate testimony, economist Lee Preston contended that "the notion of dividing these large bureaucracies into separate plants that might behave more like vigorous competitive firms is a notion that they have, in fact, discovered for themselves, and [they] have tried to invent a kind of surrogate for the market through the divisionalized structure itself within the firm." Turner adds that ascertaining what plant-scale economies exist should not prove impossible in horizontal divestitures. "I would suppose every time a company is going to build a plant and decides what plant to build, it gets a blend of engineering and cost data which gives the firm some estimate of what the best size is." And in March, 1976, Senator Philip Hart revealed on the Senate floor how Exxon had been telling state tax authorities—in order to reduce its local tax burden—that it was a company of very separate operating divisions which were not tightly welded together.

In fact, at least vertical and conglomerate deconcentration appear not at all difficult to accomplish. A recessionary economy is encouraging firms to decentralize *sua sponte*. So a $3.8 billion Sun Oil Company, the nation's 37th largest manufacturing firm, announces it would voluntarily reconstitute itself into six separate companies; two would own the oil and the other four would run the exploration, production, refining, and retailing divisions. And large conglomerates, like LTV and Litton, are deconglomerating.

Even assuming its efficacy and viability, however, the remedy of deconcentration faces yet more specific opposition. Critics often argue that deconcentration is unfair to current shareholders. These "owners" are usually innocent of the original conduct that produced the offending oligopoly, yet they stand to lose their anticipated monopoly profits, for which they may have paid a premium. It would pervert public policy, however, if the government could never again attack a societal evil once it passed out of the hands of its original owners. No shareholder has a perpetual right to exploit a continuing illegal condition, even if he or she paid for the privilege. Part of the risk of an investment is that you may earn something you didn't expect (an unexpected oil find) or you may not earn something you do (A&P was held liable for $35 million in a price-fixing case in 1974). The risk of loss comes with the territory.

Moreover, major divestitures have consistently been shown to *help* shareholders. One year after the 1911 break-up of Standard Oil into 34 separate entities, the imputed value of one share in Standard Oil had risen from $660 to $971, an increase of 47 percent while the market as a whole rose only 7.6 percent. Share increases after the industry-wide divestitures of the 1935 Public Utility Holding Company Act were even more substantial. The *Yale Law Journal* calculated in 1949 that representative common stock prices had soared from 276 percent to 914 percent above 1935 levels, with some preferred stocks up as much as 1,060 percent. Today many sophisticated analysts believe that the break-up of an IBM or AT&T could benefit investors. Splitting IBM into several rival computer firms would allow each to compete more rigorously and grow far faster. Weeden and Company's Donald Weeden paid due homage to the advantages to shareholders of greater efficiency, innovation, and vigor associated with divested firms. In testifying before the Senate Antitrust and Monopoly Subcommittee, Weeden concluded, "Deconcentration cases . . . generally have demonstrated that the sum of the parts equals and often exceeds the price of the concentrated whole."

Conservative economist Harold Demsetz, speaking for another school of criticism, argues that "Embracing the market concentration doctrine through legislation is thus very likely to penalize the success and superior performance upon which depends the progress and wealth of this nation." Demsetz wrongly assumes that if a firm is big it must be efficient, when quite often the precise opposite is the case. The chance that long-term success may result in an antitrust case logically would not deter profit-minded firms in their pursuit of markets nor their pursuit of monopoly profits earned prior to dissolution suits.

It has been pointed out that divestiture relief in the past has often failed to attain its stated objectives. This is largely true. Of 137 "structural" cases brought against firms under Section 2 of the Sherman Act between 1890 and 1969, only 24 resulted in significant divestiture of a national or large regional monopolist. Government antitrust lawyers struggle to win cases rather than to devise workable remedies *after* a case is won. (For example, when Pullman was ordered to divest itself of its sleeping car business in the late 1940s, the firm obediently did so—to a joint venture of railroads doing 95 percent of the nation's passenger service.) One major study remarks that "termination of ownership by the defendant seems to be the principal focus of Government enforcement efforts, [not] the restoration of a viable competitive market structure." This is just fine with the divesting firm, as Kenneth Elzinga pointed out in his study of antitrust relief:

It is in the divesting firm's interest to seek out or favor a buyer who will either be cooperative, phlegmatic in his rivalry, or destined to fail. It is in the public's interest that the buyer be independent, a business maverick, and destined to succeed. . . . Consequently, effective antimerger relief requires that the authorities not give the companies involved free rein in this selection.

There is little doubt that the remedy stage of a major antitrust case often appears as an afterthought to prosecutors, defendant companies, and judges. The historical low quantity and quality of the Judgments Section of the Antitrust Division supports this view. The failure of divestiture traces to its faulty implementation in litigated proceedings, not to the nature of deconcentration itself.

In our view, the doctrinal basis for a Justice Department attack on oligopolies *per se* already exists. But it is unlikely that the Justice Department or FTC will systematically move against oligopoly power. If they haven't in six or seven decades, it's hard to anticipate they will now. To them the law is uncertain, resources inadequate, and business political pressure against such cases substantial. "With the law in doubt," former Antitrust Division chief Donald Turner has said, "it is a policy decision of no little difficulty to launch a case seeking restructuring of a major industry."

It is perhaps just as well. In that elusive pursuit of a monopolistic "intent" and coercive conduct, antitrust litigation leads to the paraphernalia of The Big Case—thousands of exhibits, months of hearings, and transcripts as large as telephone books. Cases such as the ongoing IBM monopoly trial—where counsel predicted the discovery of 50 *million* documents—are, in the words of veteran antitrust lawyer Paul Warnke, "basically untryable." And even if they were, a district court judge or even five Supreme Court justices may lack the self-confidence to innovatively interpret the antitrust laws so as to restructure much of American industry.

Given the history of antitrust law, only new legislation can effectively accomplish the widespread decentralization of monopoly power. A deconcentration section of a federal chartering bill would contain sections to (a) discourage *future* anticompetitive acquisitions and (b) undo *existing* concentration:

Future Concentration—Despite Richard McLaren's initial efforts, case law against large conglomerate mergers has failed to develop. Yet these mergers can reduce competition and produce bloated and inefficient offspring—as previous sections elaborated. To arrest any historical trend toward huge multidivisional conglomerates, legislation should forbid any federally chartered firm from acquiring any firm among the largest eight firms in any industry where four or fewer firms control 50 percent or more of the market. And to the extent that such corporations *do* make any acquisitions of firms in unconcentrated industries, they must within three months of the acquisition divest themselves of an approximately equal amount of assets.

This rule would encourage so-called "toehold" acquisitions in other industries, rather than the takeovers of leading firms by major companies (e.g., a Procter & Gamble of a Clorox). And it would stop in its tracks the past quarter century growth in aggregate concentration. Since a major company would have to sell off assets approximately equal to those they acquire, no such corporation could now grow any larger via merger; of course, it could still do so via internal expansion.

This proposal avoids the strains and delays of current antimerger law. No longer would the government, after the merger, have the burden of proving the combination's anticompetitive nature and of unscrambling it. That procedure encourages companies to merge quickly and then delay antitrust proceedings as long as possible. Instead, there would be a presumption against ever larger conglomerates, though they would still be permitted to make acquisitions they deem advantageous.

Existing Concentration—A deconcentration provision of a Federal Chartering Act must be a no-fault provision: i.e., the nub of the illegality is not a subjectively evil intent but an objectively anticompetitive structure. This section would create a presumption of monopoly power if four or fewer corporations account for 50 percent or more of the sales in any important line of commerce in any section of the country in any consecutive two-year period within the most recent five years.*

The Justice Department's Antitrust Division, with substantial accumulated experience in this area, seems best suited to enforce this provision. With its new mandate and an increased budget for a new deconcentration section, the Division should become far more effective and expeditious than in its performance in earlier antimonopoly cases. It would no longer need to hope that a disgruntled secretary or executive vice president will come forward to document an intent to monopolize. It need only show the fact of monopoly or oligopoly power in a relevant market. To facilitate this judgment, the Antitrust Division would publish a list of relevant product markets within a year of the implementation of the Act. The kind of increased corporate disclosure described in Chapter V, especially for more detailed divisional and product line reporting, would enable the Division to develop these standards.

Once legislation clearly prohibited the possession of monopoly

---

* These proposals are not meant to be exhaustive in the autitrust area. Omitted, for example, is the kind of vertical divertitive of the petroleum industry noted in chapter 8 of *The Closed Enterprise System*. That earlier book contains additional proposals to restrain market power.

power, it can be expected that the leading firms in some industries would voluntarily offer a suitable divestiture plan to the Antitrust Division—so as to avoid a costly litigation they would be destined to lose. For those federally chartered firms which did choose to challenge any deconcentration effort, there would be a three-level case before a specially appointed five-judge Antimonopoly Court. Creation of such an expert and ongoing tribunal seems preferable to fortuitously leaving such momentous decisions to differing, and often economically inexperienced, federal district court judges.

Level one would consider whether the defendant possesses monopoly power. If the court, based on a strict concentration ratio formula, decides in the affirmative, the defendant can try to rebut this conclusion in level two by arguing that its market domination results solely from the ownership of valid patents, lawfully acquired and lawfully used. If it fails to establish this defense, the Antimonopoly Court will decide on the appropriate relief in level three. In this effort it will be aided by a special master. This official can ask the Antitrust Division and the defendant firm(s) to propose remedial action, but he or she can also select a group of economists—from a special pool of economists throughout the country on call for such assignments—to develop its own plan.

The authorizing legislation would make clear that once monopoly power is conclusively established, the appropriate remedy is deconcentration until four or fewer firms no longer control 50 percent or more of that relevant market. This goal can be reached by a special master's plan that either requires the defendant to sell off assets to an existing firm or to establish new "going concerns." *

---

* Predictably, defendant companies will protest the impossibility or unfairness of proposed divestitures, but the court should keep firmly in mind the Supreme Court's admonition that "Those who violate the [Sherman Act] may not . . . avoid an undoing of their unlawful project on the pleas of hardship and inconvenience."

Willard Mueller pointed out in Senate testimony why the government should treat with some skepticism the complaints of interested parties in divestiture proceedings:

When Procter & Gamble acquired Clorox . . . P&G attorneys first came in with a list of prospective acquirers, to which they wanted to sell Clorox. The FTC staff thought the potential acquirers were just as objectionable in terms of anticompetitive effects as P&G.

At the time, they brought their investment bankers along—very impres-

The plan must be careful that the defendant firm and the existing or new firm be viable competitors with an adequate market share and sufficient access to supplies and outlets. The only way a defendant firm can avoid such divestiture is if it can clearly demonstrate to the special master and court—within six months of the determination of monopoly power in level two—that significant economies of scale would make any horizontal divestiture an economically inefficient remedy. The time limit is crucial to prevent wealthy corporations hiring fleets of economists to argue for years—during which time it would retain the disputed assets. With its substantial resources and knowledge, a monopoly firm should be able to make its case, or not, within that compact a period. If an economies defense does prevail, the special master and court will then turn to other remedies to mitigate market power. They could, for example, order the defendant to divest itself of vertically integrated suppliers or dealers, order it to transfer technology or patents royalty-free to competitors, or forbid the defendant from further expansion in that industry. But since the studies of Scherer and others indicate that plant economies of scale larger than 7 percent of a market are very rare, it is unlikely that a monopoly firm will be able to justify itself by reference to its size.

In the tradition of the antitrust laws, this deconcentration proposal requires the government not to regulate an industry but to make it competitive in a one-shot transaction. Those who oppose such "big government" action effectively insulate big business depredations from public scrutiny. It takes a peculiar conservative vision to oppose government intervention for competition yet acquiesce to the private governments who dominate the industrial economy. Thurman Arnold saw the irony in the toleration of big

---

sive people—and explained why they couldn't do anything other than sell it to a going concern. They couldn't possibly divest it.

And we went right down the list and said that our recommendations to the Commission were that they could not—that we disapproved the sale of this company to them. The result was just incredible. In only a matter of weeks, which can only mean that these guys are even more ingenious that I thought, or else they had a contingency plan all along, P&G attorneys came back with a proposal for spinning it off, establishing a new company. . . . Subsequently, [Clorox was spun off and] has thrived.

business "so long as the organization was not called the government, and therefore did not disturb the smooth process of accustomed ritual." As more conservatives like Simons, Burns, and Rinfret appreciate that reduction of monopoly power helps free enterprise and renders big government less necessary, deconcentration will be at hand.

How and Why It Will Work

———————————————

VIII

Jurisdiction and
Enforcement

My strong advice to you gentlemen is to do nothing. Do not comply; resist the law with all your might.

—Attorney John Foster Dulles, advising clients
on the 1935 Public Utility Holding Company Act.

S OON AFTER THE Corporate Accountability Research Group's proposal to federally charter giant corporations was released in report form in January 1976, Wilmington's leading attorneys began a sustained attack on the scholarship of this five-year-long study. The January 25th edition of the DuPont-owned *Wilmington News Journal* quoted Delaware attorneys as labeling our work "immature . . . uninformed . . . superficial . . . distorted." "Much of the more than 400 pages contains heavily biased, badly researched diatribe," said a related editorial. Two lawyers on the Corporation Law Committee of the Delaware Bar Association published a column in the *Journal* with the breathtaking conclusion that: "Proponents of federal chartering have not advanced any valid reason to abandon our present system."

Obviously, Delaware's corporate bar does not wish to lose the goose that lays all the golden fees. The state itself has less to fear. Since this proposal would create a dual national-state chartering system, the impact even on Delaware would be initially minimal. If enacted, all corporations would continue to incorporate in a state; the federal government would additionally require the largest industrial, retail, and transportation corporations to charter in Washington.

This dual chartering system fully appreciates the constitutional principle of federalism: *viz.*, the national government should preempt a field of law only to the extent that the states can not fulfill desired public policies. It also recognizes legislative realities. Rather than asking Congress to spend several years drafting the two or three hundred separate provisions necessary for a comprehensive corporate code, it allows Congress to focus its legislative resources on enacting a law which deals with the most urgent questions of corporate power.

SCOPE

The Act would cover all industrial, retail, and transportation corporations which sold over $250,000,000 in goods or services or employed more than 10,000 persons in the United States in any one of the previous three years. These standards would apply to such privately held behemoths as Deering Milliken, Hallmark Cards, Hearst Publications, and Cargill, as well as all U.S. subsidiaries or divisions of foreign corporations which sell or employ more than the requisite standards.*

The largest industrial, retail, and transportation corporations represent the central core of the United States economy. Nonfinancial corporations annually produce approximately 52 percent of the total goods and services produced by all business, government, household, and institutional sources. The vast preponderance of this production is the work of the very largest corporations. To cite one important illustration, approximately two-thirds of all industrial sales last year were made by the 550 or so industrial corpora-

---

* Banks, insurance companies, public utilities, not-for-profit corporations, co-operatives, and all unincorporated associations would be specifically excluded from the Act, although the reforms recommended by this proposal could be tailored to the operations of the largest financial corporations in subsequent proposals. Privately held corporations and the U.S. subsidiaries or divisions of foreign corporations, such as KLM or Volkswagen, would be subject to the disclosure, employees rights, and antitrust sections of the Act if their sales or employment exceeded the requisite levels, but would not be subject to the governance section (Chapter IV) unless or until their corporation or U.S. subsidiary was listed on a U.S. stock exchange or held by 2,000 or more American stockholders.

tions with sales over $250,000,000 apiece. By employing a $250,000,000 annual sales figure as its principal criterion, the Act would bypass approximately 15,000,000 smaller business associations yet would reach some 700 industrial, retail, and transportation corporations whose immense size clearly indicates a national impact.

Since annual sales are occasionally a misleading measure of corporate social impact, however, secondary scope criteria would include any corporation which employed more than 10,000 persons in any one of the three previous years. This standard will reach the laggard giants which are experiencing depressed sales years but still retain the size and potential to affect local communities or employees as much as currently more prosperous firms.

Yet what about the problem of "corporate runaways"—companies which flee jurisdictions with strict business laws to relocate in international Delawares like Panama or the Grand Cayman Islands? As Thomas Jefferson once observed, "Merchants have no country. The mere spot they stand on does not constitute so strong an attachment as that from which they draw their gain." Modern merchants vivify Jefferson's view. Anthony Sampson, author of *The Sovereign State of ITT*, pointed out that multinationals "regard governments, like other obstacles to management, as nuisances to be circumvented or overcome." Dow Chemical's Chairman Carl Gerstacker explained at a 1972 White House Conference that he yearned for a lonely island on which he might establish the headquarters of an "anational" company, independent of allegiance to any country. More bluntly, a Mobil Oil Corporation vice president warned Senators Hollings and Hartke in March 1975 that if their proposal for elimination of the foreign tax credit on oil firms was enacted, "Oil companies would consider moving control of their international operations out of the country."

Given such disloyalty, it is probable that some United States corporations will consider fleeing abroad rather than complying with an effective new federal corporation law—if they thought they could get away with it. Under this proposal they cannot. The "previous three years" test and a related provision specifying that once a corporation is chartered under the federal corporate law, it must remain so, will insure that as long as giant American corporations wish to sell or produce in the United States, they will be subject to the chartering act. And since the U.S. market constitutes one-third to one-half the world market in many commodities, our largest firms will undoubtedly be unwilling to sacrifice this market for the privilege of a Panamanian charter.

ENFORCEMENT

In few aspects does state corporation law fail quite so completely as in the state's inability—or unwillingness—to enforce their corporation laws. Enforcement of the 1920s prohibition laws seemed vigorous by comparison. Recently, it was reported that a private travel agency run by Joseph Yeldell, Washington, D.C.'s Human Resources Director, lost its charter because it failed to file two annual reports as required by law. Unaffected, the firm has continued to do business. Similarly, in Indiana, AT&T, the nation's largest corporation, lost its licence to do business there because it failed to file an annual report. There were no hearings held and no fines assessed. Although Ma Bell had legally ceased to exist in Indiana, business continued as usual. As Marie Shultie, head of Delaware's Corporations Division, explained in an interview, her state has no enforcement wing. No steps are taken even to prevent a corporation that has lost its charter for failure to pay franchise taxes from continuing to hold itself out as a bona fide Delaware corporation. Frequently Delaware corporations pay a $25 fine rather than file a required annual report.

In September and October of 1975, we surveyed the 50 states on their enforcement and compliance programs. Of the 31 states that responded, 24 acknowledged that they did not employ a *single person* to enforce the substantive provisions of their corporations laws. Although these states had incorporated over 1,500,000 active corporations, not one could point to a single instance in which a corporation had been penalized in 1972, 1973, or 1974 for a violation of its corporations laws other than the failure to pay franchise taxes or file an annual report. And most had no idea whether the corporations they did penalize for failure to pay taxes or file reports subsequently complied with these sanctions. The Secretary of State of one state, Arkansas, estimated that no more than 40 percent of penalized corporations did so.

The enforcement record of the Securities and Exchange Commission—the existing agency we believe best suited to enforce most of the Federal Chartering Act—shines by comparison. Its existing Corporate Finance and Enforcement divisions already administer related disclosure, proxy, and remedial laws. It is the logical agency—whatever its historical warts—to enforce all provisions of the Act except the antimonopoly provisions outlined in Chapter VII. But to equip the Commission to assume this new assignment, certain institutional reforms are desirable to increase its independence and effectiveness:

● *SEC Budget requests should be routed directly to Congress rather than through the Office of Management and Budget.* Each year the SEC is required to submit its budget request to the White House's politically sensitive Office of Management and Budget (OMB). And in each fiscal year since 1972, OMB has cut an average of 8–10 percent from the SEC's budget request, despite the fact that in 1972 the OMB's own "management review" of the SEC determined "the agency had run down in numbers and strength and had not kept up with the increased workload it had been called upon to handle." Like the Consumer Product Safety Commission, the SEC should be allowed to present its budget directly to Congress. This would move industry lobbying against the SEC out of the back rooms of the White House and into the public hearing rooms of the Appropriations Committees. It would also give the Commission the opportunity to present its best case rather than operate under the constraints of an often hostile White House.

● *Industry conflicts of interest should be prohibited.* Almost as legendary as the SEC's accomplishments during the 1930s was its integrity. Explained a proud former chairman William O. Douglas, "The industry never took [the staff] to lunch or dinner. All invitations by industry-connected people to spend weekends on Long Island or elsewhere were politely turned down. . . . In my five years at the SEC only one man was dismissed, not because he had taken a bribe but because he exuded his susceptibility."

In recent years, however, one commissioner, Ralph Saul, left to become President of the American Stock Exchange; a second, James Needham, to head the New York Stock Exchange; Hamer Budge, once chairman, now works for the Investors Diversified

Services mutual fund—indeed, he initially discussed working for the fund while it was under SEC investigation; Donald Cook, also a former chairman, and Ralph McElvenny, a staff attorney in the Public Utilities Division, became chief executive officers of power companies they previously regulated.

As Justice Douglas recently wrote, it should be "unthinkable" for an SEC commissioner or staff attorney to become head of a utility company, a brokerage house, or a stock exchange—or to leave to become counsel to one of them. "The reason [is] simple: if that were the goal, even in the subconscious, regulation would suffer. The federal agent would then face the job less objectively. In form, he would be serving the public interest; in fact, he would be proving his worth to a future employer." In April, 1976, there was a classic illustration of Justice Douglas's point. Shortly before Commissioner A. A. Sommer, Jr. left the SEC to join a corporate law firm, he delivered a much publicized speech criticizing the Commission's reluctance to issue guidelines on foreign bribery as "totally unacceptable . . . a sorry situation," and then detailed his sympathy for "innumerable businessmen, attorneys and accountants" allegedly confused by the SEC's enforcement program.

Accordingly, SEC commissioners and senior staff assistants should be barred from joining a law firm with a SEC clientele or from joining a stock exchange, brokerage house, or corporation subject to its jurisdiction for two years after leaving the agency. It should be equally "unthinkable" for an SEC official to invest in the securities of a company subject to its jurisdiction; or to accept speaking honorariums, Christmas gifts, money, loans, vacations, investment opportunities, or any other favor from a corporation, broker, or exchange subject to its jurisdiction. Congress should require automatic dismissal of any SEC commissioner or employee found to have accepted such financial benefits in any form after the effective date of this Act.

● *A Fund should be established for reimbursing investors' advocates who appear before the Commission.* Industry representatives may be able to tilt the most honest agency simply by the frequency of their appearance. James Landis explained this well in his celebrated remark that "[I]rrespective of the absence of social contacts and the absence of undue hospitality, it is the daily machine-gun like impact on both agency and its staff of industry representation that makes for industry orientation on the part of many honest and capable agency members as well as agency staffs." This is a particularly great risk at an agency like the SEC, where issues, such as the more technical of the federal chartering provisions, may seem far removed from the daily experience of most consumer advocates as well as the general public. Yet, precisely for this reason, it is essential that mechanisms be established to ensure that the general interests of investors or the public be represented in rulemaking proceedings. Business should not be allowed to shape the content of federal chartering policy by default.

The Commission should have the authority to reimburse the costs of outside investors or consumer advocates who otherwise could not afford to appear in important rulemaking proceedings. This is consistent with the Supreme Court's decision in the securities case of *Mills v. Electric Auto-Lite Co.* that the federal courts may order reimbursement of the costs of counsel where "the litigation has conferred a substantial benefit on the members of an ascertainable class, and where the court's jurisdiction over the subject matter of the suit makes possible an award that will operate to spread the costs proportionately among them." And it is consistent with the recent FTC Improvement Act, which has a half million dollar appropriation for this purpose.

● *Citizens' rights of action.* Finally, investors and the public should have a right of action against the SEC itself, in addition to the right of judicial review of agency actions accorded by the Administrative Procedure Act. A citizen (or class of citizens, via expanded class action rights) should be able to (1) bring suit to order the Commission (or the Antitrust Division under the antimonopoly section) to initiate action if failure to act presents an unreasonable public harm or risk; (2) sue to enforce the SEC's statutes and rules if the Commission deliberately fails to do so; and (3) recover damages and attorneys fees in cases of injury by reason of the Commission's knowing violation of its own statutes or rules. The necessity of such a remedy being available against *every* governmental agency was made clear by the Nixon Administration. A continuing study by the Corporate Accountability Research Group has found over 1,000 separate instances where federal appeals courts have ruled that federal agencies during Nixon's administration had violated their own statute or their own regulations. As an ultimate safeguard in any democratic legal system, citizens need the power to compel government agencies to obey the law.

ENFORCEMENT IN THE FEDERAL COURTS

A federal corporations law should also end the perverse form of forum-shopping inspired by the states with the most lax corporate laws. Under current practice, a corporation and its executives—the potential defendants in civil suits—choose which state law will apply to them when they select the jurisdiction in which they incorporate. Since the number of individuals who judge corporate litigation in the principal chartering states is fairly discrete, corporate defendants also, in effect, choose their judges. And the judges in a state like Delaware are usually normatively indistinguishable from, or actually come from, the corporate world in that self-proclaimed "little home of big business." The deficiencies of such a practice were anticipated in Hamilton's *81st Federalist Paper*, when he noted the "prevalency of a local spirit . . . to disqualify the local tribunals for the jurisdiction of national causes. . . ."

Withdrawal of corporate litigation from a state like Delaware to the federal district courts, however, must be accompanied by the systematic removal of the procedural obstacles that today throttle both state corporate and federal securities litigation.

First, standing rules need to be broadened. Both federal securities and state corporation laws largely restrict the right to bring a lawsuit to those who were shareholders of a corporation at the time of the alleged wrong, even though earlier or subsequent shareholders of the corporation may be equally injured if stock prices go down. This type of standing rule is an enduring testament to the political abilities of corporate lawyers to rig the procedural rules of corporate litigation so as to reduce the liability of their clients. Far preferable would be a rule that allows a suit to be maintained by any person, association, state attorney general, or agency of the United States which alleges a violation of federal corporate or securities law. As the United States Supreme Court ruled in *Sierra Club v. Morton*, "Where a dispute is otherwise justiciable, the question whether the litigant is a 'proper party to request an adjudication of a particular issue' . . . is one within the power of Congress to determine."

This broader conception of standing would expand opportunities to litigate violations of the Federal Chartering Act toward the common law ideal that "for every wrong there is a remedy." The Michigan Environmental Protection Act of 1970, which embodies precisely such a standard, has recently been replicated in the environmental laws of seven other states; a federal version was introduced by President Gerald Ford when he was a Congressman and also by Michigan Senator Philip Hart. It should be restricted by a provision that a federal court can only award attorneys' fees and reasonable costs to plaintiff's counsel when the plaintiff prevails (in which case the reward should be mandatory). Such a limitation will fully prevent the federal courts from being flooded with nonmeritorious suits. Senate hearings in 1973 determined that of the first 50 suits filed under the Michigan Act, only one or two could be described as frivolous, and they were quickly disposed of by the courts.

Second, the statute of limitations on federal securities and federal corporation litigation should be extended to six years from the current pointlessly restrictive three years—which self-serving corporate lobbyists first secured in 1934 and have succeeded in maintaining ever since.

Third, the availability of equitable remedies under federal corporate and federal securities laws should be clarified. Inherent to every state and federal civil court is the power to fashion equitable remedies likely to deter or correct serious and ongoing harms. This authority has been historically shunned by courts, wary of becoming too directly involved in internal corporate affairs.

Recently, however, the Enforcement Division of the SEC has begun to make imaginative use of these latent powers. Against a series of corporations guilty of nondisclosure of foreign bribes or domestic campaign fund abuses—including Northrop, Phillips, and 3M—the SEC required the appointment of independent Special Review Committees to prepare and file with the Commission detailed reports on the nature of the violations, in each case reserving the right "to seek such further relief as may be necessary or appropriate" after reviewing the report. Against Mattel Corporation, which understated its pretax income in 1971 by $18.3 million, the Enforcement Division persuaded a federal court to appoint a majority of new outside directors to Mattel's board and executive committee whose integrity was deemed "satisfactory" by the Commission. Similarly, against Sanitas Service Corporation, a federal court ordered that an Audit Committee, a Legal Committee, and outside General Counsel be given the duties of overseeing financial operations and reporting to shareholders to assure an end to a four-year pattern of corporate illegality. In other civil cases, the SEC has ordered receivers, restitution of property, and disgorgement of illegally gained profits back to the corporation and its shareholders. The Federal Corporate Chartering Act should originally state that a federal court may order such equitable or ancillary relief and that it may do so on the motion of a shareholder or other individual plaintiff as well as the SEC.

TAXPAYER RIGHTS

Against those federally chartered corporations which profit by doing business with the federal government or are the recipients of direct or indirect (tax) subsidies, enforcement rules are particularly in need of redefinition.

Given the size of the federal payout to giant corporations—now over $100 billion annually—and the described abuses associated with such contract programs, any federal taxpayer should be able to bring direct suits against the corporation for tax or contract fraud and/or against the responsible federal official for failure to enforce applicable statutes, regulations, case law, or contracts upon a prima facie showing of evidence. Such suits will be facilitated by the disclosure provisions of this Act, which will make income tax returns and contracts matters of public record and which will limit corporate invocation of the protective doctrine of "trade secrecy" during the discovery phase of litigation.

As with all litigation under the Federal Corporate Chartering Act, the court shall have equitable discretion to cause the election of new directors to prevent the repetition of a substantial civil or criminal wrong; to appoint a special review committee to prepare a detailed report on the violation; or to order the return of an illegally obtained benefit. But because fraud in a corporate subsidy or contract program is in effect a fraud against the entire country, the federal district courts should be encouraged to exercise their equitable powers to order the hiring of a special financial or program executive for a temporary period to supervise the previously fraudulent operation and prevent its recurrence; order the dismissal of responsible corporate executives, counsel, or auditors; and fine responsible persons a portion or all of the fraudulently procured monies either through direct assessments or termination of otherwise vested pension or compensation rights.

SANCTIONS

Penalties for violation of the Federal Chartering Act are grounded in two basic assumptions: First, existing penalties for corporate abuse are laughably inadequate and rarely reach the culpable individual within the corporation; and second, because businessmen are sophisticated individuals who act premeditatively rather than compulsively, serious penalties can successfully deter illegality.

In the past 18 months, sources as diverse as the Burger Court, Senator John McClellan, the SEC's Enforcement Division, and Attorney General Edward Levi have come to the conclusion that stricter corporate penalties are needed. In *United States v. Park*, the Supreme Court in 1975 unanimously held a corporate executive to a standard of strict criminal liability following his firm's violation of the Food and Drug Act for failure to implement measures to insure that violations of that law not occur. Explained the Court, "the requirements of foresight and vigilance imposed on responsible corporate agents are . . . perhaps onerous, but they are no more stringent than the public has a right to expect of those who voluntarily assume positions of authority in business enterprises whose services and products affect the health and well-being of the public that supports them." Senator McClellan's massive S.1 Bill to revise the United States Criminal Code provides that the criminal liability of an executive for the conduct of his corporation in certain instances be broadened and that the liability of the corporation for the conduct of its executive also be expanded. The SEC has sought injunctions to bar corporate executives from serving with particular corporations or all public corporations upon proof of a civil violation of the securities laws. And Attorney General Levi has created a White Collar Crime Task Force to study the extent and costs of such violations and to suggest new remedies' in addition to traditional criminal sentences and fines.

More specifically, penalties for violations of the Federal Chartering Act should include the following:

• Corporate officers convicted of willful corporate-related violations of the Act should be disqualified from serving as a corporate officer or director in any American corporation or partnership for five years after a conviction, guilty plea, or *nolo contendere* plea. This is only logical. One does not re-employ an embezzler as a bank teller. Union officials under the Landrum-Griffin Act and broker-dealers under securities laws can be similarly suspended for pertinent violations. There are many positions available in a company for such a corporate law violator other than management or the board, which are peculiarly positions of trust.

• Fines should be calibrated to the size of the firm and the "size" of the violation. A violation by GM—given the firm's resources and impact—should not be penalized the same as if by Mrs. Smith's Pie (*Fortune*'s 833rd industrial firm). Instead of absolute fines, there would be percentage fines based on gross sales—so the fine would fit the criminal.

This approach has some modest precedent. A federal judge fined IBM for failure to product documents in the Justice Department's current antitrust proceeding. He analyzed the size and resources of IBM and then settled on a fine of $150,000 a day—one appropriate for IBM but not for a small firm or a streetwalker. His decision acknowledged the need to graduate fines to get a response from business, rather than employing the equivalent of a corporate traffic ticket. In Common Market nations such as West Germany, antitrust and other laws now impose fines on the basis of a percentage of the gross annual sales or profits of the firm, rather than in stated currency amounts which have progressively less sting the greater the size of a firm.

• Penalties must also increase for corporate recidivists, since by definition the company or executive has not been successfully deterred. For example, a second and third offense within a three-year period could lead to an increasing percentage fine based on gross sales. If there were more than three nontechnical violations of the Federal Chartering Act within a three-year period, a "corporate habitual offender" provision should subject the company to a SEC-supervised reorganization of existing management—which would have allowed or tolerated the continuing violations.

• In no instance should a corporation be allowed to indemnify any executive or director against any liability or penalty of a civil or criminal action. Nor should any corporation or corporate officer be permitted to purchase insurance against such civil or criminal liabilities. In actions settled by compromise or plea bargain, no indemnity should be permitted except with the approval of the court. And all indemnity payments should be disclosed to corporate shareholders.

• Finally, corporate conflicts of interest should be removed from the discretion of the boardroom and made the subject of designated civil sanctions in federal district court. Specifically, no corporate director, executive, representative or agent should be allowed to sell any real or personal property to the corporation in which he works, with the exception of the purchase or sale of the corporation's own securities as part of a geneal incentive stock, securities issuance, or redemption program. Second, no corporate director or executive should accept any employment in any other business firm while employed full time by a federally chartered corporation; nor should he or she receive remuneration or own stock or otherwise profit from any business engaged in the same lines of commerce or transacting business with the corporation for which he works. Third, no corporate executive or director should accept employment in any government agency while employed full time by a corporation subject to this act. This last provision will not only ensure singleminded loyalty to shareholders but also avoid the conflict of an executive simultaneously serving an agency with a general public interest and a corporation with a particular financial interest. If the government agency requires business advice, it may invite or compel testimony, hire former business executives, or retain more neutral experts.

In sum, business illegality has its own cost curve. If we punish companies and individuals with penalties which are the equivalent of wrist slaps, the result is predictable. If we make the cost of lawlessness sufficiently high, it should discourage many violations which are now profitable to pursue. Only then will today's corporate crime wave crest and recede short of our third century.

IX

The Case *Against*
Federal Chartering

Revolutions were made by Pharaoh, not by Moses; by the Tsar, not by Marx.

—Justin Kaplan, discussing Lincoln Steffens

WHY FEDERAL CHARTERING, such an old idea, in 1976? To summarize the previous text—because (a) our largest corporations have such harmful market and nonmarket impacts; (b) state chartering laws, downgraded by the Delaware syndrome, have failed to restrain corporate abuses; (c) the governing ethos of our giant firms more resembles an autocracy than a democracy; (d) the officers of these corporations lack individual accountability for their actions; (e) corporate secrecy has overwhelmed the need for corporate disclosure; (f) these firms routinely violate the rights of their employees; (g) widespread market concentration insulates most of our largest companies from the rigors of competition; (h) there is occurring an outbreak of corporate payoffs and other crimes; and (i) our chronic economic conditions amply demonstrate that these corporations are not performing well even by their own standards—there is an obvious need to fundamentally reform the giant corporation in America. Federal chartering is an effective means to that goal.

Of course, "federal chartering" alone is only a vehicle. One speaker at a business law conference accurately observed that "A federal incorporation act could, of course, turn out merely to be another version of the Delaware Act or the Model Business Corporation Act." The precise content of a Federal Chartering Act, then, is crucial. In the previous eight chapters, there has been presented an agenda to strengthen the legal rights of each of the giant corporation's five principal constituencies:

• *For shareholders*—The Act would increase the likelihood of efficient and profitable corporate management by requiring a full-time outside board of directors, with a full-time staff available to it, to monitor executive performance. The board would review all fundamental business decisions, hire and dismiss the chief executive, set the salary of all executives, nominate the corporation's financial auditors, and select the firm's general counsel. The board itself will be comprised of nine "constituency directors," each with the general duty to see that the corporation is profitably run and a specific duty to oversee a particular aspect of corporate management, such as "employee welfare" or "research and planning." Shareholders or shareholder groups holding more than .1 percent of the stock or who comprise more than 100 individuals may nominate up to three persons to serve as directors. In directorial elections, only beneficial or actual owners of stock would be eligible to vote, all campaign costs would be limited and assumed by the corporation and cumulative voting would be required. Shareholders must approve all "fundamental transactions" such as important mergers and the issuance of new securities. To further stimulate directors to be vigorous watchdogs of management, shareholders will receive detailed explanations of fundamental transactions, have greater access to nonprivileged corporate data, be allowed to attend portions of some directors' meetings, and have more effective legal means to bring civil suits against negligent or disloyal corporate management. Directors would also be required to disclose detailed financial information in the corporation's quarterly and annual reports and in a residual *Corporation Register*, including increased profit and loss accounting by subsidiaries and product lines.

• *For employees*—The Act would require more detailed disclosure of toxic substances in the workplace, minority employment by job and income categories, and ultimately multinational firm "job exportation." The Act would also protect the civil liberties and civil rights of both union and non-union workers by adopting an Employee Bill of Rights. Federally chartered firms would be required to observe the First Amendment requirements of freedom of expression; to respect the privacy of all employees; and not to discriminate in any transaction or occurrence on account of race, religion, creed or sex. To give teeth to these new rights, all employees would have the right to bring an action against unjust dismissal or unjust harrassment. And to the extent employees purchased stock, they would enjoy greater influence in selecting directors and guiding board policy, according to the liberalized shareholder nomination and election process noted above.

● *For consumers*—More accountable managers would be far less likely to make the kind of decisions that have led to irresponsible technology, product dangers, pollution, and monopoly practices. Specifically, the Act would require that major advertisements by federally chartered firms be substantiated, permit consumers expanded class action rights, and reduce prices generally by deconcentrating primary industries. In industries where four or fewer firms control 50 percent or more of the sales in a relevant market, chartered companies must divest themselves of sufficient assets and otherwise revamp business practices to restore competition to that market. Companies under the Act would also be prohibited from acquiring any firm among the eight largest in any concentrated industry; and any acquisitions they do make must be matched by the divestiture of a like amount of asserts.

● *For taxpayers*—The Act would require corporate disclosure of congressional and executive lobbying contacts and federal tax returns and contracts. In cases of fraud or waste in federal contracts, taxpayers would have standing to bring suits either against the corporation or the responsible government official or agency.

● *For neighboring communities*—The Act would require disclosure of polluting plant discharges and compliance schedules and the issuance of a "community impact statement" when a plant is relocated. If three directors or three percent of the voting shares find a corporate facility is causing a health hazard, the affected community will vote on a corporate referendum to decide how to contain the hazard.

Since the TNEC hearings in the late 1930s, the subject of the federal chartering of America's major corporations has hardly been prominent in political dialogue. Ralph Nader advocated it in the late 1960s. Morton Mintz and Jerry Cohen discussed it in their 1971 book *America, Inc.* Senator Henry Jackson's Interior Committee issued a volume of articles on the subject in 1974. The next year Rep. James Stanton introduced a bill with federal chartering elements and the American Bar Association sponsored a conference on federal corporate law at Airlie House in Virginia. While these events still did not make federal chartering a household word, they did inspire occasional comment and criticism from politicians, businesspersons, and the business press. What follows is a discussion of the most prevalent past, and probable future, criticisms of federal chartering:

• *Isn't this just more regulation?* With public figures from Jerry Ford to Jerry Brown denouncing federal government interference in our lives, it is predictable that critics will attempt to paint federal chartering with an antiregulation brush.

But political slogans cannot obscure the already articulated *raison d'être* of federal chartering—more competition, more democracy, less crime—goals which even reflexive conservatives can embrace. One of its premises, in Franklin Roosevelt's words, "is not that the system of free private enterprise has failed . . . but that it has not yet been tried." According to the late Walton Hamilton, the author of *The Politics of Industry* and a Yale Law School professor, "If the focus is shifted to market structure, then it seems to me the federal role is appropriately limited once the limitations in the charter are agreed to. Then competition, rather than extensive regulation, could determine the direction of our economy."

Nor will it require huge new bureaucracies to accomplish these goals. The Federal Chartering Act has largely self-regulating provisions with objective standards: e.g., a company must release minority hiring data by plant; it must utilize cumulative voting. If federally chartered firms fail to obey such provisions, empowered employees or shareholders can initiate legal action to enforce the Act. Or a reinforced SEC and Antitrust Division will enforce clear standards of the law. Historically, these two agencies have made the market process work better, rather than substituted for it. Indeed, it is when the market fails to perform as expected and when such agencies fail to take corrective action that we get truly burdensome regulation like wage and price controls.

• *Won't the federal chartering agencies be captured by business, just as other regulatory agencies have?* This anxiety is an extension of the first one, and is based on a comparable misperception. Federal chartering is unlike existing regulatory agencies in three fundamental respects. First, while New Deal agencies were delegated vast discretion under vague statutes to regulate "in the public interest," federal chartering is far more narrowly circumscribed; its mission is specific, not open-ended. It will decide whether a company within its scope has a "shareholder director"; it will not decide what a transporter can charge to ship a tomato from Fresno to Albuquerque. Thus, there is less temptation and room for business interests to try to lobby and shape agency decisions. The original legislation would have shaped these decisions already.

Second, existing regulatory agencies have lacked outside stimuli and pressures to vigorously enforce their laws. Federal chartering, however, specifically encourages citizens to intervene or sue, if necessary, to insure that the Act's provisions are followed; interested constituencies, therefore, can be expected to bring substantial pressure on their companies and on the SEC and Antitrust Division to enforce the Act's provisions. And third, existing regulatory agencies each have a particular industry lobbying it. Truckers and railroads can expend all their effort on the Interstate Commerce Commission, and natural gas producers on the Federal Power Commission. Because federal chartering cuts across many industries, no one of them will be able to control enforcement or monopolize access to it.

• *Won't federal chartering make it harder and more costly to conduct business; won't it add to the already great paperwork of business?* "Most regulations of business necessarily impose financial burdens on the enterprise for which no compensation is paid," former Justice William Douglas once wrote, "Those are part of the costs of our civilization." Or to put it another way, any costs entailed in complying with a Federal Chartering Act must be compared with the costs of *not* complying. Air pollution alone assesses damages of $23 billion annually on our society; Frederic Scherer estimates monopoly-related waste at $87 billion annually; more prosaically, excessive executive compensation and managerial and directorial conflicts-of-interest are commonplace. By promoting competition and obedience to laws, federal chartering will reduce such costly activities. Fine-tuning our largest 700 firms should make them more, not less, efficient.

Consider, for example, the burdens of disclosing information to the federal government. As of March 31, 1975, the Office of Management and Budget's computer system already showed a total of 2,149 regular questionnaire forms to business, with approximately 115 million responses; in addition, 123 single-shot forms were in use, involving some 600,000 business firms. Yet as business supporters groan that such paperwork could fill 50 football stadiums, they invariably fail to mention the benefits of corporate disclosure—recited in detail in Chapter V—which make the economy work more effectively. Federal chartering disclosure will preempt and consolidate many existing, and often overlapping, agency information programs.

Finally, existing agency information requirements can indeed be burdensome—but mostly to small businesses. It is they who, lacking annual sales in the hundreds of millions of dollars, labor under the reporting requirements of government. And it is they who have to disclose details of their single-line operations, while giant companies don't have to disclose such data for each of their subsidiaries—which gives big business an unfair competitive advantage over small business. By focusing on the largest and most prosperous corporations, federal chartering would require additional disclosure from those who can best afford and deserve it, to the advantage of those who already disclose.

● *It is unfair for the federal government to now manipulate these rights of private property; it is especially unfair to Delaware.* In 1940, Edward Clark, the Secretary of State of Texas, told the Temporary National Economic Committee that "We would like by your consent to be let alone and permitted to run unmolested what modest little business an all-wise, all beneficient Providence has bestowed upon us."

This view seriously misperceives the role of law. Unlike monarchies, private property is based not on divine will but legal standards. The Delaware General Corporation Law is not an immutable text, but only current law, revisable by due process of law. The law creates and protects that bundle of rights called property or the corporation, and this same law can rearrange that bundle of rights if it is in the public interest. Or as Benjamin Franklin put it in 1783, "Private property is a creature of society, and is subject to the calls of that society, whenever its necessities shall require it. . . ."

Delaware's particular and obvious concern over a Federal Chartering Act evokes, we must admit, little sympathy. That state is fortunate it is not compelled to pay compensation to the other 49 for seizing so much of the chartering business for itself, given the manner in which its government has debased the law over the years.

● *We don't need new law but a renewed emphasis on corporate social responsibility.* Even if the formal mechanisms of accountability failed to harness corporate power, it has been said, we could at least depend on the social responsibility of business managers to act in the public interest.

This is an approach with a long lineage. In the medieval period, the church denounced the unalloyed pursuit of profit and St. Thomas Aquinas wrote that business enterprise could be justified if directed "for a definite purpose, namely, the good estate of the household [community]." Even Adam Smith, in a work preceding *The Wealth of Nations*, posited as a precondition for capitalism that competitors should be restrained in their actions by "sympathy" and "moral sentiments." A 1921 book entitled *U.S. Steel: A Corporation with a Soul* argued that U.S. Steel was a socially responsible monopoly—unlike, for example, the earlier Standard Oil monopoly.

In 1953, the Supreme Court of New Jersey, in a seminal decision, upheld the right of corporate officers to make reasonable charitable contributions largely on the basis of simple corporate good citizenship. In the late 1960s, former Gulf Oil chairman Bob Dorsey (who in the next decade would admit paying $4 million in bribes to South Korean officials) told the Columbia Graduate School of Business that "the first responsibility of business is to operate for the well-being of society." By 1971, a *Harvard Business Review* survey showed that 61 percent of its readers recognized a corporate duty to serve not only the interests of owners but also those of employees, customers, and the public.

There are, to be sure, critics of this viewpoint, most notably Professor Milton Friedman. He argues that "there is one and only one social responsibility of business—to use its resources and engage in activities designed to increase its profits." This view is forceful, but empirically unfounded. Friedman's argument rests upon a fiercely competitive economy which simply doesn't exist for most major American corporations. And it is the rare businessperson who will so bluntly admit to such a narrow and unpopular sounding motive as pure profit.

To a limited extent, corporate social responsibility can be a useful concept. If companies believe it is in their long-run interest to develop good will and a good image by good works, few would complain. So it seems a commendable use of discretionary business power when Aetna Life & Casualty takes on a black director and increases its pretax charitable contributions from 1 percent to 1½ percent of profits, or when Xerox releases employees for a year's community service, or when IBM sponsors *Long Day's Journey into Night* on television (without commercials!). More significantly, responsible corporations may work to correct a problem they created whether or not the law compels them to do it—e.g., a few pulp and paper mills reduced their pollution of waterways before an Environmental Protection Agency was created.

On balance, however, corporate social responsibility seems more hyperbole than fact. First, it is not clear that General Motors has acted significantly more responsibly following its much touted selection of black minister Leon Sullivan for its board of directors; the insurance industry in 1967 pledged, with much fanfare, a $2 billion dollar plan for low income housing and related projects, a plan that has fizzled out. The late Whitney Young, executive director of the Urban League, once complained that "Many companies limit their concern to press releases, empty speeches, or less."

Second, corporations rarely scrutinize their actual products with the corporate responsibility ethic in mind. So the auto industry rejected shatterproof glass, collapsible steering columns, non-eggshell bumpers and less polluting or fuel-efficient cars until legal or political pressure persuaded them otherwise. Contributions to local charities or minority business is one thing, but safer products another.

Third, corporate responsibility will remain a marginal benefit, the philosophic equivalent of last hired, first fired. In January 1975, the *Wall Street Journal* reported that in the crunch of a severe recession, "executives have become less interested in looking for broader responsibilities . . . the present state of the economy makes it imperative for corporations to return to their primary responsibilities."

What is imperative is that neither businesspeople nor legislators nor the public be lulled into depending on corporate social responsibility as an all-purpose solution. At best, corporate social responsibility is a fair weather volunteer. To address the problems of corporate power catalogued in Chapter I requires more than corporate voluntary virtue. With the collapse of corporate law and ineffectuality of corporate responsibility, we need a new mechanism to shape corporate behavior.

● *Why is there one conglomerate of a bill to cope with governance, disclosure, employees rights, and concentration, instead of dealing with each substantive problem separately?* Corporate reform legislation has been historically piecemeal and trivial, attacking the results of corporate abuse but rarely its causes. After great effort, a reform bill becomes law once in a generation—a Clayton Act; the securities acts. Invariably, however, its proponents come to realize that the problem of unaccountable corporate power is far larger than any narrow remedy. To contain that power requires a systemic, integrated approach like federal chartering.

By systemic we mean a reform that confronts causes and not effects, that addresses fundamental issues of the legitimacy and accountability of corporations in a constitutional democracy. By integrated, we mean that the various solutions to corporate abuse are in fact interrelated—as they were in the early 1800s, when chartering laws simultaneously dealt with a company's absolute size, its internal governance, and disclosure. For example, less concentrated and more competitive markets require broad disclosure to inform consumers, competitors and potential competitors. In turn, more competition would inspire more comparative advertisements, which would disclose more pertinent facts about a firm's product. Increased competition and disclosure should improve the way a corporation is governed, for challenge and exposure tend to discourage the vast waste and autocratic abuses that flourish in giant firms. Governance rules to encourage more democracy should lead to the elevation of more competent and responsible corporate leaders, which will lead to more law-abiding decisions generally. A comprehensive Federal Chartering Act would depend on the "internal" checks of corporate democracy and the "external" checks of disclosure, competition, and constituency remedies to safeguard against corporate abuses. The omission of any prop weakend the entire structure.

● *It can't pass.* Unless one is a Rip Van Winkle, it is impossible to ignore the precipitous decline in public confidence in business. Given the recent performance of our major companies in the economy and in court, this trend should hardly be surprising. Opinion Research Corporation polls found that while in 1965 52 percent of the public thought there was too much power concentrated in a few companies, 75 percent thought so in 1973; and while 37 percent thought that large corporations should be broken up in 1965, 53 percent believed so in 1973. According to Louis Harris, 55 percent of the public had "great" confidence in major companies in 1966; by 1974 that had fallen to 18 percent. Another Harris survey in 1973 found 77 percent of the public wanted the Nixon Administration to be "tougher on business" in the next four years. Finally, in September 1975, pollster Peter Hart found that 49 percent of those surveyed agreed that "big business is the source of most of what's wrong in this country today" while 45 percent disagreed; and, by 49 percent to 39 percent, poll respondents agreed it would do "more good than harm" to "develop a new political movement to challenge the influence of big business."

Even Congress seems to be getting the message. The 45 Senators who voted to break up the oil industry in October 1975 were merely reflecting the widespread sense that an oligopolistic oil industry, profiting in conjunction with the parallel OPEC cartel, could no longer hide behind the slogan of a free enterprise system. As for federal chartering itself, support could come from benefiting consumer, shareholder, labor, taxpayer, and small business groups. John Tunney, a liberal Democratic Senator, supports federal chartering; so do moderate Democratic legislators such as Senator Henry Jackson (for oil companies) and Rep. James Stanton; so did former Senator Marlow Cook, a conservative Republican. Indeed, even the speakers at a June 1975 conference of 130 securities lawyers, according to *The New York Times*, "reached a consensus that there is a need to provide new controls to curb wrongdoing by corporate management."

● *Federal chartering will lead to the federal takeover of business, or to socialism.* Federal chartering is approximately as socialistic as federal charters for banks, which have existed since 1864, or the Justice Department proposal in 1975 to shift regulation of insurance from the states to Washington. This matters little to proponents of such an argument. With each overdue legislative constraint on business, those with something to lose predict catastrophe. In 1934 Richard Whitney, then president of the New York Stock Exchange, warned that the enactment of that year's securities act would lead to the nationalization of all industry. The next year Wendell Willkie, who was president of the Commonwealth & Southern Corp., a utility holding company, said that the Public Utility Holding Company Act would destroy the value of investments in utility stocks. This syndrome has its more modern variants—usually regarding the costs of additional safety and pollution controls—but its essential character is unchanged: those with an investment in the status quo have a self-interest to exaggerate the costs of change. That federal chartering's premise of more decentralized competition is the precise opposite of socialism will probably not blunt the contention of people who equate corporate oligarchy with the Republic.

If anything, the precise reverse of federal chartering could lead to a federal takeover. As big business grows bigger, less accountable, and less law-abiding, government will be compelled to extend its authority over this rogue elephant in our midst. "Big business collectivism in industry," Franklin Roosevelt observed, "compels an ultimate collectivism in government." In 1905, Boston attorney Louis Brandeis, more dramatically, made a similar point:

The greatest factors making for communism, socialism, or anarchy among a free people are the excesses of capital, because as Lincoln said of slavery,

"Every drop of blood drawn with the lash shall be requited by another drawn with the sword." . . . [E]very excess of capital must in time be repaid by the excessive demands of those who have not the capital. Every act of injustice on the part of the rich will be met by another act or many acts of injustice on the part of the people. If the capitalists are wise, they will aid us in the effort to prevent injustice.

In our view, the issue is whether the competitive enterprise system can be made to work equitably and efficiently. Federal chartering can help attain this end. Grounded in competition and the Constitution, federal chartering is easily compatible with the principles that are supposed to govern our society and economy. "It is not creative minds that produce revolutions," wrote H. G. Wells in *The Salvaging of Civilization*, "but the obstinate conservation of established authority. It is the blank refusal to accept the idea of an orderly evolution toward new things that gives a revolutionary quality to every constructive proposal."

Notes on Sources

I. The Corporate Impact

Data on largest corporations: Fortune, May, 1975, at 208. See also Ralph Nader, Mark Green, and Joel Seligman, *Constitutionalizing the Corporation: The Case for the Federal Chartering of Giant Corporations* (hereinafter referred to as *Constitutionalizing*) (The Corporate Accountability Research Group, 1976), Appendix A, at 498–500.

Examples of corporate managers' power: See Vandiver, "Why Should My Conscience Bother Me?" in *In the Name of Profit* (R. Heilbroner, ed.) (1972), and M. Mintz and J. Cohen, *America, Inc.* 257–260 (1971).

Analysts who perceive large corporations to be like private governments: A. A. Berle, *The 20th Century Capitalist Revolution* (1954); W. Hamilton, *The Politics of Industry* (1957); Dahl, "Governing the Giant Corporation," in *Corporate Power in America* 10 (R. Nader and M. Green, eds.) (1973); Latham, "The Body Politic of the Corporation," in *The Corporation in Modern Society* 220 (Mason, ed.) (1959); R. Eells, *The Government of Corporations* (1962); J. K. Galbraith, *The New Industrial State* (1967); A. Miller, *The Supreme Court and American Capitalism* (1968).

Friedmann view: Friedmann, "Corporate Power, Government by Private Groups, and the Law," 57 *Columbia Law Review* 155, 176 (1957).

INDUSTRIAL POLLUTION

U.S. Steel coke plant: The New York Times, August 27, 1972, III, at 3.

Anita Summers observation: Summers, "Hidden Charges: The Costs Corporations Don't Bear," 10 *Business and Society Rev.* 85 (Spring, 1974).

1946–1971 increase in levels of pollution: B. Commoner, *The Closing Circle* 143–145 (1971).

Industrial pollution accounts for one-third of all solid waste, one half of all air pollution, and one half of total water pollution: Council on Economic Priorities, *Guide to Corporations* 14 (1974).

Cancer Institute and World Health Organization find pollution causes cancer: Washington Post, February 16, 1975, at K1, K8.

Health and property costs of pollution: See section on Pollution in Chapter V.

TOXIC SUBSTANCES

B. F. Goodrich—vinyl chloride example: Page and Munsing, "Occupational Health and the Federal Government: The Wages are Still Bitter," 38 *Law and Contemporary Problems* 651–2 (1974).

Johns-Manville plant: Washington Post, May 22, 1972, at 1.

PHS survey on beryllium: "Beryllium," *Environment*, April, 1974, at 35–6; *see also*, "The Disease of the Century," *Time*, October 20, 1975, at 67.

Maximum liability only $12,500: K. W. Kapp, *The Social Costs of Private Enterprise* (2nd edition, 1970).

DISCRIMINATION

Only 15 women among 2,500 senior executives: Business Week, November 24, 1975, at 58.

Only six women among 1,008 directors of 67 largest California firms: "Power to Which People?" *New Republic,* February 20, 1971, at 9.

Black, female income differentials: U.S. Dept. of Commerce, *The Social and Economic Status of the Black Population in the United States* 1973 2 (1974); U.S. Dept. of Labor, *Women Workers Today* 6 (1974).

Brimmer on new drift toward inequality: Washington Post, February 24, 1976, at A16.

WHITE COLLAR BLUES

Blue collar blues: See generally, The Department of HEW's report of December, 1972, *Work in America,* and R. Sennett and J. Cobb, *The Hidden Injuries of Class* (1973).

Job alienation found by American Management Association: New York Times, June 3, 1973, IV, at 12.

John DeLorean: Quoted in, Loving, Jr., "The Automobile Industry Has Lost Its Masculinity," *Fortune,* September, 1973, 187, 264, 268.

Wilmington conference on business management: Washington Post, May 14, 1972, at F1.

Business Week on the breakdown in innovation: Business Week, February 16, 1976, at 56.

POLITICAL POWER

Wertheimer on "explosion" of corporate money in politics: Washington Post, March 10, 1976. at A12.

Elmer Bobst's friends in high places: Washington Post, January 29, 1972, at A2.

On lobbying generally: See sources to Chapter V section on lobbying.

THE CORPORATE WELFARE SYSTEM

$3.2 billion in cash subsidies; $21.2 billion in tax subsidies paid to corporations: See *Federal Subsidy Programs,* A Staff Study prepared for the use of the Subcommittee on Priorities and Economy in Government of the Joint Economic Committee (October 18, 1974).

Ferguson studies of the Maritime industry: cited in H. Saxner, "On Troubled Waters: Subsidies, Cartels, and the Maritime Commission," in M. Green (ed.) *The Monopoly Makers* (1973).

Congressman Vanik analysis: Cong. Rec., October 7, 1975 at 1.

DISC: S. Surrey, "Tax Subsidies as a Device for Implementing Government Policy: A Comparison with Direct Government Expenditures," in The Economics of Federal Subsidy Programs, A compendium of papers submitted to the Joint Economic Committee, Part I, 74–105 (May 8, 1972). More recent illustrations of Surrey's criticisms may be found in R. Brandon, J. Rowe and T. Stanton, *Tax Politics* (1976).

$39.5 billion for defense procurement. "100 Companies—Companies receiving the Largest Dollar Volume of Military Prime Contract Awards, Fiscal Year 1975," issued by Department of Defense (November 21, 1975).

Criticisms of defense contracts: L. Ellsworth, "Defense Procurement: 'Everyone Feeds at the Trough,' " in M. Green (ed.), *The Monopoly Makers* (1973).

Cost of ICC, CAB, FCC regulation: See M. Green, "Uncle Sam the Monopoly Man," in *id.*

Conclusion of the Joint Economic Committee: Federal Subsidy Programs, supra, at 3.

PRIVACY INVASIONS

Senator Edward Long's hearings: See generally, E. Long, *The Intruders* (1966).

Senate Subcommittee on Constitutional Rights: "Privacy, Polygraphs, and Employment," a study prepared by the Staff of the Subcommittee on Constitutional Rights of the Committee on the Judiciary, U.S. Senate, 93rd Cong., 2d. Sess., (November, 1974).

LOCAL SWAY

Union Camp manager: J. Fallows, *The Water Lords* 95 (1971).

U.S. Steel in Gary, Indiana: On the Impact and Administration of the Property Tax, Hearings before the Subcommittee on Intergovernmental Operations of the Senate Government Operations Committee, 92nd Cong., 1st Sess. (June 26, 1972).

Dorgan on largest corporations avoidance of state tax liabilities: Rosapepe, "Corporations and State Taxes: The Big Ones Get Away," *The Washington Monthly,* January, 1975, at 14.

Studies of lack of civic involvement: See generally, "The Bifurcation of Power in a Satellite City," in *Community Political Systems* (M. Janowitz, ed.) (1961); and K. David and R. L. Blomstrom, *Business, Society and Environment Social Power and Social Response* 267–268 (1971).

C. Wright Mills: Small Business and Civic Welfare: Report of the Smaller War Plants Corporation to the Special Committee to Study Problems of American Small Business, U.S. Senate, 79th Congress, 2nd Sess., Doc. No. 135 (1946). *See also,* a study that same year finding similar correlations between large scale corporate farming and farming communities. *Small Business and the Community—A Study in Central Valley in California on Effects of Scale of Farm Operations,* Report of the Special Committee to Study Problems of American Small Business, U.S. Senate, 79th Cong., 2nd Sess., Comm. Print No. 13 (1946).

DECEPTIVE INFORMATION

Top 100 advertisers spent $3.6 billion in 1974: Advertising Age, May 12, 1975, at 76.

Study of limiting advertising expenditures to three percent of sales revenues: Comanor and Wilson, *Advertising and the Distribution of Consumer Demand* (Stanford Graduate School of Business, Res. Paper No. 160) (1973).

Potlatch Forests picture of clear water river: R. Heilbroner (ed.), *In the Name of Profit* 252–253 (1972).

Television manufacturers ads 60 percent inadequately substantiated: Advertising for Television Sets: A Public Interest Evaluation, Committee Print by The Institute for Public Interest Representation, the Senate Commerce Committee, 92nd Cong., 2nd Sess. (December, 1972).

PRODUCT SAFETY

Drug overprescription: See, Washington Post, May 21, 1974, at A2.

Cosmetics injure 60,000 annually: New York Times, February 6, 1972, at 66.

DC 10 cargo doors: Wall Street Journal, March 3, 1975, at 17.

Report of the National Commission on Product Safety: Final Report of the National Commission on Product Safety 1 (June, 1970).

CORPORATE CONCENTRATION

Judge Learned Hand dictum: United States v. Aluminum Co. of America, 148 F.2d. 416, 427 (2d Cir. 1946).

Galbraith's market system and planning system: J. Galbraith, *Economics and the Public Purpose* (1973).

Data on increasing concentration: See sources to Chapter VII.

Federal Trade Commission estimate of higher prices: See, Scanlon, "FTC and Phase II: The McGovern Papers," 5 *Antitrust Law & Econ. Rev.* 19, 33 (Spring, 1972).

Scherer on waste: F. M. Scherer, *Industrial Market Structure and Economic Performance* 405 (1970).

MULTINATIONAL CORPORATIONS

AFL-CIO on job exportation: "An American Trade Union View of International Trade and Investment," in *Multinational Corporations: A Compendium of Papers,* Senate Finance Committee, at 62 (1973). *See,* Chapter II in R. Barnet and R. Muller, *Global Reach* (1974) (hereinafter Barnet and Muller).

U.N. study of profits taken out of Latin America: Cited in, Barnet and Muller, at 139, 152, and 153.

Transfer-pricing: See, Nader and Green, "Is the 'Worldcorp' Above the Law? Time for the U.N. to Move," *War/Peace Report,* September/October, 1973, at 4.

Multinationals prefer capital-intensive production to labor-intensive production needed in underdeveloped nations: E. L. Schumacher, *Small is Beautiful* (1971). *See also,* R. Ledogar, *Hungry for Profits* (1975).

CONCENTRATION OF WEALTH AND INCOME

Wealth, income maldistribution: See, J. Pechman and B. Okner, *Who Bears the Tax Burden?* (1974); W. Bell, R. Lekachman and O. Schoir, *Public Policy and Income Distribution* (1973); B. Moore, Jr., *A Modest Proposal for the Reform of the Capitalist System* 1 (1974).

BUSINESS CRIME

Sutherland on business leaders as subversives: E. Sutherland, *White Collar Crime* (1949).

Special Prosecutor's Office prosecutions for violations of campaign finance laws: New York Times, August 24, 1975, III, at 7; an additional firm was subsequently convicted.

The Securities and Exchange Commission's disclosure cases: Chairman Roderick Hills testimony before the Senate Banking Committee, March 3, 1976.

Internal Revenue Service to question 1,200 firms: Washington Star, April 8, 1976, at D-8.

Nine grain companies shortweighing: See, e.g., Washington Post, March 3, 1976, at 1.

W. T. Grant executives alleged kickbacks: Business Week, February 24, 1975, at 74.

60 percent of Fortune 1000 respondents agree "many price-fix": M. Green, B. Moore, Jr., and B. Wasserstein, *The Closed Enterprise System* 472 (1972).

II. The Collapse of State Corporation Law

English origins of corporate law: S. Williston, "History of the Law of Business Corporations Before 1800," 3 *Harvard L. Rev.* 105 and 149 (1888); J. Davis, *Essays in the Earlier History of American Corporations* (1917), II, at 3–33 and 291–330. *See also,* W. Cary, *Corporations* 1–5 (1969).

At most 40 business corporations chartered prior to Constitutional Convention: Davis, *supra,* at 3–33.

Rostow calls them "puny": E. Rostow, "To Whom and for What End Is Corporate Management Responsible?", in E. S. Mason (ed.), *The Corporation in Modern Society* 50 (1959).

Economy "addicted to agriculture": Alexander Hamilton's celebrated complaint, *The Federalist Papers*, No. 11. *See also*, Hamilton's *Report on the Subject of Manufacturers* (1791).

Colonial capital formation unusual outside of the family: See, e.g., D. Bell, "The Breakup of Family Capitalism" in his collection of essays, *The End of Ideology* (1960). On the role of the corporation in the colonial economy, *see generally*, S. Bruchey, *The Roots of American Economic Growth* (1968); V. Clark, *History of Manufacturers in the United States*, 1607–1860 (1929); O. and M. Handlin, *Commonwealth, A Study of the Role of Government in the American Economy, Massachusetts, 1774–1861* (1969); R. Robertson, *History of the American Economy* (1964); and A. Schlesinger, Jr., "Ideas and the Economic Process" in S. Harris (ed.), *American Economic History* (1961).

Almost overnight corporation become an important instrument of economic development: Handlin, *supra* 61–63, 78–80, 98–99, and 106–114 and Davis, *supra*, 326–328.

The number of incorporations soared: Davis, *supra*, 26 and 291.

Dodd on chartering of manufacturing corporations during War of 1812: E. Dodd, "Corporations" in the *Encyclopedia Britannica*, VI, at 524 (1971).

The privilege of limited liability: E. Dodd, *American Business Corporations Until 1860 With Special Reference to Massachusetts* (1954).

THE JACKSONIAN REACTION

Jackson vetoes the Act to extend the term of the Second Bank of the United States: Jackson's Veto Message *quoted in* A. Schlesinger, *The Age of Jackson* 90 (1945). *See also*, Handlin, *supra*, at 218.

Gouge's attack on all corporate privileges: Gouge *quoted in*, J. Hurst, *The Legitimacy of the Business Corporation* 30 (1970).

Industrialization accelerated between 1830–1860: Robertson, *supra*, 197–202; Bruchey, *supra*, 194–207, 83–87, and 139–140; and Dodd, *American Business Corporations Until 1860*, 258, 376, and 338–339.

Jacksonian politics transformed the nature of the business corporation: Dodd, *American Business Corporations Until 1860*, 287–288 and 283; *Liggett v. Lee*, 288 U.S. 517, 541 n. 4 (Brandeis, J., in dissent) (1933); R. Larcom, *The Delaware Corporation* 2–3 (1937).

General incorporation acts imposed size, line of business, capital, term, and geographic limits: See, Brandeis dissent in *Liggett v. Lee*; A. Bickel (ed.), *The Unpublished Opinions of Mr. Justice Brandeis* 142–144 (1957); Dodd, *American Business Corporations Until 1860*, at 317–318, 325; and A. Berle and G. Means, *The Modern Corporation and Private Property* 119–140 (Rev. Ed., 1968) (hereinafter, Berle and Means).

Shareholder powers explicitly established: Berle and Means, at 122–129, and E. Dodd, "Statutory Developments in Business Corporations Law, 1886–1936," 50 *Harv. L. Rev.* 27, 33 (1936).

Brandeis on Jacksonians fear of corporate power: Bickel *supra*, at 140–141.

THE TRUSTS

Jacksonian economy atomized: See, A. Chandler, "The Beginning of 'Big Business' in American Industry," 33 *Bus. Hist. Rev.* 1, 4 (1959).

The genesis of a national railroad system and the expanded urban market: Id. at 4–5, and 28–29; and Robertson, *supra*, at 280–282.

Lloyd on railroads: H. D. Lloyd, *Wealth Against Commonwealth* 11 (1936).

Gentlemen's agreements and output pools: W. Stevens, *Industrial Combinations and Trusts* 1 (1913); and H. Faulkner, "Consolidation of Business" in E. Rozwenc (ed.), *Roosevelt, Wilson, and The Trusts* (1950).

Rockefeller secures railroad rebates in 1871: Lloyd, *supra*, at 9–10; and I. Tarbell, *The History of the Standard Oil Company* 33, 38–52 (1925).

Tarbell on the collapse of independent oil interests in Cleveland: Tarbell, *supra,* at 67–68; Lloyd, *supra* at 43–44; and *Standard Oil Co.* v. *United States,* 221 U.S. 1 (1911).

U.S. Congress condemns South Improvement Company: Tarbell, *supra,* at 100.

Rockefeller secures control of 95 percent of all refined oil shipments: Id. at 145–146; and Faulkner, *supra,* at 10–11.

The formation of the Standard Oil Trust: Faulkner, *supra,* and Tarbell, *supra,* at 224–229.

The formation of other trusts: Stevens, *supra,* at 13; Faulkner, *supra,* at 7; and H. Wilgus, "Need of A National Incorporation Law," 2 *Michigan L. Rev.* 358, 368 (1903).

1877 Supreme Court decision on constitutionality of railroad regulation: Munn v. *Illinois,* 94 U.S. 113 (1877). Other state laws described in Robertson, *supra,* at 289–291.

State antitrust laws through 1890: Faulkner, *supra,* at 15; and *Report of the United States Industrial Commission* (1900–1902), II, Table following page 264.

New York court rules trust illegal, 1887–1892: On legal issues concerning the early trust cases, *see* S.C.T. Dodd's partisan—through informative—article, "The Present Legal Status of Trusts," 7 *Harv. L. Rev.* 157 (1893).

Ohio Supreme Court holding in Standard Oil case: State ex rel. Attorney v. *Standard Oil Company,* 49 Ohio St. 137, 30 N.E. 279.

Rockefeller's alleged violations of law: see, e.g., Tarbell, *supra,* II, at 129–140 and 256–269.

NEW JERSEY—"THE TRAITOR STATE"

Rockefeller analogy of the growth of a large business to the American Beauty Rose: Rockefeller remark *quoted in* J. Galbraith, *The Affluent Society* 71–72 (Rev. Ed., 1969). On history of corporate law in New Jersey, *see,* J. Dill, "National Incorporation Laws for Trusts," 11 *Yale L. Jour.* 273 (1902) and L. Steffens, "New Jersey: A Traitor State," 25 *McClure's* 41 (1905).

Bribery of Governor of New Jersey: Steffens, *supra,* at 41–45. For evidence supporting Steffens charge, *see,* original shareholder list in Corporation Trust Company of New Jersey certification of incorporation on file with Secretary of State, Trenton, New Jersey. *See also,* H. Stoke, "Economic Influences Upon the Corporation Laws of New Jersey," 30 *Jour. of Pol. Econ.* 551 (1930). For a more benign explanation, *see,* E. Keasbey, "New Jersey and the Great Corporations," 13 *Harv. L. Rev.* 198, 264 (1899).

New Jersey's 1891 Act: Steffens, supra, at 46–48; Stoke, *supra* note 51, at 571; and Larcom, *supra,* at 60–62.

New Jersey repeals Antitrust Law in 1892: Stoke, *supra,* at 209.

Dill chairs Revision Committee which produces 1896 Act: Steffens, *supra,* at 45–48; and Stoke, *supra,* at 572.

1896 Holding Company provision: Statute *quoted in* Steffens, *supra,* at 47. Other 1896 provisions affecting corporate size and purposes in Stoke, *supra,* at 572–573; and Keasbey, *supra,* at 208.

1896 statute revises capitalization requirements: Steffens, *supra,* at 48; *Report of the United States Industrial Commission* (1900–1902), I. at 248–249, 251, and 1080–1081; and W. Ripley, *Main Street and Wall Street* 101, 205 (1927).

Shareholder control eviscerated by 1896 Act: S. McReynolds, "The Home of Trusts," 4 *World's Work* 2526 (1902), and *Report of the United States Industrial Commission,* I, at 243.

After 1896 Act the largest corporation flock to New Jersey: For detailed presentation of this data, see *Constitutionalizing* at 46. Sources: McReynolds, *supra;* Stoke, *supra,* at 574; Steffens, *supra,* at 49; and G. A. Evans, *Business Incorporations in the United States 1800–1943* 59 (1948).

Montague estimates 95 percent of major corporations chartered in New Jersey by 1900: Montague *quoted in* Stoke, *supra,* at 574.

U.S. Steel incorporated in New Jersey in 1901: J. Moody, *The Truth About the Trusts,* 453 (1904).

Moody's Greater Industrial Trusts: Id. at 453–468, and 486.

Livermore's combinations, 1888–1905: S. Livermore, "The Success of Industrial Mergers," *Quarterly Journal of Economics* (November, 1935).

Kaplan's major trusts: A. D. H. Kaplan, *Big Enterprise in a Competitive System* (1954).

New Jersey's only concern, according to Steffens, "Does it Pay?": Steffens, *supra.*

Governor brags about state surplus: Id. at 50; and Stoke, *supra,* at 574–575.

1886 Supreme Court decision: Santa Clara County v. Southern Pac. R.R., 118 U.S. 394.

New Jersey's retaliatory statutes: Stoke, *supra,* at 576; Dill, *supra,* at 284–285, and 287; and *Report of the United States Industrial Commission,* I, at 227.

West Virginia, Maine, Delaware, Maryland and Kentucky enter the chartermongering business: Report of the United States Industrial Commission, I, at 241, 247–248, and 1078–1079; Stoke, *supra,* at 575–576; and Keasbey, *supra,* at 201–202. Actually West Virginia had sent its Secretary of State to New York City to sell corporate charters before New Jersey went into the business. But he was not received very enthusiastically, both because West Virginia had retained a $5,000,000 capital stock limitation and because "tramp" corporations—those organized in one state to do business in another—were still considered suspect.

Law review note describes survival of unfit state laws: Note, "State Laws: Survival of the Unfit," 62 *University of Pennsylvania Law Review* 509, 510, and 514 (1914).

Massachusetts and New York gut their laws to reduce attractions of New Jersey: Dill, *supra,* at 282; and Dodd, 50 *Harvard Law Review* at 34–39.

1904 Committee on Uniform Incorporation Law conclusions: quoted in Note, 62 *University of Pennsylvania Law Review* at 511–512.

By 1912 New Jersey had reshaped the corporate law of virtually every state in its image: J. Baker, "The Evil of Special Privilege," *Yale Law J.* 220, 222–223 (1912).

Wilson criticizes New Jersey corporate laws: Wilson quoted in 96 *The Nation* 91 (January 23, 1913).

Penitent legislature enacts Seven Sisters Act in 1913: Id. at 91; and Stoke, *supra,* at 577–579.

DELAWARE—OPERA BOUFFE

Marvel's pamphlet advertising Delaware's 1899 law: Quoted in Note, "Little Delaware Makes A Bid for the Organization of Trusts," 33 *Am. L. Rev.* 418 (1899). *See generally,* E. Latty, "Why Are Business Corporation Laws Largely 'Enabling'?" 50 *Cornell Law Quarterly* 599, 602–603 (1965); Larcom, *supra,* at 9–10, and *Report of the United States Industrial Commission,* I, at 241, 248, 1079, and 1119–1123.

Delaware Assembly amends constitution to conform to 1899 corporate law: Larcom, *supra,* at 84–88.

Wall Street initially shuns Delaware: See, Moody, *supra,* on number of major corporations chartered in Delaware through 1904. On reaction of New York bar, *see,* Note, 33 *American Law Review* 418; Note, "Delaware Missionary Enterprise," 33 *American Law Review* 794 (1899); and Book Review, "Smith's Delaware Corporation Law," 33 *American Law Review* 945 (1899).

1899 Law Review note derides Delaware legislative: Note, 33 *American Law Review* at 418.

Delaware retained features of New Jersey law which permitted economic concentration: Larcom, *supra,* at 60–62.

Delaware also permitted stock pyramiding: Berle and Means, at 184–185 and 68–70; J. Bonbright and G. Means, *The Holding Company* (1932); and Larcom, *supra,* at 70.

Dodd calls Delaware "The happy hunting ground for corporate promoter": Dodd, 50 *Harvard Law Review* at 27.

Shareholders disenfranchised by non-voting stock: A. Berle, "Investors and the Revised Delaware Corporation Act," 29 *Columbia Law Review* 563 (1929); A. Berle, "Corporations and the

Public Investor" 20 *American Economic Review* 54 (1930); Berle and Means, *supra;* Hurst, *supra,* at 148–149; Ripley, *supra,* at 84–85, 52–53, and 123–124; and W. H. S. Stevens, "Stockholders Voting Rights and the Centralization of Voting Control," *Quarterly Journal of Economics,* May, 1926, at 353.

Dividend rights prejudiced: Berle, 20 *American Economic Review,* at 61–65; and Berle and Means, at 136–138.

Blank stock created: Berle, 29 *Columbia Law Review,* at 563–564; and J. Flynn, "Why Corporations Leave Home," *The Atlantic Monthly,* September, 1932, at 268.

Similarly, stock purchase options could be issued: Berle, 29 *Columbia Law Review,* at 565–570; Berle, 20 *American Economic Review,* at 64; and Berle and Means, at 167–170.

Berle on "The Power of Confiscation": Berle, 29 *American Economic Review,* at 65.

Delaware home for one-third of New York Stock Exchange in 1932: Flynn, *supra,* at 270. See also, Larcom, *supra,* at 175–176; and C. Ward, "Delaware's 'Black Flag': An Answer to John T. Flynn's Article in September (1932) Atlantic Monthly Entitled 'Why Corporations Leave Home,' " a pamphlet published by the Corporation Service Company, Wilmington, Delaware (1932). Proxy holders charade described throughout the Flynn article.

Delaware's legislature never questioned the propriety of revisions suggested by New York bar, 1913–1934: G. Harrington, *The Legislative History of the Delaware General Incorporation Act 1899 to 1933,* 1933, (Masters Thesis on file with Harvard Law School Library, Cambridge, Massachusetts).

Corporate franchise taxes averaged 31 percent, 1913–1934: Constitutionalizing, at 535–536.

Judge Landis would have indicted Delaware if he could: Landis quoted in Ripley, *supra,* at 32–33.

DELAWARE FOREVER

By 1963 other states more competitive: W. Cary, *Corporations,* at 10–11; W. Cary, "Federalism and Corporate Law: Reflections Upon Delaware," 83 *Yale Law Journal* 663, 665–668 (1974); and E. Folk, "Some Reflections of a Corporation Law Draftsman," 42 *Connecticut Law Journal* 409, 409–410, and 419 (1968).

Secretary of State Dukes troubled by events of 1963: Interviews with Samuel Arsht, partner, Morris Nichols, Arsht & Tunnell, Wilmington, Delaware, January 15, 1975 and Margaret Storey, Executive Vice President, Corporation Service Company, Wilmington, Delaware, January 16, 1975. Monthly compilations of incorporations tabulated by Division of Corporations, Secretary of State, Dover, Delaware.

Governor Carvel warns against "wrangling": Wilmington Morning News, March 5, 1963.

Legislature appropriates $25,000 to revise law on December 31, 1963: Comment, "Law for Sale: A Study of the Delaware Corporation Law of 1967," 117 *University of Pennsylvania Law Review* 861 (1969).

Dukes appoints himself and nine others to Revision Committee: Id. at 864–865.

Commission delegates its authority to a three man Drafting Committee: Id. at 864–865. The two attorneys still living who were on the three man Drafting Committee have disputed this. See, S. Arsht, "A History of the Delaware Corporation Law", 1 *Journal of Delaware Corporate Law* 1 (1976); and *Wilmington News Journal,* January 25, 1976, at 1.

Professor Folk excluded from deliberations of Drafting Committee: Comment, 117 *University of Pennsylvania Law Review* 865–869.

Committee corresponded with leading corporate law firms: Id. at 867–868.

Revisions written in Arsht's office: Id. at 867–869.

Corroon expected little trouble with Delaware General Assembly: R. Corroon, "The Proposed New Delaware Corporation Statute", 20 *Jour. of Legal Ed.* 522 (1968).

The Commission never expected the legislature to do anything but pass the law: Comment, 117 *University of Pennsylvania Law Review*, at 869.

Delaware "home" for 448 of 1,000 largest corporations: See detailed treatment in *Constitutionalizing*, Appendix B, at 501–531. Delaware's income from corporate related fees and taxes is detailed in *Constitutionalizing*, Appendix C, at 532–538.

1974 report to Governor on franchise tax revenues: Governor's Franchise Tax Study Committee, *Final Report to the Governor* 6 (1974).

Court decision granting incumbent management power to cause corporation to re-purchase shares to avoid a take-over: Cheff v. Mathes, 41 Del. Ch. 494, 199 A.2d 548 (1964).

Decision eliminated appraisal rights if merger labelled a sale of assets: Hariton v. Arco Electronics, Inc., 41 Del. Ch. 74, 188 A.2d 123 (1963).

Decisions prejudicing rights of minority shareholders in subsidiaries in deference to business judgment rule: Chasin v. Gluck, 282 A.2d 188 (Del. Ch. 1971); *Sinclair Oil Corp. v. Levien*, 280 A.2d 717 (Del. Ch. 1971); and *Getty Oil Co. v. Skelley Oil Co.*, 267 A.2d 883 (Del. Ch. 1970).

Decision furthering decline of the board of directors: Graham v. Allis-Chalmers Mfg. Co., 40 Del. Ch. 335, 182 A.2d 328 (Ch. 1962), *aff'd.* 41 Del. Ch. 78, 188 A.2d 125 (1963).

New York attorney explains Delaware legislature will do anything it can for management: New York attorney *quoted in Business Week*, June 8, 1968, at 40.

Delaware Supreme Court dominated by corporate bar: Cary, 83 *Yale Law Journal* at 690–692.

Cary analysis of Ward v. Village of Monroeville: Id. at 697–698.

Folk's eulogy of state corporation law: E. Folk, "Does State Corporation Law Have a Future?", *Georgia State Bar Journal*, February, 1972, at 311–312.

III. The Federal Chartering Alternative

Stone on arranging things so that people who call the shots do not bear full risks: C. Stone, *Where the Law Ends* 46 (1975).

Business executives convicted of Watergate campaign finance violations not discharged: The New York Times, August 24, 1975, III, at 1.

Chayes on corporations as first successful claimant of unregulated power since the nation state: Chayes, "The Modern Corporation and the Rule of Law," in E. S. Mason (ed.), *The Corporation in Modern Society* (1959) at 37.

Hamilton on irresponsible power: W. Hamilton, "Foreword to the DuPont-General Motors Decision: The Merger Problem in a New Perspective," 46 *Georgetown Law Journal* 561, 563 (1958).

Government minority stockholder in First and Second Banks of the United States: See, L. Watkins, "Federalization of Corporations," 13 *Tennessee Law Review* 89, 92, and 95 (1935) and *McCulloch v. Maryland*, 4 Wheat. 316 (1819).

American government acquired all shares of Panama Railroad: Watkins, *supra*, at 95–96.

World War I federally owned corporations: Id. at 96.

China Trade Act: 15 U.S.C. 141.

1924 Inland Waterways Corporation: Watkins, *supra*, at 97.

Tennessee Valley Authority did what private capital would not: 16 U.S.C. 831–31dd.

The Confederation granted a national charter to Bank of America in 1781: Watkins, *supra*, at 95.

Dispositive 1964 Supreme Court decision: Heart of Atlanta Motel, Inc. v. United States et al., 379 U.S. 241.

Madison proposed Constitution empower Congress to grant charters: See, Note, "Federal Chartering of Corporations: Constitutional Challenges," 61 *Georgetown Law Journal* 123, 125–126 (1972).

Jefferson anxious First Bank would overawe the States: H. Wilgus, "Need of a National Incorporation Law," 2 *Michigan Law Review* 358, 379–380 (1904).

Roosevelt on need for publicity of facts regarding giant industrial combinations: quoted in G. Leinwand, *A History of the United States Federal Bureau of Corporations* (1903–1914) 1962 (doctoral dissertation, New York University) at 56.

New York Times criticism of Bureau of Corporations legislation: Id. at 80.

Theodore Roosevelt refers to work of Bureau as "tentative": Id. at 108.

Between 1903 and 1914 Roosevelt, Taft and Wilson supported federal chartering: Leinwand, *supra,* at 142–144; and Note, *supra,* 61 *Georgetown Law Journal* at 126.

Wickersham drafted federal licensing bill and proposed it to Congress in 1910: Leinwand, *supra,* at 142–143; and Watkins, *supra,* 13 *Tennessee Law Review* at 93.

Wall Street Journal favors federal chartering in 1908: Quoted in Federal Trade Commission, *Report on Utility Corporations,* No. 69-A, September 15, 1934, at 56.

Three officials of National Association of Manufacturers favors federal chartering: Id. at 56–57.

Support for federal chartering bills, 1904–1914: Id. at 32–45.

Taft changes his mind on federal chartering in 1912: Id. at 9–10.

Senate Commerce Committee concludes federal incorporation neither necessary nor desirable: Id. at 10.

Eight bills introduced between 1915 and 1932: Id. at 42.

Franklin Delano Roosevelt regarded NRA as a form of federalization of corporations: S. Rosenman (ed.), 2 The Public Papers and Addresses of Franklin D. Roosevelt 202 (1938) ("A Recommendation to the Congress to Enact the National Industrial Recovery Act to Put People to Work, May 17, 1933").

Brief talk of replacing NRA with federal chartering: Watkins, *supra,* at 94–95.

O'Mahoney promotes National Charters for National Business: See, Temporary National Economic Committee, Final Statement of Senator Joseph C. O'Mahoney, "The Preservation of Economic Freedom" 10 (March 11, 1941); and J. O'Mahoney, "Federal Charters and Licenses for Corporation," 22 *J. of National Educational Association* 27 (1938).

IV. Who Rules the Corporation?

The statutory image of corporate governance (otherwise known as the legal norm); W. Cary, *Corporations* 150, and 190–192 (1969); D. Vagts, *Basic Corporation Law* 307–309 (1973); M. Mace, *Directors: Myth and Reality* 6–7 (1971); R. Gordon, *Business Leadership in the Large Corporation* 116 (1961); J. Bacon and J. Brown, *Corporate Directorship Practices: Role, Selection and Legal Status of the Board* 13–15 (1975); and *Lee v. Jenkins Bros.,* 298 F.2d 357, *cert. den.,* 361 U.S. 913 (1959).

Sampson's description of ITT meeting: A. Sampson, *The Sovereign State of ITT* 99–100 (1973).

Miller on decade of bad business decisions: quoted in J. Ross and M. Kami, *Corporate Management in Crisis: Why the Mighty Fall* 19 (1973).

W. T. Grant: New York Times, February 13, 1976, at 1; and *Fortune,* March, 1976, at 28.

Daylin: Business Week March 17, 1975, at 62; and July 28, 1975 at 30.

Chrysler: Fortune, May, 1975, at 176.

RCA: Fortune, December, 1975, at 17.

Rock Island Railroad: Business Week, September 29, 1975.

Bowman Instruments: Business Week, June 11, 1975, at 23.

Good Hope Industries: Business Week, December 2, 1975, at 24.

Airlines on the brink: TWA: Business Week, July 7, 1975 at 52; *Pan Am: Business Week,* July 28, 1975, at 30; *Eastern: Business Week,* December 22, 1975, at 40. See, generally, *Fortune,* February, 1975, at 59.

Gulf and Royal-Dutch Shell joint venture in General Atomic Company: Wall Street Journal, February 25, 1976, at 7.

Westinghouse: New York Times, February 1, 1976, at F4.

Pacific Gas and Electric: New York Times, February 1, 1976, at 24.

Genesco: Business Week, July 7, 1975, at 66.

U.S. Industries: Business Week, July 7, 1975, at 38.

Rapid American: Business Week, November 3, 1975, at 66.

Singer Company: Business Week, June 30, 1975 at 106; July 28, 1975, at 30 and January 12, 1976 at 30; and *Fortune,* December, 1975, at 100.

Consolidated Foods: Business Week, March 3, 1975, at 24.

General Foods: Business Week, April 21, 1975 at 34.

Ryder Systems: Business Week, April 14, 1975, at 25.

Mattel: Business Week, April 21, 1975, at 34.

Rockwell: Business Week, November 3, 1975, at 92.

ITT: Fortune, May, 1975 at 201 and June, 1975 at 110.

Gulf Corporation bribery revelations: Report of the Special Review Committee of the Board of Directors of Gulf Oil Corporation (December 30, 1975).

Northrop: Report to the Board of Directors of Northrop Corporation on the Special Investigation of the Executive Committee (July 16, 1975).

3M: Report of the Special Agent to the Board of Directors of 3M Company (October 29, 1975).

Ashland Oil: Report of the Special Committee to the Board of Directors of Ashland Oil, Inc. (June 26, 1975).

THE LEGAL BASIS OF MANAGEMENT POWER

Attendance at Campaign GM's first shareholder meeting: D. Schwartz, "The Public Interest Proxy Contest: Reflections on Campaign GM," 69 *Michigan Law Review* 419, 429 (1971).

99.7 percent of director elections uncontested: 39th Annual Report of Securities and Exchange Commission. Aggregate data for years 1956–1973 from 22nd–39th *Annual Reports* and presented in chart form in *Constitutionalizing* at 91.

THE BEST DEMOCRACY MONEY CAN BUY

Aranow and Einhorn on follow-up letters: E. Aranow and H. Einhorn, *Proxy Contests for Corporate Control* 234 (1968).

Northern State buys back an election: The saga of CAPUR is recounted in *The Progressive,* July, 1974, at 19–23; *Business and Society Review,* Winter 1974–1975, at 106; and Investor Responsibility Research Center, Analysis No. 3, Supplement No. 1, March 14, 1975 at 3–16.

Campaign GM pamphlet: Schwartz, 69 *Michigan Law Review* at 428.

Management's army in a proxy war: Aranow and Einhorn, *supra,* at 260 and 272–279; *The Wall Street Journal,* February 23, 1967, at 1; and *The New York Times,* February 23, 1969, III, at 1.

Only a dozen instances of insurgents matching management expenses in past 25 years: M. Eisenberg, "Access to Corporate Proxy Machinery," 83 *Harvard Law Review* 1489, 1501 (1970); Aranow and Einhorn, *supra,* at 262, note 43 and 543–544; and J. Livingston, *The American Stockholder* 144, note 7 (1958).

Incumbent management can use corporate personnel to campaign on its behalf: Attorney Louis Nizer memorably described the thousands of Loew's employees who made telephone calls on behalf of MGM President Vogel in Nizer's *My Life in Court* (1961). Attorneys Edward Aranow and Herbert Einhorn describe a similar contest involving an unnamed "large national corporation" in which a substantial part of the sales force was mobilized on a national scale to contact designated shareholders. Aranow and Einhorn, *supra,* at 270.

State corporate law has done nothing to correct the inequality of campaign resources: Aranow and Einhorn, *supra,* at 547–564; M. Eisenberg, 83 *Harvard Law Review* 1489; and L. Machinger "Proxy Fight Expenditures of Insurgent Shareholders," 19 *Case Western Law Review* 212 (1968).

MANAGEMENT CONTROL OF INFORMATION

Neither state nor federal law places any meaningful restrictions on amount of money management may spend reporting to shareholders: W. Cary, "Federalism and Corporate Law, Reflections Upon Delaware," 83 *Yale Law Journal* 663, 667 (1974).

Lockheed only admitted it would have collapsed after Congressional subsidy voted: 1970 Lockheed Annual Report.

SEC claims proxy rules aid corporate democracy: M. Caplin, "Shareholder Nominations of Directors: A Program for Fair Corporate Suffrage," 39 *Virginia Law Review* 141, 145–146 (1953).

Items shareholders cannot find out under SEC disclosure program: See, e.g., Comment, "Law for Sale, A Study of the Delaware Corporation Law of 1967," 117 *University of Pennsylvania Law Review* 861, 886–887, and 895 (1969).

Shareholders right to know under state law is potentially broader: Theoretically, shareholders may also seek access to corporate data under state common law, or what might more precisely be termed shareholder "inherent" rights. *See,* S. Williston, "A History of the Law of Corporations Before 1800," 2 *Harvard Law Review* 105, 149 (1888). In practice, this alternative does not add one iota to shareholders rights. Although the shareholder common law right of inspection was originally quite broad, the trend of post-World War II decisions has been to limit this "inherent" right to the same restrictions of "proper purpose", "good faith" and minimum ownership specified by the statutes. Cary, *Corporations* at 1020–1022.

Shareholders right to examine shareholder lists: Durnium v. Allentown Fed. Savings & Loan Assn., 218 F. Supp. 716 (D.C. Pa. 1963).

Courts deter excessive "stockholder agitation": See, e.g. *Martin v. Columbia Pictures Co.,* 133 N.Y.S. 2d 469, 476 (Sup. Ct. 1953).

Court power to limit shareholders to reasonable requests: See, e.g. *Delaware General Corporation Law,* section 220(c).

A&P shareholder access denied: In re McKintosh Foundation, New York Law Journal, March 18, 1974, at 2 (Sup. Ct., 1st Dept.).

Ralston Purina Shareholder access denied: State v. Ralston Purina Co., 358 S.W. 2d 772 (Mo. 1962).

Gulf Sulphur Shareholder access denied: State of Delaware ex rel. Armour v. Gulf Sulphur Corp., 233 A2d 457 (Del. Super. Ct. 1967), *aff'd.* 231 A.2d 470 (Del. Sup. Ct. 1967).

MANAGEMENT CONTROL OF THE LAW

Cumulative voting generally: Aranow and Einhorn, *supra,* at 331–347.

Professor Williams finds proxy contests twice as frequent with cumulative voting: C. Williams, *Cumulative Voting For Directors* 62–69 (1951).

23 states required cumulative voting by 1955: J. Bacon, *Corporate Directorship Practices: Membership and Committees of the Board* 8 (1973); and *Model Business Corporation Act Annotated,* section 53.

Attorney is frustrated by Wisconsin refusal to enact cumulative voting in 1950: G. Young, "The Case For Cumulative Voting," 1950 *Wisconsin Law Review* 49.

States drop cumulative voting after 1955: Compare *Wolfson v. Avery,* 126 N.E. 2d 701, 726 (Ill. 1955) with Investor Responsibility Research Center, Analysis No. 3, Supplement No. 1, March 14, 1975, at 3–14.

Cumulative voting not required in Delaware and 32 other states: Bacon, *Corporate Directorship Practices: Membership and Committees of the Board* at 8. See, *Delaware General Corporation Law,* section 214; and *Model Business Corporation Act Annotated,* section 33.

Only 15 percent of corporations in states with permissive cumulative voting provide for it: Williams, *supra,* at 13; and Bacon, *Corporate Directorship Practices: Membership and Committees of the*

Board, at 7. Conference Board statistics indicate that 17 percent of the sample had cumulative voting. However, this included a number of privately held corporations in which cumulative voting is more common. *See*, Investor Responsibility Research Center, Special Report No. 5, July 8, 1973.

In Delaware, a simple majority may repeal cumulative voting: Maddock v. Vorclone Corp., 17 Del. Ch. 39, 41–43, 147 A. 255, 256 (Ch. 1929). But c.f. *Western Air Lines, Inc. v. Sobieski*, 191 Cal. App. 2d 399, 12 Cal. Rptr. 719 (1961).

Delaware and 42 other jurisdictions allow "classification" of board: Delaware General Corporation Law, section 141(b); and *Model Business Corporation Act Annotated*, section 37. *See generally*, L. Adkins, "Corporate Democracy and Classified Directors," 11 *Business Law* 31 (1955); and E. Sell and L. Fuge, "Impact of Classified Corporate Directorates on the Constitutional Right of Cumulative Voting," 17 *University of Pittsburgh Law Review* 151 (1956).

Management may issue nonvoting stock: Delaware General Corporation Law, section 151(a).

Ford Motor Company example: Cary, *Corporations* at 409.

Only Illinois and a few other states forbid nonvoting stock: People ex rel. Watseka Tel. Co. v. Emmerson, 134 N.E. 707 (Ill. 1922). *See also*, W. Pittman, "Nonvoting Shares in Missouri," 26 *Missouri Law Review* 117 (1961); and Vagts, *supra*, at 356–357.

Stock exchanges do not list corporations without voting stock: N.Y.S.E. *Company Manual*, section A-15, at A-280; and A.S.E. *Guide*, CCH sections 10,045 and 10,003. But *see*, statements in N.Y.S.E. *Company Manual*, section A-15, at A-281–A-282.

Fifty percent of stock voted by financial intermediaries: R. Soldofsky, *Institutional Holdings of Common Stock 1900–2000* Michigan (1971). *See also*, Investor Responsibility Research Center, Special Report B., March 18, 1974, at 65; *New York Stock Exchange Fact Book* (1974), at 52; P. Blumberg, "Reflections on Proposals for Corporate Reform through Change in the Composition of the Board of Directors: 'Special Interest' or 'Public Directors'," 53 *Boston University Law Review* 547, 555–556 (1973); M. Eisenberg, "The Legal Roles of Shareholders and Management in Modern Corporate Decision Making," 57 *California Law Review*, 1, 46–48 (1969); and *Disclosure of Corporate Ownership*, prepared by the Subcommittee on Intergovernmental Relations and Subcommittee on Budgeting, Management, and Expenditures of the Committee of Operations, U.S. Senate (March 4, 1974), at 7.

The Wall Street Rule: M. Eisenberg, 57 *California Law Review*, at 46.

Recent shareholder proposals directed at social issues: Investor Responsibility Research Center, Special Report No. 5, July 8, 1973; and Special Report D, August 15, 1974. *See also*, D. Schwartz 69 *Michigan Law Review*, at 502–508; and Council on Economic Priorities newsletters entitled "Annual Meetings Preview."

Financial institutions have shown only a negligibly greater willingness to oppose management: See, *Constitutionalizing*, at 113.

MANAGEMENT CONTROL OF OTHER FUNDAMENTAL
CORPORATE DECISION MAKING

Historic shareholder rights: A. Berle and G. Means, *The Modern Corporation and Private Property* (Rev. Ed. 1968); and Eisenberg, 57 *Columbia Law Review*, at 86–90.

Delaware's rout of shareholder powers replicated by other states: Eisenberg, 57 *Michigan Law Review*, at 66–67; and *Model Business Corporation Act Annotated*.

Delaware shareholder rights during a merger subverted by three conventional loopholes: Two are statutory. Section 251 (f) eliminates the shareholder vote of the corporation surviving a merger as long as: (a) the certificate of incorporation is not amended; (b) stock rights are not altered; and (c) no more than 20 percent of the common stock of the surviving corporation outstanding immediately before the merger is delivered to the shareholders of the acquired corporation to effectuate the merger. Under this provision, a big corporation like ITT can gobble up lots of small corporations without the approval of its shareholders. Similarly, the "short form" merger provisions of section 253 permit a parent corporation owning at least 90 percent of the shares of each class of stock of a subsidiary to merge upon the mere resolution of the board. Eisenberg, 57 *Michigan Law Review*, at 69–70. *See also*, V. Brudney and M. Chirelstein, "Fair Shares in Corporate Mergers and Takeovers," 88 *Harvard Law Review* 297, 300–303 (1974).

The third loophole is judicial. Under a celebrated series of Delaware Court decisions (*See, Heilbrunn v. Sun Chem. Corp.*, 38 Del. Ch. 321, 150 A.2d 755 (Sup. Ct. 1959); *Hariton v. Arco Electronics, Inc.*, 41 Del. Ch. 74, 188 A.2d 123 (Sup. Ct. 1963); *and Orzeck v. Englehart*, 41 Del. Ch. 361, 195 A.2d 375 (Sup. Ct. 1963); rejecting the so-called "de facto" merger doctrine, a Delaware corporation may buy all of the assets or all of the stock of another corporation—and thus accomplish the ends of a merger—without being subject to the requirements of a merger vote.

Most large industrial corporations are highly diversified: See, e.g., *Fortune*, June, 1967, at 175.

Section 271 only Delaware statute concerning corporate divisions: Eisenberg, 57 *Michigan Law Review*, at 150–180.

Firms go private: See, Wall Street Journal, October 18, 1974, at 7.

Super majorities before Mergers: Wall Street Journal, April 4, 1975, at 31.

WHITHER/ WITHER THE BOARD OF DIRECTORS

Board of Directors legal role: The Model Business Corporations Act and every jurisdiction except Arizona (which has no provision on the power and qualifications of directors), Hawaii, and Maine provide that the business and affairs of a corporation shall be managed by a board of directors. *Model Business Corporation Act Annotated*, section 35. See also, R. Gordon, *supra*, at 116; The National Industrial Conference Board, *Corporate Directorship Practices* (1967); and E. Folk, *The Delaware General Corporation Law* at 611–613.

Douglas—"Directors Do Not Direct": W. O. Douglas, "Directors Who Do Not Direct," 47 *Harvard Law Review* 1305 (1934).

Drucker view: P. Drucker, *Management* 628 (1973).

Townsend's analysis: R. Townsend, *Up the Organization* 31 (1970).

Executive tells Mace nine hundred and ninety-nine times out of a thousand, the board goes along with management: M. Mace, *Directors: Myth and Reality* 46–47.

Another executive can't think of a single time board failed to support management: Id. at 47.

President chooses his successor finds Mace: Id. at 70.

Corporate president states he will tap his successor: Id. at 67.

RCA ouster of Sarnoff: Business Week, November 24, 1975, at 76.

Conference Board on failure of board to monitor chief executive: Bacon and Brown, *supra*, at 21.

Compensation committees are not decisionmaking bodies: Mace, *Directors: Myth and Reality* at 181.

Decorum at the Penn Central contributed to collapse: See, J. Daughen and P. Binzen, *The Wreck of the Penn Central* (1971).

House Banking and Currency Committee conclusion: The Penn Central Failure and the Role of Financial Institutions, Staff Report of the Committee on Banking and Currency, House of Representatives, 92nd Congress (January 3, 1972), at vii.

Board creature of chief executive: Business Week, May 22, 1971, at 50, 51 and 56.

Our survey of 200 largest industrial corporations' boards: Constitutionalizing, Appendix D, at 539–554.

Corporate president observes it is a little bit like being knighted to be a director of GM: Mace, *Directors: Myth and Reality*, at 88.

Corporate president explains you pick personal friends with prestige titles: Id. at 99.

Another executive agreed: You sure as hell are not going to ask Ralph Nader: Id. at 99.

Outside director system like a private club: Id. at 89.

An exception, Leon Sullivan at 1971 GM meeting: Wall Street Journal, May 24, 1971.

Choreography of directors meetings: Mace, *Directors: Myth and Reality* at 10–13.

Havemeyer testimony: quoted in W. Ripley, *Wall Street and Main Street* 158 (1927).

Directors little better informed today than brethren who slept before them: See, R. Townsend, Book Review of J. Daughen and P. Binzen, *The Wreck of the Penn Central, The New York Times,* December 12, 1971 (Book Review section) at 3. *See also,* M. Eisenberg, "Legal Models of Management Structure in the Modern Corporation: Officers, Directors, and Accountants, 63 *California Law Review* 375, 380 (1975).

Goldberg on monolithic recommendations: Business and Society Review, Spring 1973, at 38; and Interview, February 18, 1975, Washington, D.C.

Eisenberg on executives denying directors any access to certain categories of information: M. Eisenberg, 63 *California Law Review* at 380.

1971 survey: Cited in Id. at 380.

Directors fees: J. Bacon, *Corporate Directorship Practices: Compensation,* 1–6 and 46–47 (1973).

Our survey of 200 largest corporations: Constitutionalizing, Appendix D, at 539–554.

McMullen's description of executive committees: J. McMullen, "Committees of the Board of Directors," 29 *Bus. Law* 755, 761–762, and 766–767 (1974). *See,* also, J. Bacon and J. Brown, *Corporate Directorship Practices: Role, Selection and Legal Status of the Board* 54–56, and 61 (1975); and *Model Business Corporation Act Annotated,* section 42.

THE LIMITATIONS OF SHAREHOLDER LITIGATION

STATE LAW: THE NON-DUTY OF CARE

1867 ultra vires decision: Zabreskie v. Hackensack & N.Y.R.R., 18 N.J. Eq. 178.

Fletcher's Cyclopedia of Corporations on discarding the theory of ultra vires: Fletcher's Cyclopedia of Corporations, IV, section 3413 (Permanent Edition, 1974). *See, also, Model Business Corporation Act Annotated,* section 7; and *Delaware General Corporation Law,* section 124.

New York's statute on negligence: Business Corporation Law, section 717.

Bishop review of case law on duty of care: J. Bishop, "Sitting Ducks and Decoy Ducks: New Trends in Indemnification of Corporate Officers and Directors," 77 *Yale Law Journal* 1078, 1099 (1968). Professor Biship's conclusion was corroborated by the Wyatt Company's 1974 Directors & Officers Liability Survey. The Wyatt Company surveyed 1,321 industrial companies (including 425 on the Fortune 1000 leading industrials list) about claims of action brought against them during a six year period, 1968–1973. Not one allegation of negligence was reported.

Various grounds on which state courts will hold directors or executives liable: D. Dykstra, "The Revival of the Derivative Suit," 116 *University of Pennsylvania Law Review* 74, 77–78 (1967); and S. Klaw, "Abe Pomerantz is Watching You," *Fortune,* February, 1968, at 144.

Security for expenses provisions: See *Model Business Corporation Act Annotated,* section 49. The case for the first security for expenses provision was made in F. Woods, *Survey and Report Regarding Stockholders' Derivative Suits* (1944). *But, see,* G. Hornstein, "New Aspects of Stockholders' Derivative Actions," 47 *Columbia Law Review* 5 (1947).

Rules respecting attorneys' fees: E. Folk, *The Delaware General Corporation Law,* at 491–492; and Note, "Attorneys' Fees in Shareholder Derivative Suits: The Substantial Benefit Rule Reexamied," 60 *California Law Review* 164 (1972).

FEDERAL SECURITIES LAWS: "TAKING OVER THE UNIVERSE GRADUALLY?"

Wall Street Journal editor on perils of outside directors: Quoted in M. Gartner, "Are Outside Directors Taking Outside Chances?," *Juris Doctor,* March, 1973, at 37.

Loss on great Rule 10b-5: L. Loss, "The American Law Institute's Federal Securities Code Project," 25 *Business Law* 27, 34 (1969).

Supreme Court emphasizes securities laws do not reach internal mismanagement: Superintendent of Insurance v. Bankers Life & Casualty Co., 404 U.S. 6, 12–13 (1971).

Federal securities laws will not reach executive decision to engage in an unprofitable line of business: Medical Committee for Human Rights v. Securities and Exchange Commission, 432 F.2d 659 (1970). *But, see,* new SEC proxy rules promulgated thereafter, 17 C.F.R. 240.14a-8(c) (1972).

Cary's Complaint: Cary, 83 *Yale Law Journal*, at 700.

NULLIFYING THE JUDGMENT: INDEMNIFICATION INSURANCE

Seventeen states permit corporations to purchase indemnification insurance: McMullen, 29 *Business Law* at 755–776.

Words of a typical policy: Quoted in, Bishop, 77 *Yale Law Journal*, at 1078.

76.1 percent of corporations listed on New York Stock Exchange carry indemnification insurance: Wyatt Company, 1974 *Directors & Officers Liability Survey*, at 1, and 15.

Delaware's provision allows corporations to insulate officers from all liabilities: Insurance policies now in force proceed on the assumption that anything goes. Typically, coverage is two-fold. Under Part I of a Director And Officers Liability Insurance Form, the insurance company agrees to reimburse the corporation for all indemnification losses on expenses that the corporation is required to make to directors and officers. Under Part II, the insurance company agrees to indemnify the directors and officers for everything else. This is then followed by a series of exclusions. The insurance company "except insofar as the Company [meaning the corporation paying for the insurance] may be required or permitted by law" will not indemnify a Director or Officer for loss in connection with any claim of: 1) libel or slander; 2) unlawful personal profit; 3) unlawful remuneration; 4) purchase and sale of the corporation's stock within 6 months in violation of section 16(b) of the 1934 Securities Exchange Act; or 5) a final judgment of deliberate dishonesty. Except for violations of section 16(b) of the 1934 Securities Exchange Act, none of these "exclusions" really excludes. Few indemnified corporate officers allow suits against them to go to trial. After they settle a case, they may demand reimbursement from the insurance company on the theory they were not really guilty of the excluded item. This gives insurance corporations the choice of paying up or taking the officers to court and proving their guilt. Since the court alternative runs the risk of a judicial decision holding that aspects of corporate indemnification insurance are in violation of the legal principle against insuring deliberate wrongful acts, the insurance companies generally pay-off the corporate officers, in whole or in part, rather than litigate through to a full court determination on the merits.

CONFLICTS OF INTEREST

Brandeis on interlocking directorates: L. Brandeis, *Other Peoples' Money* 35 (1913).

Antitrust Subcommittee criticizes enforcement of section 8 of the Clayton Act: Antitrust Subcommittee, *quoted in* P. Dooley, "The Interlocking Directorate," *American Economic Review*, June, 1969, at 314, 319.

Dooley's research: Id. at 315, 317, and 319.

Our survey of interlocks: See, *Constitutionalizing*, Appendix E, at 555–566.

Center for Science analysis of oil company interlocks: Center for Science in the Public Interest Study, "Interlocking Oil: Big Oil Ties With Other Corporations," excerpted in Hearings Before the Subcommittee on Budgeting, Management and Expenditures and the Subcommittee on Intergovernmental Relations of the Committee on Government Operations, United States Senate, 93rd Cong., Second Sess. on *Corporate Disclosure*, April 23, 24, and May 20, 21, 1974, II, at 1009–1050.

Gibson description of Minneapolis interlocks: R. Gibson, "The Men in the Board Room," *Minneapolis Star*, January 18, 19, 20, and 21, 1971.

Top executive explains risk of putting investment banker on board: Mace, *Directors: Myth and Reality* at 140.

Juran and Louden instance of investment banker guiding company into poor investment: J. M. Juran and J. Louden, *The Corporate Director* 202 (1966).

Investment banker insisted on being involved in loan: Mace, *Directors: Myth and Reality* at 147.

Corporate president criticizes operation stakeout: Id. at 144.

New York law firms prohibit partners from becoming directors: Gartner, *Juris Doctor*, March, 1973, at 4–5.

1971–1972 study of 12,000 companies finds one in six employs outside counsel as director: W. Hudson, *Outside Counsel—Inside Director* (1973).

1846 Supreme Court decision on conflicts of interest: Michoud v. Girod, 4 How. 503, 554.

Marsh on history of conflicts decisions: H. Marsh, "Are Directors Trustees? Conflict of Interest and Corporate Morality," 22 *Business Law* 35 and 32 (1966).

Scholar terms conflict principle fundamental law: Brandeis, *Other Peoples' Money* at 38–39.

New Jersey court on fraud that is too cunning: Stewart v. Lehigh Valley R.R. Co., 38 N.J. Law 505, 522–523 (Ct. Err. & App. 1875).

Folk analysis of Delaware law regarding self-dealing: Folk, *The Delaware General Corporation Law* at 75–76.

1974 executive compensation of highest paid executive was $400,000: See, *Constitutionalizing*, Appendix F, at 567–591.

1963 salary: W. Lewellen, *Executive Compensation in Large Industrial Corporations* 23, and 137 (1968). $145,000 figure determined by subtracting 31 percent stock related income from "Average Before-Tax Salaries and Bonuses" figure to produce comparable figure.

AVERAGE DISCLOSED REMUNERATION AND STOCKHOLDINGS,
FIVE HIGHEST PAID EXECUTIVES
AT THE FIFTY LARGEST INDUSTRIAL CORPORATIONS
(*Inherited and founders stockholdings deleted*)

	Direct Remuneration	Direct Remuneration Plus Dividend Income	Value of Shareholdings Oct. 1, 1975	Estimated Annual Retirement Benefits
Highest Paid Executive	$401,954	$462,336	$1,566,009	$133,910
Second Highest	$295,531	$331,950	$ 718,911	$ 96,505
Third Highest	$238,635	$265,398	$ 599,139	$ 79,589
Fourth Highest	$214,659	$237,341	$ 448,233	$ 70,238
Fifth Highest	$197,347	$219,071	$ 536,726	$ 71,405

Lewellen on 1970–1973 salaries: W. Lewellen, "Recent Evidence on Senior Executive Pay," *National Tax Journal* 159 (1975).

1960–1963 capital gains of $220,087 per year: W. Lewellen, *The Ownership Income of Management* 75 (1971).

Our survey of annual retirement benefits: See, *Constitutionalizing* Appendix F, at 567–591.

List of executive perquisities and amenities: See, *Business Week*, May 12, 1975, at 90.

REMEDIES

REVAMPING THE BOARD

Environmental impact statements required by National Environmental Policy Act: See, C. Stone, *Where the Law Ends* 217–227 (1975).

Douglas proposal for professional directors: W. Douglas, *Democracy and Finance* 46–55 (1940).

ELECTION OF THE BOARD

Chayes on voting rights for those affected by the corporation: A. Chayes, "The Modern Corporation and the Rule of Law," in E. Mason (ed.), *The Corporation in Modern Society* 40–41 (1959).

Dahl holds a similar view: R. Dahl, *After the Revolution* 123, and 138–139 (1970).

Stone recommends public directors: Stone, *Where the Law Ends* (1975).

Criticisms of co-determination statute: See, R. Dahl, "Governing the Giant Corporation," in R. Nader and M. Green (eds.), *Corporate Power in America* 10–24 (1973). *See also*, D. Vagts, "Reforming the 'Modern' Corporation: Perspectives from the German," 80 *Harvard Law Review* 23 (1966); and G. Alperovitz, "Noted Toward a Pluralist Commonwealth," in P. Brenner, et al. [eds.], *Exploring Contradictions* (1974).

Sullivan on GM board: See, *e.g.*, *Business Week*, April 10, 1971, at 100.

Giovacchini at Gillette: Wall Street Journal, December 12, 1975, at 1.

Firms which already pass-through votes: P. Blumberg, *The Megacorporation in American Society: The Scope of Corporate Power* 126–128 (1975).

V. Corporate Disclosure

Kefauver hearings on drug firms produce curious coincidence: Hearings of Antitrust and Monopoly Subcommittee of the Senate Committee on the Judiciary, 86th Cong., 2nd Sess. (1960).

Bell Telephone footdragging: Statement of the Trial Staff, August 29, 1973, FCC Docket No. 19129.

OMB questionnaires ask 'Does agency pledge confidentiality?': See, Appendix for Standard Form No. 83 and accompanying instructions.

GAO adopts OMB standard question: The GAO also calls upon the Business Advisory Council for assistance in its supervisory functions over the administrative agencies, and consults trade associations whose members are involved in supplying data.

International Trade Commission will not disclose chemical firm annual reports: See, *e.g.*, Production and Sales in 1974, Sunthetic Organic Chemicals, Form No. CD-A1 (Budget Bureau No. 73R0002), Approval Expires August 1975. Relatedly, section 1905 of Title 18 provides that any employee of the U.S. Government who makes any unauthorized disclosure of "information coming to him in the course of his employment or official duties" shall be subject to a fine of not more than $1,000 or imprisonment for not more than one year, or both.

Bureau of Mines Director explains his Bureau's policy of confidentiality: Letter from Thomas V. Falkie, Director of the Bureau of Mines, April 3, 1975.

Bureau of Census utilizes both mandatory and voluntary data collection methods: The basic eco-

nomic censuses and most of the annual surveys in the economic area are collected under mandatory authority (13 U.S.C. 9); the bulk of the quarterly and monthly surveys are dependent upon
the voluntary cooperation of the business community.

Census Bureau Director says all data accorded confidential treatment: Letter dated April 11,
1975 from Vincent P. Barabba, Director, Bureau of the Census.

Supreme Court case agreeing with FTC data request: St. Regis Paper Co. v. U.S., 368 U.S. 208
(1961).

Business lobby pressures Congress to nullify Supreme Court decision: The applicable section of 13
U.S.C. 9, enacted into law October 1962, states: "No department, bureau, agency, officer, or
employee of the Government, except the Secretary (Department of Commerce) in carrying out
the purposes of this title, shall require, for any reason, copies of census reports which have been
retained by any such establishment or individual. Copies of census reports which have been so
retained shall be immune from legal process, and shall not, without the consent of the individual
or establishment concerned, be admitted as evidence or used for any purpose in any action, suit,
or other judicial or administrative proceeding."

Council on Wage and Price Stability Reports "immune from legal process": Sec. 5(f) (1) and (2) of
Public Law 94–78. The law became effective August 15, 1975.

*Mueller argues governments are often woefully uninformed of corporate affairs: Role of Giant
Corporations*, hearings before Subcommittee on Monopoly of Senate Select Committee on Small
Business, 92nd Cong., 1st Sess., Pt. 2, at 1096 (Nov. 9, 1971).

Federal Trade Commission notes critical role of information in free enterprise economy: Id., Pt. 2
at 596.

Marshall definition of a corporation: Dartmouth College v. Woodward, 4 Wheat 518, 636 (1819).

Supreme Court decision written many years later: Hale v. Henkel, 201 U.S. 43, 74 (1906).

Burger's view of trade secrecy: The Chief Justice's view is found in the main opinion in
Kewannee Oil Co. v. Bicron Corp. 94 S.Ct. 1879 (1974). *See also* Note, "Limits of Trade Secret Law
Imposed by Federal Patent and Antitrust Supremacy," 80 *Harvard Law Review* 1432 (1967).

*Supreme Court limits on privileges which conflict with copyright and patent clause: See especially,
Sears, Roebuck & Co. v. Stiffel*, 376 U.S. 225 (1964); and *Compco Corp. v. Day-Brite Lighting, Inc.*,
376 U.S. 234 (1964).

High standards required of proxy solicitations: See, section 14(a) of the 1934 Securities Exchange Act and regulations promulgated thereunder.

SOCIAL IMPACT DISCLOSURE

POLLUTION

One-third of streams and all rivers polluted: Council on Economic Priorities, *Guide to Corporations* 14 (1974).

Reserve Mining asbestos discharges: See, D. Zwick and M. Benstock, *Water Wasteland* 140–
166 (1971).

General Electric PCB discharges: Natural Resources Defense Council letter to Russell Train,
EPA Administrator, August 24, 1975. *See also, New York Times*, November 21, 1975, at 24.

90 percent of 3,000 industrial sources issued permits: Interview with officials at Environmental
Protection Agency.

Londoner who violated soot decree paid for it with his life: H. Hesketh, *Understanding and Controlling Air Pollution* 1 (1974).

Impossible to see more than 50 feet in Monongahela Valley: The New York Times, November 20,
1975, at 1; and *The New York Times*, November 21, 1975, at 24.

Galaxy Chemical plant fumes cause cancer rates to soar: Washington Star, November 28, 1975, at
B1.

Kepone poisoning: See, Washington Star, November 30, 1975, at 1; and *Washington Star,* December 10, 1975 at 1.

National Cancer Institute estimate of environmental causes of cancer: P. J. Bernstein, "Cancer Pollution Link Seen," *Washington Post,* February 16, 1975 at K1, K2, and K8; B. Richards, "Pollution-Cancer Link is Suggested," *Washington Post,* April 4, 1975, at A1, and A6; and "Chemical Carcinogens: A Long-Neglected Field Blossoms," *Science,* March 8, 1974 at 940; and also, H. R. Menck, J. T. Casagrande, B. E. Henderson, "Air Pollution: Possible Effects on Lung Cancer," *Science,* January 18, 1974 at 210–11.

Aerosol spray cans deplete ozone layer: Business Week, February 17, 1975, at 50.

Study of job gains because of pollution laws: Washington Post, December 30, 1975, at A1.

Securities and Exchange Commission new environmental disclosure regulations: Securities Exchange Act of 1934 Release No. 11733, October 14, 1975.

SEC narrow interpretation of environmental disclosure: Id. at 38.

OCCUPATIONAL SAFETY AND HEALTH

Udall states workplaces among most lethal environments: Quoted in F. Walleck, *The American Worker: An Endangered Species* 25 (1972).

NIOSH estimates there are over 25,000 toxic substances: General Accounting Office, *Report to the Senate Committee on Labor and Public Welfare: Slow Progress Likely in Development of Standards for Toxic Substances and Harmful Physical Agents Found in Workplace* 16 (1973).

27 cases of angiosarcoma linked to vinyl chloride: New York Times Magazine, October 27, 1974, at 23.

Lloyd predicts vinyl chloride occupational disease of the century: New York Times Magazine, October 27, 1974, at 23.

Allied and Dow report high cancer levels among workers handling arsenic: J. Page, "Toward Meaningful Protection of Worker Health and Safety," 27 *Stanford Law Review* 1345, 1356 (1975).

Rubber workers dying of cancer at 50–300 percent rate greater than general population: L. Agran, "Getting Cancer on the Job," *The Nation,* April 12, 1975, at 434.

Alexandria, Virginia company records mercury and arsenic sufficient to kill 70 people: Washington Post, February 23, 1976, at A1.

Nuclear Regulatory Commission prepared to revoke license: Washington Post, February 23, 1976 at A1.

50 percent of uranium miners expected to die of cancer: L. Agran, "Getting Cancer on the Job," *The Nation,* April 12, 1975, at 434.

Wagoner on asbestos take home risk: Washington Post, March 25, 1975, at A1.

NIOSH has produced only 26 criteria documents: Interview with Mary Win O'Brien.

OSHA has produced only three standards: The President's Report on Occupational Safety and Health (1973).

NIOSH officials concede need for criteria documents for 1,000–2,000 toxic substances: Congressional Quarterly, August 24, 1974, at 2291.

1975 budget for occupational cancer: Interview with NIOSH staff, January 7, 1976.

Fewer than 800 inspectors: Washington Post, November 8, 1975, at A27.

Only two firms convicted of criminal violations: Id.

The average fine has been $25: Id.

Hynan sees no cause for alarm: Interview with John Hynan, December, 1975.

Forms available to employees: Department of Labor, Bureau of Labor Statistics Report No. 412, "What Every Employer Needs to Know About Recording and Reporting Under OSHA."

Six months to develop comprehensive list of sources of mercury: Zwick and Benstock, *Water Wasteland* at 246.

EMPLOYMENT DISCRIMINATION

Black males paid 69 percent of white males: U.S. Department of Commerce, *The Social and Economic Status of the Black Population in the United States* 59 (1973).

Equal Employment Opportunity Commission found 25 percent employ no blacks: "25% of Firms with 100 Workers Employ No Blacks Brimmer Reports," 12 *Fair Employment Report* 83 (1974).

Blacks double unemployment: Employment and Earnings, January 1975, at 6.

Only 18 percent of nonwhites hold white collar jobs: U.S. Equal Employment Opportunity Commission, *Employment Profiles of Minorities and Women in 20 Large SMSA's* 3 (1974).

Female income 59 percent that of males: U.S. Department of Labor, *Women Workers Today* 6 (1974).

96 percent of private jobs paying more than $15,000 held by white males: J. K. Galbraith, et al., "The Galbraith Plan to Promote the Minorities," *New York Times Magazine,* August 22, 1971 at 9.

Kellogg on women among senior executives: Business Week, November 24, 1975, at 58.

EEO–1 information kept confidential: But, see, Legal Aid Society of Alameda County v. Schultz, 349 F. Supp. 771 (No. Cal. 1972).

Equal Employment Opportunity Commission back pay cases: Data supplied by the Equal Employment Opportunity Commission Public Information Office.

EEOC's efforts handicapped by cumbersome statute: Report of the U.S. Commission on Civil Rights, *The Federal Civil Rights Enforcement Effort,* V, (1974).

Private enforcement also discouraged: Ind. at 542–543. *See,* C. Wyman, "Striking Back: How to File a Complaint with the EEOC" *Woman's World,* September–October, 1975, at 13.

McDonnell-Douglas trade secret: Hearings before the Subcommittee on Monopoly of the Senate Committee on Small Business, 92nd Cong., 1st Sess., on "The Role of Giant Corporations in the American and World Economies," II-A, at 1362 (1971).

Montgomery Ward, Sears, and J. C. Penny definitions of officials: "Help Wanted Minorities and Women in the Retail Trade," *Economic Priorities Report,* V, No. 3, at 19 (1974).

CORPORATE ADVERTISING

U.S. advertisers paid 50 percent more than all other nations in 1972: Advertising Age, February 17, 1975, at 52.

1976 expenditures equal $31 billion: Wall Street Journal, December 24, 1975, at 18.

Advertised aspirin, etc. sells for more: See generally, B. Moore, *A Modest Proposal for the Reform of the Capitalist System* 15–26 (1974).

Brand name canned fruit 20 percent higher prices: National Commission on Food Marketing, *Special Studies in Food Marketing,* 47, 65 (Tech. Study No. 10) (1966).

Denenberg estimates consumers could save $3 billion on insurance policies: Pennsylvania Insurance Commission, *Shoppers' Guide to Life Insurance* (1972).

Federal Trade Commission substantiation program: Antitrust and Trade Regulation Report, March 20, 1973 at A-18, December 19, 1972 at A-1, July 13, 1971 at A-24, August 24, 1971 at A-20, October 19, 1971 at A-5, February 1, 1972 at A-8, January 4, 1972 at A-9, May 30, 1972 at A-5, September 26, 1972 at A-8, July 21, 1972 at A-9, August 1, 1972 at A-15, November 28, 1972 at A-10, May 30, 1973 at A-3, and June 19, 1973 at A-17.

Independent firm examined 54 claims by automakers: C. Dietrich and D. Miller, *Engineering Analysis to Documentation Submitted by Manufacturers to Substantiate 54 Advertising Claims FTC Advertising Substantiation Program,* 127 (1972) submitted to Bureau of Consumer Protection, Federal Trade Commission.

FTC found 30 percent raised questions about adequacy: Staff Report to The Federal Trade

Commission on the AO Substantiation Program together with Supplementary Analysis of the Submissions and Advertisers Comments, Committee on Commerce, United States Senate, 93rd Cong., 2d. Sess., (Comm. Print) 2 (1972).

FTC believes program curbs most blatant false claims: Antitrust and Trade Regulation Report, January 8, 1974 at AA-1.

Commission unwilling to challenge image advertising: The Nation, December 20, 1975, at 646.

Selectivity of program: J. R. Ferguson et al., "Consumer Ignorance as a Source of Monopoly Power: FTC Staff Report on Self Regulation, Standardization and Product Differentiation II," 5 *Antitrust Law and Economic Review* 55, 68 (1972).

Lack of real sanctions: Id.

Purposes of FTC program: Antitrust and Trade Regulation Report, June 15, 1971, at D1.

CORPORATE LOBBYING

What is the Business Roundtable: Business and Society Review, Spring 1976.

Common cause found oil lobby represented by 229 lobbyists: Testimony of D. Cohen, President, Common Cause, in support of H.R. 15 before the Committee on Standards of Official Conduct, House of Representatives, December 3, 1975.

Standard Oil letter to shareholders and employees: Washington Post, January 8, 1975, at A1 and A9, and January 9, 1975, at A1 and A8.

Supreme Court upheld constitutionality of Federal Regulation of Lobbying Act in 1954: United States v. Harris, 347 U.S. 612 (1954).

Deakin estimates $200 spent for every dollar reported: J. Deakin, *The Lobbyists* (1966).

National Association of Manufacturing list of 14,000 plants: Testimony of Fred Wertheimer, Vice President of Operations, Common Cause, before the Subcommittee on Administrative Practice and Procedure of the Committee on the Judiciary, United States Senate, April 14, 1975.

FINANCIAL DISCLOSURE

THE SEC'S DISCLOSURE SYSTEM

The SEC's required disclosures: Description of disclosure requirements derived from 1933 Securities Act and 1934 Securities Exchange Act and regulations promulgated thereunder.

Commission empowered to prescribe rules in the public interest: See, section 7, 8a, 8c, 10a, 10b, 10c of the 1933 Act and Sections 5, 6, 9b, 9c, 10, 11, 12, 13, 14, 15, 15a, 16 and 17 of the 1934 Act.

SEC interprets public interest to mean protection of investors: Securities Exchange Act of 1934 Release No. 11733, October 14, 1975.

Metcalf 1972 findings on top 30 shareholders: Cong. Rec., April 25, 1972, at E4242.

Frequent use of street names by Bank of America and others: Cong. Rec., June 19, 1972, at S9622–9625.

Cede largest holder in several airlines: Id.

Third layer of street names is comprised of banks: Cong. Rec., April 25, 1972, at E4243.

SEC entertaining comments on regulations to disclose 30 shareholders for each class of voting stock: Washington Post, August 26, 1975, at D7.

SEC regulations on significant subsidiaries: Item 4(a) of 10-K instructions require designation by "appropriate symbols (a) subsidiaries for which separate financial statements are filed; (b) subsidiaries included in consolidated financial statements; (c) subsidiaries included in group financial statements filed for unconsolidated subsidiaries; and (d) other subsidiaries, indicating briefly why financial statements of such subsidiaries are not filed."

SEC left determination of accounting standards to accountants in 1937: W. Douglas, *Go East, Young Man* 275 (1974).

Soon SEC turned over disciplinary questions to AICPA: R. Chatov, *Corporate Financial Reporting, Public or Private Control* 127 (1975).

AICPA implores management to stipulate standards: Id. at 187–188.

This is like batter calling the balls and strikes: Quoted in M. Eisenberg, "Legal Models of Management Structure in the Modern Corporation: Officers, Directors, and Accountants," 63 *California Law Review* 375, 418 (1975).

Only AICPA restraint generally accepted accounting principles: Quoted in Id. at 418.

Institute's official view: Quoted in Id. at 420.

Eisenberg explains the net result: Id. at 418–419.

Boothe Corporation fires Andersen: Id. at 426, note 180.

Spacek criticizes the roulette wheel: "A. Smith," *Supermoney* 206 (1972).

Adam Smith on massaging the numbers: Id. at 206–207.

By 1972, the game was no longer such fun: Id. at 211.

Thomas O'Glove on the worthless signature: Id. at 211.

David Norr expressed the same sentiment: Id. at 214–215.

Courts warn legal profession to beware: Id. at 215.

Head of drug company on one good accountant: Id. at 215.

Lybrand lawsuit: U.S. v. Simon, 425 F.2d 796 (2d Cir. 1969), *cert. denied* 397 U.S. 1006 (1970).

Peat, Marwick guilty: Eisenberg, 63 *California Law Review* at 429.

Andersen censured: Id.

500 claims by 1973: Id.

Settlements ranged from $300,000 to $5,000,000: Id.

SEC regulations require explanations of changes in accounting practices: 17 C.R.R. 210.3–07.

Disparities between reports to shareholders and to IRS: Tax discrepancies are disclosed in the 10-K Form and can be fascinating. Exxon informed its shareholders it paid taxes at a rate of 71.3 percent of profits in 1974 before deducting depletion allowances, investment tax credits, and "other" items to reveal its actual effective rate of 32.7 percent on domestic operations.

Explain dismissal of accountant: Securities Act of 1933, Release No. 5550 (December 20, 1974).

Congress creates FASB: See, Chatov, *Corporate Financial Reporting, Public or Private Control.*

Commission takes this unlikely time to look to private sector: SEC, Statement of Policy on the Establishment and Improvement of Accounting Principles and Standards, Accounting Series Rel. No. 150, September 20, 1973.

FASB directly funded by Financial Executives Institute: Chatov, *Corporate Financial Reporting, Public or Private Control* at 236.

Business executives on Standards Council: Id. at 305–306.

Federal Trade Commission on attracting potential entrants: Quoted in National Journal, February 10, 1973 at 185.

Price Commission had no reliable data: W. Mueller, "Corporate Secrecy vs. Corporate Disclosure," in R. Nader and M. Green (eds.) *Corporate Power in America* 113 (1973).

SEC recognized product line data essential in 1939: Quoted in D. Schwartz, "Financial Reporting of Diversified Companies: Legal Implications," 20 *Hastings Law Journal* 119, 126 (1968).

Honeywell report: Hearings before the Subcommittee on Monopoly of the Senate Committee on Small Business, 92nd Cong., 1st sess., on "The Role of Giant Corporations in the American and World Economies," IIA, at 1552 (1971).

General Telephone on Sylvania: Id., II, at 1125.

LTV in 1970: Washington Post, November 8, 1971, at A2.

ITT in 1970: Mueller, "Corporate Secrecy vs. Corporate Disclosure," in R. Nader and M. Green (eds.) *Corporate Power in America* at 115–120.

General Motors is a single line of business: Formerly the largest and now the second largest industrial firm, GM's total sales in 1974 amounted to $31.5 billion. Total U.S. sales were $26 billion, of which $23.4 billion constituted "automotive products."

1969 Cabinet Committee estimate: Studies by the Staff of the Cabinet Committee on Price Stability, *Study Paper Number 2, Industrial Structure and Competition Policy* 87 (January, 1969).

TO THE RESCUE, THE FTC

FTC rarely distinguished itself: See, E. Cox, R. Fellmeth, and J. Schulz, *The Nader Report on the Federal Trade Commission* (1969).

In mid-1950s FTC sought funds for line of business program: Hearings before the Subcommittee of the House Committee on Appropriations, Independent Offices Appropriations for 1957, 84th Cong., 2nd Sess., 1956, at 1294.

Recent statement of the Commission on Quarterly Financial Report: FTC, Quarterly Financial Report for Manufacturing, Mining, and Trade Corporations, First Quarter 1975, at 8.

FTC staff report on four food industries: FTC, Price and Profit Trends in Four Food Manufacturing Industries, Staff Report by A. Masson and R. C. Parker, July 1975.

Serious deficiencies in data: Interview with Frederic M. Scherer, Director, FTC Bureau of Economics, *Washington Post*, August 22, 1975.

Special rider forbids FTC study: For fuller details see M. Green, B. Moore, and B. Wasserstein, *The Closed Enterprise System* 369 (1972).

Mueller testified corporate secrecy enemy of a market economy: Role of Giant Corporations, hearings before Subcommittee on Monopoly of Senate Select Committee on Small Business, 92nd Cong., 1st Sess., Pt. 2, at 1094 (Nov. 9, 1971).

Heilbroner on what corporations know about each other: R. Heilbroner, Introduction to *Guide to Corporations, A Social Perspective* (1974).

Nelson on competitive advantage of largest corporations: See, e.g., Senator Gaylord Nelson press release, November 7, 1971, distributed by Senate Small Business Committee (SSBC #6303.)

GAO initially not enthusiastic: Report to Comptroller General Approving Federal Trade Commission's Proposed Annual Line of Business Report (Form LB), prepared by Philip S. Hughes, Assistant Comptroller General. The approval date was May 11, 1974.

Judge Weinfeld decision: Aluminum Co. of America et al. v. FTC, 390 F. Supp. 301 (S.D.N.Y. 1975). The New York case involved, in addition to Alcoa, GE, GM, Goodrich, International Paper, Owens-Illinois and Union Carbide. The opinion, dated Feb. 19, 1975, also refused to order FTC to give notice it may lack authority to prevent public disclosure of the information supplied under the Freedom of Information Act.

Judge Schwartz decree: A. O. Smith Corp. v. FTC. 396 F. Supp. 1108 and 1125 (D. Del. 1975). In additon to A. O. Smith, defendants were Inland Steel, Northwest Industries, Oscar Mayer, Merck, Hobart Corp., Goodyear Tire & Rubber, Thomas J. Lipton. Eight separate suits were consolidated for judgment.

Corporate patterns survey: Statistical Report, Value of Shipments Data by Product Class for the 1,000 Largest Manufacturing Companies of 1950, Staff Report to the Federal Trade Commission, Jan. 1972.

TOWARD A NEW FINANCIAL DISCLOSURE PROGRAM

Scholar could not identify Standard Oil investments: W. Mueller, "Corporate Secrecy vs. Corporate Disclosure," in R. Nader and M. Green (eds.) *Corporate Power in America* at 126 (1973).

Wisconsin allowed examination of corporate tax returns: Id at 125.

CASB now covers NASA: Chatov, *Corporate Financial Reporting, Public or Private Control* at 298.

French comprehensive accounting system: Id. at 298.

Belgium and West German systems: Id. at 298.

Chatov criticizes SEC policy: Id. at 293.

Bureau of Economic Affairs authority under Bretton Woods Agreement: Washington Post, December 22, 1974, at B3.

Japanese corporations give same profit figures to tax collector and shareholders: Barnet and Muller, *Global Reach* at 370.

Subpart F adopted in West Germany and Great Britain: Id. at 370.

VI. An Employee Bill of Rights

Supreme Court holds the Corporation should be considered a person: See, A. S. Miller, *The Supreme Court and American Capitalism* (1968).

Berle anticipates extension of Marsh doctrine: A. Berle, "Constitutional Limitations on Corporate Activity—Protection of Personal Rights from Invasion through Economic Power," 100 *University Pennsylvania Law Review* 933 (1952). *See Jackson v. Metropolitan Edison Co.,* 419 U.S. 345 (1974); *Hodgeus v. NLRB,* 96 S. Ct. 1029 (1976).

Recent High Court case concerning public utility: See, The New York Times, December 24, 1974, at 1.

Even more recent case concerning picketing: See A. S. Miller, "The Constitution in Retreat," in *The Nation,* April 10, 1976 on implications of *Hudgens v. National Labor Relations Board.*

Earlier case overruled: Amalgamated Food Employees Union Local 590 et al. v. Logan Valley Plaza, Inc., 391 U.S. 308 (1968).

Hanan view: M. Hanan, "Make Way for the New Organization Man," *Harvard Business Review,* July–August 1971, at 128.

Other advocates of job power: See, especially, Report of a Task Force to the Secretary of Health, Education, and Welfare, *Work in America* (1973).

FIRST AMENDMENT RIGHTS

Supreme Court decision balancing property rights and First Amendment liberties: Marsh v. Alabama, 326 U.S. 501, 509 (1945).

Cases of corporations firing employees who participated in political activity: See especially, P. Petkas and K. Blackwell, *Whistle Blowing* (1972). *See also,* A. Berle, *The 20th Century Capitalist Revolution* 83–102 (1954); P. Blumberg, *Corporate Responsibility in a Changing Society* 101–136 (1972); and R. Heilbroner, *In the Name of Profit* (1972).

Only five states protect non-union freedom of expression: Note, "California's Control on Employer Abuse of Employee Political Rights," 22 *Stanford Law Review* 1015 (1970). Statute citations at 1019, note 28.

George Geary fired: Petkas and Blackwell, *supra* at 154–156.

Henry Durham forced out of Lockheed: Id. at 152–154.

Colt workers feared being blackballed: Id. at 140–146.

GM engineers pressured: Id. at 158–161.

Carl Houston fired: Id. at 148–151.

Vandiver and Lawson forced to leave: R. Heilbroner, *In The Name of Profit* 3–31, (1971).

No state action for malicious discharge: Petkas and Blackwell, *Whistle-Blowing* at 210–211.

GE executive states employees must be willing to resign: New York Times, February 22, 1976.

RIGHTS OF PRIVACY

Supreme Court rules views of individual are made inviolate: Schneider v. Smith, 390 U.S. 17 (1968).

Census taker enjoined from questions: A. R. Miller, *The Assault on Privacy* 113 (1971).

No person compelled to answer polygraph machines: See Schmerber v. California, 384 U.S. 757 (1966).

Eighty percent of largest corporations subject applicant to a battery of tests: Note, "Legal Implications of the Use of Standardized Ability Tests in Employment and Education," 68 *Columbia Law Review* 691, 696 (1968). Compare W. Whyte, *The Organization Man* 192 (1957). In 1952, one-third of U.S. corporations used personality tests. By 1954, Whyte estimated 60 percent did so.

Job applicant must answer non-job related inquiries: Whyte, *The Organization Man*, at 110–111, and 115; and V. Packard, *The Naked Society* 68–71 (1964).

Fidelifacts or Bishop's Service talks with neighbors: Packard, *The Naked Society* at 49.

PEI's get into man's home for a look around: Id. at 53–54.

Bishop's Service 1964 questionnaire: Id. at 55.

American Security Council card file: "The 'Lie Detector'—Guilty until 'Proven' Innocent," pamphlet published by AFL–CIO Maritime Trades Department (1970).

Lie detector widely promoted for screening job seekers: Packard, *The Naked Society*, at 56–59.

1974 Senate Subcommittee study of polygraphs: "Privacy, Polygraphs, and Employment," a study prepared by the staff of the Subcommittee on Constitutional Rights of the Committee on the Judiciary, U.S. Senate, 93rd Cong., Second Sess., November 1974, at 2–3.

1971 AFL–CIO publication: "The Worker's World: Privacy and the Need to Know," published by the AFL–CIO Maritime Trades Department, November 16, 1971, at 50.

Packard estimates 13,500,000 employees scrutinized: Packard, *The Naked Society*, at 25.

American Broadcasting similar estimate: Quoted in "The Worker's World: Privacy and the Need to Know," published by the AFL–CIO Maritime Trades Department, November 16, 1971, at 42.

Long impressed by 1962 survey of industrial espionage: E. Long, *The Intruders* 208–209 (1966).

1967 New Republic article on GM document: The New Republic, February 18, 1967, at 18.

Within five years, computer data banks: Miller, *The Assault on Privacy* at 48.

Newsweek on bug boom: Newsweek, September 3, 1973.

Corporate employment of outside specialists: See, "The Great Game of Corporate Espionage," *Dun's Magazine*, October 30, 1970, at 30.

Wood explains about government and business: General Wood *quoted* in Petkas and Blackwell, *Whistle-Blowing*, at 1.

Most surveillance techniques probably lawful: K. Greenwalt, "The Right of Privacy," in Dorsen (ed.), *The Rights of Americans*, at 318 (1970).

13 states limit polygraph tests: Washington Star September 12, 1975, at E–6.

Miller concludes injured persons frequently held to waive rights: Miller, *The Assault on Privacy* at 200.

EQUAL RIGHTS

Berle on access to business opportunity: Berle, 100 *University of Pennsylvania Law Review* at 953–954.

Why protect auto dealers but not other dealers: Arguably the Robinson-Patman Act, 15 U.S.C. 13 *et seq.*, provides some protection. Section 2, 15 U.S.C. 13, prohibits certain price discriminations. 15 U.S.C. 14 makes criminal predatory price cutting. Neither really is in point. Neither section prevents a corporation from terminating a supply or distribution relationship.

Similarly, the Sherman Act only prohibits a refusal to deal where it is part of an attempt to monopolize. *See,* P. Areeda, *Antitrust* 287–317 (1967).

1970–1974 gasoline shortage hurt independents: Newsweek, March 18, 1974, at 94.

AN EMPLOYEE BILL OF RIGHTS

IBM recognizes propriety of this right: Indeed, a recent IBM policy memorandum indicates that corporation has established an elaborate system to allow employees to inspect and verify facts in personnel files.

1884 Tennessee court decision: Payne v. Western & A.R.R., 81 Tenn. 507 (1884).

Labor Act permits unions to insert just cause provisions in collective agreements: L. Blades, "Employment at Will vs. Individual Freedom: On Limiting the Abusive Exercise of Employer Power," 67 *Columbia Law Review* 1404 (1967).

VII. Corporate Monopoly: Failure in the Marketplace

A SKETCH OF LAW AND LAW ENFORCEMENT

Jefferson writing to Madison: The Writings of Thomas Jefferson 329 (1853).

1888 observer: Cited in, G. W. Stocking and M. W. Watkins, *Monopoly and Free Enterprise* (1951).

Government lost six of first seven cases: A. D. Neale, *The Antitrust Laws of the U.S.A.* 16 (Second Edition, 1970).

Olney did not file a single case: L. Huston, *The Department of Justice* 98 (1967).

Two seminal Supreme Court decisions in 1911: Standard Oil Co. of New Jersey, et al. v. United States, 221 U.S. 1 (1911); *United States v. American Tobacco Co.,* 221 U.S. 106 (1911).

Roosevelt attack on muckrakers: R. Hofstadter, *The Age of Reform* 246 (1956).

LaFollette criticism of Roosevelt: R. M. La Follette, *La Follette's Autobiography* 479 (Wisconsin Press Edition, 1960).

1909 Senate Judiciary Report: Cited in 221 U.S. 1, 96 (1911).

U.S. Steel and International Harvester cases: United States v. United States Steel, 251 U.S. 417, 451 (1920); *United States v. International Harvester,* 274 U.S. 693, 708 (1927).

Hand's 1945 Alcoa decision: United States v. Aluminum Co. of America, 148 F.2d 416, 424, 432 (2d. Cir. 1945).

1962 Supreme Court decision confirmed purpose of Celler-Kefauver Act: Brown Shoe Co. v. United States, 370 U.S. 294, 315 (1962).

Mason on appropriations: "Current Status of Monopoly Problem," 62 Harv. L. Rev. 1265, 1284 (1949).

Eastland, Celler, and Dirksen pressured Justice Department: See, M. Green, B. Wasserstein and B. Moore, Jr., *The Closed Enterprise System* 35–37 (1972) (hereinafter cited as Green).

Katzenbach on getting a political benefit: Id. at 33.

1955–1974 average fines: Clabault and Burton, *Sherman Act Indictments* (1967). Their study covered 1955–1965.

Cost-Benefit analysis of antitrust crime: H. N. McMenimen, Jr., *High Profitability—The Reward for Price-Fixing* 1 (1969). (His statistics do not take account of the 1969 Tax Reform Act, which permitted only one-third of the treble damages to be deductible.)

Phillips on success of antitrust: Quoted in, "Is John Sherman's Antitrust Dead?", *Business Week,* March 23, 1974, at 849.

THE ROAD TO MONOPOLY

2,653 consolidations 1898–1902: S. R. Reid, *Mergers, Managers and the Economy* 38 (1968). This study provides much of the data for subsequent textual discussion of merger waves.

By 1904, 319 trusts had 2,400 firms: A. Nevins and H. S. Commager, *A Short History of the United States* 307 (1969).

Brandeis on combination: Address by Louis D. Brandeis, "Social Justice and the Trusts," before the Undergraduates of Harvard University (December 18, 1912).

Rostow on quest for monopoly power: Rostow, "The New Sherman Act: A Positive Instrument of Progress," 14 *University of Chicago Law Review* 567–8 (1947).

Journal article on personal bargaining: Wall Street Journal, August 28, 1968, at 1.

FTC on uncollected taxes: Federal Trade Commission, *Economic Report on Corporate Mergers* 143 (1970).

Effect of advertisements on price competition: H. Skornia, *Television and Society* 90 (1965).

1966 study of 1,697 advertisements: Hearings on Possible Anticompetitive Effects of Sale of Network Advertising, Senate Antitrust and Monopoly Subcommittee of the Senate Judiciary Committee, 89th Cong., 2nd Sess., Part I, at 245 (1966).

Big firms obtain discounts on advertisements: Id. at 41; and *see*, Leonard, "Network Television Pricing: A Comment," *Journal of Business*, January, 1969, at 93–103.

Blair study of 33 consumer goods industries: J. Blair, *Economic Concentration: Structure, Behavior and Public Policy* 322–323 (1972) [hereinafter cited as Blair].

Turner on advertising and profitability: Address on "Advertising and Competition," before the Briefing Conference on Federal Controls of Advertising and Promotion, June 2, 1966.

Shepherd and Barber calculations of oligopoly control: W. Shepherd, *Market Power and Economic Welfare* 106 (1970); and R. Barber, *The American Corporation* 22 (1969).

Four firm concentration ratios for bread and cement: Blair at 10; *See also*, J. Blair, *Industrial Organization* 126–127 (second ed., 1968).

Measday on drug industry: Measday, "The Pharmaceutical Industry," in W. Adams (ed.), *The Structure of American Industry* 167 (4th ed. 1971).

Average four firm price ratio: See, F. M. Scherer, Industrial Market Structure and Economic Performance, 63 (1970) [hereinafter cited as Scherer].

Blair found for 209 industries: Blair at 22–23.

U.S. Steel acquired iron-ore deposits: Blair at 26.

Supreme Court landmark GM-DuPont decision: U.S. v. E. I. DuPont de Nemours & Co., 353 U.S. 586 (1957).

200 Manufacturing Corporations' share of total manufacturing assets in 1968: Federal Trade Commission Economic Report on Corporate Mergers at 173 (1969).

Mueller testimony before the Senate Antitrust Subcommittee: The Conglomerate Merger Problem, Pt. 8, hearings before the Antitrust and Monopoly Subcommittee of the Senate Judiciary Committee, 91st Cong., 2nd Sess., at 4550 (November, 1969).

Chevalier on commercial banks: Chevalier, "The Problem of Control in Large American Corporations," *Antitrust Bulletin*, Spring, 1969, at 165.

THE COST OF CONCENTRATION

Grymes on big corporations: Quoted in Business Week, March 23, 1974 at 46, 56.

Gerstacker on advantage of size: Speech by Carl Gerstacker, "Rebalancing the Corporation," delivered at the White House Conference on the Industrial World Ahead, Washington, D.C., February 7–9, 1972, at 274.

1974–1975 car prices up while sales down: "Detroit's Dilemma on Prices," *Business Week,* January 20, 1975, at 82.

Adams on steel industry: W. Adams (ed.), *The Structure of American Industry* 104 (4th edit., 1970) (hereinafter cited as Adams). Steel imports increased from 4.7 percent in 1960 to 16.7 percent in 1968, as Adams notes at page 84.

Prices and profits quite predictably higher: H. Goldschmid, M. Mann and J. F. Weston (eds.) *Industrial Concentration: The New Learning,* chapter by Weiss, "The Concentration-Profits Relationship and Antitrust" at 84 (1974) (hereinafter cited as Goldschmid). For contrary views *see* chapter by Demsetz, "Two Systems of Belief about Monopoly" at 164 (1974); Brozen, "Bain's Concentration and Rates of Return Revisited," 14 *Journal of Law & Economics* 351 (Oct. 1971).

Business Week on something strange in corporate America: "Are Some Key Industries Pushing Up Inflation?" *Business Week,* October 6, 1975, at 46.

Studies by Blair on price rise in concentrated and unconcentrated industries: Blair at 452–457; and Blair, "Market Power and Inflation: A Short-Run Target Return Model," 8 *Journal of Economic Issues* 453, 459 (June, 1974).

Means looked at 12 months beginning September, 1973: "High Hopes, High Prices," *Newsweek,* September 29, 1975, at 67. *See,* G. Means and J. Blair, *The Roots of Inflation* (1974).

Other economists hotly dispute Blair's latest study: Weiss, "The Role of Concentration in Recent Inflation," appendix to the testimony of Richard W. McLaren in *The 1970 Midyear Review of the State of the Economy,* Hearings before the Joint Economic Committee, 91st Cong., 2nd Sess., Pt. 1 at 109 (1970); for a good summary of the case against Blair and Means, *see,* Beals, "Concentrated Industries, Administered Prices and Inflation: A Survey of Recent Empirical Research," prepared for the Council on Wage and Price Stability (June 17, 1975).

Weiss on differences during cost-push and demand-pull inflation: Cited in Mueller, "Industrial Concentration: An Important Inflationary Force," in Goldschmid, at 293.

Scherer estimate of lost production: F. M. Scherer, *Industrial Market Structure and Economic Performance* 408 (1970). Final estimate based on wasteful promotional efforts, operations at less than optimal scale, pricing distortions in regulated sectors, monopoly inefficiencies due to insulation from competition, excess capacity due to cartelization and the stimulus of collusive profits, and transportation costs associated with distorted locational decisions. For a related and much disputed study, *see,* Kamerschen, "An Estimation of the 'Welfare Losses' from Monopoly in the American Economy," 4 *Western Economic Journal* 221 (1966). Estimate based on discrepancy between price and marginal cost in a variety of industries. Thus, his six percent does not include substantial losses from monopoly inefficiency—having high costs because incentive is lacking to keep them down—and from planned obsolescence, which is, effectively, a plot to waste resources.

Idle capacity means idle workers: See Okun, "Potential GNP: Its measurement and significance," in *Papers and Proceedings of the Business and Economics Statistics Section of the American Statistical Association* 98–104 (1962), which describes how for every percent reduction in unemployment, the GNP increases approximately $40 billion.

FTC study computes consumers overpay $15 billion: Scanlon, "FTC and Phase II: The McGovern Papers," 5 *Antitrust Law and Economic Review* 19 (Spring, 1972).

Shepherd and Scherer on Income Transfer: W. Shepherd, *Market Power and Economic Welfare* 212 (1970); and Scherer at 409.

Comanor and Smiley on distribution of wealth: Comanor and Smiley, "Monopoly and the Distribution of Wealth," Research Paper No. 156, Stanford University School of Business (May, 1973).

Bain study of 20 industries: Barriers to New Competition 111 (1957). A study by William Comanor and T. A. Wilson similarly concluded, in 24 of 29 industries studies, "the average size of the four largest firms exceeds the size which exhausts all economies of scale . . . and in 13 of these the differences are statistically significant." (Comanor and Wilson, "Advertising the Advantages of Size," *American Economic Review*, May, 1969, at 91). The Cabinet Committee on Price Stability agreed: "existing concentration levels in many industries are greater than necessary to achieve economies of scale in production, research and innovation" (Cabinet Committee Report at 81); *see also*, Saving, "Estimation of Optimum Size of plant by the Survivor Technique," 75 *Quarterly Journal of Economics* 569 (1961).

Economists studied 26 British industries: C. F. Pratten, *Economies of Scale in Manufacturing Industry* (1971).

Another study of 12 American industries: F. M. Scherer, A. Beckenstein, E. Kaufer and R. D. Murphy, *The Economics of Multi-Plant Operation: An International Comparisons Study* (1975).

Scherer conclusions on concentration: Scherer, "Economies of Scale and Industrial Concentration," in Goldschmid, at 28.

Lanzillotti thought there was room for at least 10 car manufacturers: Lanzillotti, "The Automobile Industry," in Adams at 273.

Bethlehem may benefit but society will not: As an example of this problem, *see*, statement of George Romney, former head of American Motors, *Hearings on Administered Prices*, before the Senate Antitrust and Monopoly Subcommittee, Pt. 6, at 2854 (1958).

Scherer on firm size and management quality: Scherer, "Economies of Scale and Industrial Concentration," in Goldschmid, at 51 and Scherer, *Industrial Market Structure and Economic Performance* 408 (1970).

Cobbs on dilemma: Business Week, January 27, 1975, at 16.

Galbraith on "benign providence": J. Galbraith, *American Capitalism* 86 (1952).

1955 study of R & D employment: Hearings on Economic Concentration, Senate Antitrust and Monopoly Subcommittee of the Senate Judiciary Committee, *supra*, pt. 3, at 1194–1198.

Standard Oil et. al. fail to develop patents: Blair at 231.

Weiss on size and research intensity: Weiss, "Econometric Studies of Industrial Organization" at 48 (paper done while resident economist at Antitrust Division, on file with authors).

Scherer studies of size and innovation: Scherer, "Economies of Scale and Industrial Concentration," in Goldschmid, at 49.

Jewkes study of invention: J. Jewkes, D. Sawers, R. Stillerman, *The Sources of Invention* (1958).

Three steel breakthroughs: W. Adams, *The Structure of American Industry* 105 (4th ed.) (1971). *See also*, Adams and Dirlam, "Big Steel, Invention and Innovation," *Quarterly Journal of Economics*, May, 1966.

Domestic companies wrong investment in open hearth furnace: Adams at 105.

McLouth Steel introduced oxygen steel process: Id.

1964 Steel R & D: Cited in, id., at 105.

Frey on last major innovation in auto industry: For description of poor innovation by the auto industry, *see*, R. Maclaurin, *Capital Formation and Economic Growth* 554, 557 (1955).

Domestic firms suppressed antipollution auto device: More fully described in Green at 254–263.

Quinn experiences at G.E.: T. K. Quinn, *Giant Business* 116–117 (1953).

Rabinow on automatic regulator: Testimony of Daniel De Simone, in *Hearings on Economic Concentration*, Senate Antitrust and Monopoly Subcommittee of the Senate Judiciary Committee, *supra*, pt. 3, 1097–1101.

Thorelli on Sherman Act: H. Thorelli, *Federal Antitrust Policy* 227 (1954).

Hand on costs of monopoly beyond economic costs: 148 F.2d 416, 428 (2d Cir. 1945).

Less discrimination in competitive firms: Shepherd, "Market Power and Racial Discrimination in White Collar Employment," 14 *Antitrust Bulletin* 141–161 (Spring, 1969); R. Straus, *Discrimination Against Negroes in the Labor Market* (Ph.d. Dissertation, Univ. of Wisconsin, 1970).

Douglas in 1949: Standard Oil Company of California v. United States, 337 U.S. 293, 319 (1949).

Oligopolies impair government ability to operate in public interest: Hart, Speech to the Lawyers

Club in Ann Arbor, Michigan, April 8, 1969. For ways big business can influence the political process, *see,* Green et al., *Who Runs Congress?* Chapters 1 and 2 (2d edition, 1975); M. Mintz and J. Cohen, *America, Inc.* (1971).

1950–1962 comparison of firms producing 16–50 products: Blair at 59.

Conglomerates accounted for 72.8 percent of large mergers 1948–1971: FTC, *Large Mergers in Manufacturing and Mining, 1948–1971* 7 (1972). For useful summaries of the conglomerate problem, *see, Report on Investigation of Conglomerate Corporations,* Antitrust Subcommittee of the House Judiciary Committee, 92nd Cong., 1st Sess., especially 78, 164, 361 (Comm. Print 1971); and Bryan, "Conglomerate Mergers: Proposed Guidelines, 11 *Harvard Journal on Legislation* 31, 33 (1973).

FTC finds little evidence of toehold acquisitions: FTC, *Conglomerate Merger Performance: An Empirical Analysis of Nine Corporations* 132 (1972).

70 percent of acquiring conglomerates larger than $400 million: FTC, Large Mergers in Manufacturing and Mining, 1948–1971 7 (1972).

No relationship between conglomerates and efficiency: See, *Economic Concentration Hearings* referring to studies by Professors Reid (at 4603), Kelly (at 4642), Hogarty (at 4647), Eslick (at 4702), and Arnould (at 4679).

Adams on ITT aggregate power: Adams, "Corporate Power and Economic Apologetics: A Public Policy Perspective," in Goldschmid, at 368.

Effect of Clorax acquisition by Procter and Gamble in 1957: Federal Trade Commission v. Procter & Gamble, et al., 386 U.S. 568, 578 (1967).

Edwards on forebearance: Economic Concentration Hearings, Part 1, at 45.

THE DECONCENTRATION ALTERNATIVE

Neal's endorsement in 1968: Report cited in Price Discrimination Legislation—1969, Senate Antitrust and Monopoly Subcommittee, 91st Cong., 1st Sess., at 30 (1969).

Simons criticism of gigantic corporations in 1948: H. Simons, *Economic Policy for a Free Society* 52, 59 (1948).

Rinfret endorsed Hart's bill: The Industrial Reorganization Act, hearings before the Antitrust and Monopoly Subcommittee of the Senate Judiciary Committee, 93rd Cong., 1st Sess., 321, 325 (March 30, 1973).

Burns says urgent need to revitalize competition: Id. at 43.

Blake on first antitrust statute: Blake, "Legislative Proposals for Industrial Deconcentration," in Goldschmid, at 340, 341.

Hale discusses divestitures: Hale, "Trust Dissolution: 'Atomizing' Business Units of Monopolistic Size," 40 *Columbia Law Review* 615, 631 (1940).

16 holding companies controlled 92 percent of all power: "Federal Regulation of Holding Companies: The Public Utility Act of 1935," 45 *Yale Law Journal* 468, 471 (1936).

Preston on divisionalized structure: The Industrial Reorganization Act, hearings before the Antitrust and Monopoly Subcommittee of the Senate Judiciary Committee, 93rd Cong., 1st Sess. 312 (March 30, 1973).

Turner on ascertaining plant-scale economies: Goldschmid, at 420.

Litton de-conglomerating: "Thinking small," *Newsweek,* June 2, 1975, at 59.

Standard Oil stock rose 47 percent after 1911 break-up: Business Week, March 17, 1975 at 66.

Analysts see break-up of IBM or AT&T as bonanza: Business Week, March 17, 1975, at 66.

Weeden pays homage to divested firms: Testimony cited in *id,* at 66.

Demsetz on penalizing success: Demsetz, "Two Systems of Belief About Monopoly" in Goldschmid, at 179.

Only 24 of 137 structural cases resulted in divestitures: Posner, "A Statistical Study of Antitrust Enforcement," 13 *Journal of Law & Economics* 365, 406 (1970).

Study remarks Government focuses on termination of ownership: Pfunder, Plaine and Whittemore, "Compliance With Divestiture Orders Under Section 7 of the Clayton Act: An Analysis of the Relief Obtained," 17 *Antitrust Bulletin* 19, 49 (Spring, 1972).

Elzinga on divesting firm: K. Elzinga, *The Effectiveness of Relief Decrees in Anti-merger Cases* (doctoral thesis, Michigan State University, Department of Economics) (1967); published in part in "The Antimerger Law: Pyrrhic Victories?" 12 *Journal of Law & Economics* 43, 65 (1969).

Doctrinal basis for attack on oligopolies already exists: Interstate Circuit, Inc. v. United States, 306 U.S. 208 (1939). *See also, American Tobacco Co. v. United States,* 328 U.S. 781 (1946); *United States v. Schine,* 334, U.S. 110 (1948); *Federal Trade Commission v. Cement Institute,* 333 U.S. 683 (1948); *Standard Oil Co. v. United States,* 337 U.S. 293 (1948).

Turner on law in doubt: The Industrial Reorganization Act, hearings before the Antitrust and Monopoly Subcommittee of the Senate Judiciary Committee, 93rd Cong., 1st Sess. 279 (March 30, 1973).

Warnke finds cases untryable: For the judicial tribulations of a big case, *see,* testimony of District Court Judge Philip Neville, *id.* at 353.

Judges often inexperienced: For an indication of judicial inexperience and lack of confidence on major antitrust cases, *see,* Green, at 474.

Supreme Court admonition to those who violate the Sherman Act: United States v. Crescent Amusement Co., 323 U.S. 173, 189 (1944).

Mueller skepticism of Procter & Gamble: Industrial Reorganization Act at 59–60.

Arnold on irony of big business: T. Arnold, *The Folklore of Capitalism* (1938).

VIII. Jurisdiction and Enforcement

SCOPE

Gerstacker favors a national company: Gerstacker, *quoted in* Barnet and Muller at 16.

Mobil Oil warning to Senators: New York Times, March 25, 1975, at 49.

ENFORCEMENT

Yeldell company lost charter: Washington Post, December 12, 1974, at A1.

Delaware companies pay $25 fine rather than file report: See Wilmington News Journal, March 23, 1971.

Douglas on SEC integrity during the 1930s: W. Douglas, *Go East, Young Man* 269 (1974).

A. A. Sommer speech: "A Parting Look at Corporate Bribery," distributed by Securities and Exchange Commission, April 2, 1976.

Landis celebrated remark: J. Landis, *Report on Regulatory Agencies to the President-Elect,* reprinted as a Committee Report by the Senate Committee on the Judiciary, 86th Cong., 2nd Sess. (1960), at 71.

ENFORCEMENT IN THE FEDERAL COURTS

Standing rules need to be broadened: See, Birnbaum v. Newport Steel Corp., 193 F.2d 461, 464 (2d Cir. 1952).

Ford, Hart supported Michigan Environmental Act: The New York Times, January 26, 1975, I, at 32. See also, J. Sax, *Defending the Environment: A Strategy For Citizen Action* (1971); and J. Sax and J. Dimento, "Environmental Citizen Suits: Three Years Experience Under the Michigan Environmental Protection Act," 4 *Ecology Law Quarterly* 1 (1974).

Senate hearings on Michigan Act: Hearings on S.1104 before the Subcommittee on the Environment of the Senate Committee on Commerce, 93rd Cong., 1st Sess., (1973), at 69.

Statute of limitations pointlessly restrictive: See, Section 13 of the 1933 Securities Act.

SEC case against Mattel: SEC v. Mattel Inc., Civ. #74-2958-FW (C.D. Cal., filed 1974).

SANCTIONS

S. 1 Bill criminal liability of executive and of corporation: Proposed sections 403 and 402.

IBM fine: Antitrust Trade Reporter, August 7, 1973, at 2.

IX. The Case Against Federal Chartering

Speaker at conference observed a federal act could turn out to be like Delaware's: Stanly Kaplan, "Fiduciary Responsibility in the Management of the Corporation," Airlie House, June, 1975.

Jackson issued volume on federal chartering in 1974: Federal Charters for Energy Corporations—Selected Materials, Senate Committee on Interior and Insular Affairs, 93rd Cong., 2nd Sess. (1974); *see also,* a valuable symposium on federal chartering in 61 *Georgetown Law Journal* (1972).

Stanton introduced a bill: H.R. 7481, *Cong. Rec.,* H. 4648 (May 22, 1975).

Roosevelt on trying free enterprise: Presidential Message on Concentration of Economic Power (1938).

Hamilton talk on federal chartering: Text of his talk on file with the authors.

Douglas on costs of our civilization: Day-brite Lightning, Inc. v. Missouri, 342 U.S. 421, 424 (1952).

Number of business questionnaires in Budget Office computer: Data supplied by Statistical Division, OMB, April 1975.

Corporate officers can make charitable contributions: A. P. Smith Mfg. Co. v. Barlow, 13 N. J. 145 (1953).

Dorsey explains the first responsibility of business: Quoted in Business and Society, August 25, 1970, at 3.

Friedman's viewpoint: Friedman, "The Social Responsibility of Business is to Increase Profits," *The New York Times Sunday Magazine,* September 13, 1970, at 146.

Journal reports executives less interested in broader responsibilities: Wall Street Journal, January 17, 1975, at 10; *see also, Wall Street Journal,* January 16, 1975, at 1.

Consensus of 130 securities lawyers: The New York Times, June 16, 1975, at 39.

Business, observes Roosevelt, compels collectivism in government: Quoted in R. Hofstader, *The American Political Tradition* 337 (1954).

Brandeis made a similar point: Louis Brandeis to the Massachusetts State Legislative Committee in 1905, in E. Mason, *Brandeis: A Free Man's Life* 130 (1946).

INDEX

Index

298 / *Index*